NINE LIVES

NINE LIVES

AIR COMMODORE
Alan C Deere
DSO OBE DFC and Bar

A Goodall paperback
from
Crécy Publishing Limited

Printed in Malta by Melita Press

A Goodall paperback
published by

Crécy Publishing Limited
1a Ringway Trading Estate, Shadowmoss Road, Manchester M22 5LH
Tel: 0161 499 0024   Fax: 0161 499 0298
www.crecy.co.uk

Contents

To
Joan
Jacqueline
and
John

Foreword

By Air Chief Marshal Lord Dowding, GCB GCVO CMG

NINE LIVES. What a title! Alan Deere must have had an exceptionally efficient Guardian Angel who, even so, must have been hard put to it to extricate his charge from the apparently hopeless predicaments in which he was constantly finding himself.

It is perhaps as a treatise on Courage that this book is principally noteworthy. In two wars I have had grim opportunities of seeing human endeavour stretched to its limits – and sometimes beyond. I was commanding the Fighter Wing in France before and during the Battle of the Somme in 1916; and there a pilot's or air-gunner's average expectation of life was one month, and at that time there were no rest periods for tired and depleted squadrons.

During the Battle of Britain I was farther away from the fighting squadrons, and too desperately busy to do much visiting; but I shall never forget the pall of gloom under which each day's casualties were scanned.

Even after all these years I can scarcely bear to be brought back to the atmosphere of those days because of the almost intolerable memory of stress and sadness which it engenders.

People are apt to talk of a very brave man as if his courage were some sort of Divine Dispensation which prevented his ever feeling afraid; but I have yet to meet the man who never in his heart knew the fear of death or, perhaps worse, of mutilation.

The brave man never lets his fear be seen, never permits his mind to dwell aimlessly on present or future dangers and never allows his actions to be influenced by his fears.

Of course the bravest nature can in the course of time be undermined by battling with inferior material against superior numbers and by lack of opportunities for sleep and rest, and we see this process at times wearing down even

7

Alan Deere's endurance; he never cracked – perhaps his was one of those rugged characters which never *would* crack this side of death; and relief came just in time.

I refrain from joining issue with the author in those few instances where our opinions differ concerning equipment or the conduct of operations; he may perhaps quote Kipling at me:

> The toad beneath the harrow knows
> Precisely where each nail point goes.
> The butterfly upon the road
> Preaches contentment to the toad.

(though I don't think I ever preached contentment to anyone engaged in the Battle of Britain).

There is, however, one episode upon which I can throw light. I refer to the 'Battle of Barking Creek' described on pages 38–39.

The large radar stations of the RDF Chain, as it was then called, were capable of giving plots of aircraft both to the east and to the west, but would give precisely the same indication for each. As they were intended to plot tracks to the eastward only, an electrical 'screen' was installed to smother all echoes from the westward. Aircraft flying inland were plotted either by the Observer Corps or the Sector Operations Rooms.

What happened on this occasion was that a refugee aircraft from Holland flew in without due notice and a section was sent off to intercept. The electrical screen at Canewdon RDF Station had somehow failed and this section appeared on the screen as coming from the east.

More aircraft were sent up to meet this non-existent attack, and more again to intercept them. Finally the table was covered with plots of incoming raids and yet no bomb had been dropped nor had any raid been picked up by the Observer Corps on reaching the coastline.

His Majesty the King had chosen this inopportune time to

honour my Headquarters with a visit, and I fear that he must have found me a most distrait host, for I was itching to find out what it was that had gone wrong.

Another story concerning this false alarm was that the Prime Minister (then Neville Chamberlain) was hastily bundled into a subterranean shelter within minutes of having made his dramatic announcement on the radio that war had been declared. There he remained forgotten for some hours until his staff were reminded of his incarceration by some question requiring a ruling from him.

Alan Deere will always stand to me as an example of the best type of Fighter Pilot whose endurance and determination brought this country of ours through the greatest immediate danger which has threatened it since Napoleon's armies stood along the Channel shore. May Britain and the Commonwealth never lack such sons.

Introduction

IN 1939, as a headstrong young man of twenty-one, I welcomed war as a glorious adventure. In 1945, war weary and wiser, I greeted peace with a fervent, "Thank God."

When the war in Europe ended I was deep in Germany as a member of the 2nd Tactical Air Force. For the past year I had followed in the wake of the conquering Allied armies as they swept through France, Belgium, Holland and into Germany. I had driven through the rubble of Caen; picked my way around the debris-strewn outskirts of Rouen; by-passed a bomb-scarred Amiens; driven through a practically undamaged and festive Brussels; gazed on the shattered Antwerp docks; crossed the still intact Nimejen bridge; trundled through the pot-holed Reichwald forest, whose shell-splintered trees bore witness to the last bitter resistance west of the Rhine; crossed this famous river into the heap of bricks and mortar that had been Wesel; finally to break out into the north German plains and so on to Celle, just fifty miles from Luneberg where Field Marshal Montgomery accepted the surrender of a defeated and demoralized German nation.

Three months later, Japan surrendered. And now there was peace. Soon the trials of war would be replaced by the struggle for post-war rehabilitation. After nearly nine years in uniform could I adapt myself to civilian life? Did I want to? Would I be given the opportunity to make the service my career? When, in October 1945, I was offered a permanent commission in the Royal Air Force, I accepted. I had come to love the RAF in peace and was proud of it in war; I knew by then that there was no other life for me.

Two months after the war in Europe ended I returned to England to get married, an event long planned when peace returned. As the post-war years merged one into the other the horrors of war fast became, for me, but fading memories, to be stirred into life only occasionally by the sight of a familiar place which sent the mind racing back across the years to scenes of triumph and tragedy. One such occasion occurred on Battle of Britain Saturday, 1953, when, as the leader of a formation of Meteor jets, I found myself over Hornchurch airfield, the scene of many exploits recounted in these pages.

As the formation thundered towards the airfield on its run across I looked forward expectantly to my first sight of the familiar station landmarks. Then they came into view: first, the tall laundry chimney to the north-east, a good circuit check point in bad weather; then the three hangars, once the proud homes of Spitfire squadrons, but now used for storage; and the landing ground itself, a small square patch of green whose grassy surface would never again thrill to the caress of operational aircraft. All this I took in at a glance, and as we passed overhead I looked down on the crowds packed on the tarmac, a scene reminiscent of a similar occasion fifteen years previously when, as a pilot in a Spitfire squadron, I flew over Hornchurch on Empire Air Day in 1939.

Now we were beyond the airfield and turning for the final run, but my thoughts were no longer concerned with the Meteors I was leading; I was thinking of the past. Hornchurch and the Spitfire; an airfield and an aircraft, vital partners in a great air battle to save a nation, both now symbols of a past era. Why not tell their story? The idea flashed through my mind, and lingered long after the event.

In the years that followed 1953, overseas postings and the diversions of a young family afforded scant opportunity for writing. In 1957, now back in England again, I sat down to write. In the intervening years many war books on the Royal Air Force were written, but none has covered the whole gamut of fighter operations in Europe. I therefore decided to drop my original intention of writing about Hornchurch and the Spitfire and to broaden the scope of my story. The result is an autobiography of a fighter pilot in peace and war, from the Munich crisis to the invasion of France. In particular, it is a personal account of fighter operations over Dunkirk and in the Battle of Britain; the first, I believe, to be written by one of The Few.

CHAPTER ONE

A Seed is Sown

FOR a breathless second I travelled forward with my crippled Spitfire. Then I began to fall. Immediately my body was sucked into the slipstream and hurled somersaulting towards the tailplane. There was barely time to observe this lethal obstruction pass above my head before I began to drop rapidly earthwards. Now for my rip-cord. The groping fingers of my right hand clawed at my left side until rewarded by the reassuring touch of cold steel thus dispelling a momentary flutter of alarm at the thought of not being able to locate the handle.

I was now clear of the aircraft and all set to pull the rip-cord. But the opening of my parachute must be delayed until I was also clear of the battle area and danger. My forced exit was made at 18,000ft at which height the air battle raged fast and furious. If I could will myself to delay the 'chute opening until I was down to a height of 10,000ft it would ensure that I was reasonably safe from stray bullets and aggressive Hun fighter pilots, and also allow time for any emergencies.

On my climb up some thirty minutes earlier I had noted that the cloud tops were at 8,000ft and I determined to wait until this sky marker was reached before pulling the rip-cord. What in reality was but a few seconds seemed an hour before my hurtling body sped past the drifting cloud banks. Whispering a silent "Please God" I pulled the rip-cord. Almost immediately the 'chute opened and my mad rush earthwards was abruptly halted, as if a giant hand had reached out from the nearby cloud and unceremoniously grabbed me by the collar. The first sensation was one of violence, followed by one of relief as I felt myself swaying gently and safely in the parachute harness.

Drifting slowly earthwards, my protecting canopy of silk forming an umbrella against the sun, I marvelled at the ease with which the seemingly difficult feat of a parachute jump had been accomplished. How many lives, I pondered, would have been saved in World War I had this instrument of survival been the rule and not the exception in the Royal Flying Corps?

Ruminating on this point, my thoughts should have channelled off into the present war, the expected invasion, the air battles of the moment and sundry other vital issues confronting England. Not so, the very jolt from the opening parachute had catapulted them across a span of fourteen years, back to the very day on which, as a boy of eight, I had resolved to be an aviator. Once diverted, they continued to wander recapturing those early years and the events which led up to the predicament in which I now found myself.

It was a glorious summer's day, and the little New Zealand town of Westport, at the foot of the Southern Alps, was bathed in warm sunshine. Three little barefooted boys were crouched around a circular patch of clay engrossed in a game of marbles. As they played, a new and puzzling sound gradually intruded upon their little world, faintly at first but growing louder and more insistent, until it filled the air with a strange persistent throb. Almost simultaneously, three heads jerked upwards and three pairs of eyes gazed skywards seeking an answer to this unwanted intrusion. One glance was sufficient; a tiny bi-plane droned overhead, its whirling propellor glinting in the bright sun.

To three small boys, whose only contact with this mechanical bird had been through the medium of picture books and models, this was an event of the first importance. That aeroplanes could fly was never in doubt; the fact that one was now overhead, seemed unbelievable. Where did it come from? Who was the pilot? Where was it going to land? The latter question was soon answered by a change in course as the aeroplane, having first circled the town, headed off in the direction of the coast with the obvious intention of landing on the long, firm stretch of sand which fringed the water's edge. Discussion and agreement were unnecessary;

with one accord the three set off on a four-mile run to the beach. As the youngest of those three boys – the others were my elder brothers – I was hard pressed to keep up the furious pace set to the beach. With each sobbing breath I willed myself to keep going knowing that should I falter no compassion would be shown, and I would be left behind.

At last we were there. Before us stood the small silver bi-plane surrounded by a knot of curious sightseers many of whom were, no doubt, seeing an aeroplane for the first time at close range. Feverishly my eyes sought for the figure of someone who measured up to my childish ideal of what a pilot should look like; alas, no tall, helmeted and gloved individual was to be seen. The pilot had been driven off in a waiting motor-car.

For long hours we stood and gazed in silent wonder at the aeroplane until eventually our persistence was rewarded by an invitation to look into the cockpit. There within easy reach was the 'joy stick,' as it was then called, the very sound of the word conjuring up dreams of looping and rolling in the blue heavens. And there, too, above a fascinating row of tiny dials, was the speedometer, the only instrument I could recognize.

As I gazed at these innermost secrets of the pilot's cockpit, there gradually grew within me a resolve that one day I would fly a machine like this and, perhaps, land on this very beach to the envy and delight of my boyhood friends. That night in bed I could think of nothing else, and for many weeks afterwards my desire to fly was fed with boyish imagination until the seed, which had been sown from the moment I first sighted the aeroplane, firmly took root.

For months after the event the ambition to become a pilot was uppermost in my mind. As, however, the months stretched into years, and with no further incidents to nourish it, the desire grew less and less but never died completely. Rather, it was stored in an undisturbed corner of a small head – filled with the joy and excitement of the adventurous open air life of a New Zealand youngster.

I was one of six boys, both my parents being of Irish stock their respective parents having emigrated to New Zealand from County Limerick in the days of the Irish troubles. The town in which we lived, situated as it was in the remoteness of the sparsely populated area of the rugged west coast, and astride some of the most beautiful and wild bush country in New Zealand, offered limitless opportunities for adventure and exploration. The summer months, in particular, were crowded with adventures. There was the beautiful Buller river, swift flowing and abounding in fish, in which to boat and swim; the seemingly endless miles of seashore with its gleaming white sand, on which to frolic and build our sand castles; the wide acres of brushland in which to build our 'dens' and the towering trees from which to hew our canoes and if these delights were not sufficient to satiate our boyhood desires, there was the harbour with its tramp steamers and their constant escort of screaming gulls battling for the floating refuse before it could be claimed by the shoals of waiting herrings which we caught in their hundreds, fishing from perilous perches on the slippery wooden cross-beams in the murky light underneath the wharf.

Our house was within a few hundred yards of the Buller river which has its source high up in the Alps, a lofty range of mountains stretching almost unbroken down the centre of New Zealand's South Island. Spring tides coinciding with an unusually prolonged rainy season often produce heavy flooding of the river particularly when an early thaw of the snow-laden Alps aggravates these conditions. In 1926, when I was eight, the river had been in flood for weeks with the steadily rising water inundating farms and homesteads whose lands adjoined its banks at lower levels. My brothers and I became intensely excited as day after day signs of the devastation further upstream made it more and more apparent that the river was still rising. What had formerly been a mass of seething, twisting logs soon became a jostling collection of dead cattle, farm appliances and domestic bric-à-brac. There would go a henhouse rubbing elbows with a pigsty, the former crowned by a bedraggled rooster still sufficiently alive to crow defiance, the latter closely followed by a drowned pig seemingly chasing its former home as if seeking re-entry before being finally swept into the sea and salty extinction. Then would come the remains of a small farmhouse, which had been swept unceremoniously from its wooden foundations, heaving and jostling for pride of place in the mad rush seawards. The gravity of the situation, especially to our own home, did not enter our heads. We were to learn only too soon what it was like to suffer the fate experienced by up-river settlers whose homesteads and belongings we had so often seen carried downstream in the swirling flood waters.

My father woke me in the early hours of the morning. "Wake up, wake up," he said, "the river has burst its banks." He tugged me from my warm bed and carried me down the passageway to join my brothers on the big kitchen table.

For hours we huddled there in the feeble light of a few spluttering candles as the water rose steadily until eventually we were forced to seek safer refuge on the kitchen sideboard and on the tops of cupboards. The pitch black night, the roaring of the floodwaters as they swirled around the house, the howling of the wind and the incessant drumming on the tin roof, added further to our terror and misery. In our remote situation – there were only two other houses in the vicinity – with no telephone and no means of escape, all seemed lost.

In the grey light of dawn, when the water level had almost risen to our final places of refuge, help arrived. A splash of oars heralded the approach of a rowing-boat and the comforting sound of a male voice calling "anybody at home," announced the presence of rescuers. Safely aboard and wrapped in warm blankets, we were ferried to a hotel in the centre of the town out of reach of the flood waters.

It was some days before the waters receded sufficiently to allow access to our house, and many months before it was fit for re-occupation. At its highest point, the water level had reached about half-way up the walls and the furniture and fittings were beyond salvage; everything was caked in brown mud when finally brought from the house.

Just three years later catastrophe again visited the little town, this time in the form of a severe earthquake. The air had been close and still for some time, and a strange feeling of foreboding persisted. At 10.30am on June 17th the first tremor hit the town, followed by shocks of extraordinary violence. I was in school at the time, and in a matter of seconds there was chaos as the intensity of the shaking increased and children fought to get through the narrow classroom door to safety.

Outside the whole earth seemed to be erupting as if some giant mole was burrowing up for air. Chimneys toppled, telegraph poles swayed, buildings collapsed and church bells rang with the heaving earth. Children were lying flat on their faces in the school yard or clutching desperately at the school fence for support. This was surely the end of the world.

Terrified, I clung to the school fence from where I could see the clock tower of the post office swaying drunkenly. Slowly a gaping crack opened up at the base and suddenly the whole edifice came hurtling down sending bricks and mortar flying in all directions. I was so absorbed in this spectacle that I hadn't noticed the alarming fissures now appearing in the ground around about. Huge cracks were opening up immediately in front of me and not twenty yards away a great rent in the road was slowly widening; I watched fascinated as it began to close again swallowing crumbling earth and asphalt, the jagged edges like the jaws of some giant monster closing inexorably on its prey.

As suddenly as it had begun the trembling ceased, and a deathly calm followed as the church bells stopped ringing and the sounds of tumbling masonry subsided. We were assembled in the school grounds and instructed to return home immediately avoiding, where possible, the centre of the town where damage was thought to be considerable. The most direct route to our house did not entail going through the town centre but on this occasion, despite being briefed to the contrary, I took the longer route, drawn by a morbid curiosity to see the remains of the clock tower, the collapse of which had so fascinated me. The main shopping street was a shambles of broken glass and dust covered rubble; fruits and sweets strewn across the street adding to the excitement of the adventure. In my childish delight at such an unexpected windfall of free sweets I gave little thought to material damage, stopping only long enough to stuff my pockets with fruit and sweets before hurrying homewards, unnoticed in the confusion about me.

The centre of the shock was at Murchison, a small farming centre several miles from Westport. It was virtually destroyed, and its population evacuated. A cloudburst produced torrential rain, and swollen rivers, diverted from their courses by landslides, made roads impassable. In Westport practically the whole of the population spent the next two nights camping in the open, our family among them, afraid to go back into buildings of any kind so long as the ground continued to rock and shake; this it continued to do for many days.

In early 1930 my family moved to Wanganui, New Zealand's fifth city, on the west coast of the North Island. Thus I had spent the twelve most formative years of my childhood in a sparsely populated part of New Zealand where my character had been moulded and toughened in a pioneering atmosphere of independence and adventure. But now in the more sophisticated surroundings of my new home town, schooling was to play the central part of my existence.

My interest in flying, long dormant through lack of opportunity, was re-awakened in Wanganui by a visit to the Town's airport by Sir Charles Kingsford-Smith in his famous tri-plane the *Southern Cross*. This pioneer aviator who had thrilled the world with his record-breaking flights, particularly across the Tasman Sea, was making a triumphant tour of New Zealand, and short passenger trips were being given at 10/- per head. After weeks of hoarding I had the necessary capital to undertake my first flight.

The great day arrived, and it is impossible to describe my thoughts as the aircraft became airborne. My dreams had come true. Suffice it to say that the seed sown in that summer nine years earlier had been fertilized, and was to grow through the ensuing years until it finally came to bloom in far away England in the winter of 1937.

At about this time Dr Kendrick Christie, our family doctor who was a qualified pilot, had spoken to me about flying and the opportunities open to a young man in the Royal Air Force. An announcement in the newspapers that the RAF was about to carry out a big expansion seemed to present me with my special opportunity and I applied to join.

I knew my father would be against the idea and that he would probably refuse to sign the application as he was required to do; I was eighteen at the time. Rather than risk refusal by asking him I persuaded my mother to sign the papers, and she reluctantly agreed. Thus it was that my application was submitted under an illegal signature; my father was not aware of the plan until official notification that I was to attend a selection board was received.

The selection board consisted of two Royal New Zealand officers and Wing Commander Hon. R. A. Cochrane of the Royal Air Force (later Air Chief Marshal) as chairman. I managed to answer all the questions put to me, and the Board seemed satisfied with my answers. I felt fairly confident of my chances as I had the necessary educational qualifications and in the sporting sphere was playing first class cricket and rugby and, in addition, had represented Wanganui at the New Zealand Boxing Championships. Most important of all I was desperately keen to fly. My confidence was justified for a few months later I was notified of my selection, subject to medical fitness. In a matter of weeks I was on my way to England.

CHAPTER TWO

Pilot Under Training

THERE were twelve of us selected for pilot training in the Royal Air Force, and I looked forward to meeting the other successful applicants in Auckland, where we were instructed to assemble for briefing prior to our departure for England. I found eleven young enthusiasts whose ages ranged from eighteen to about twenty-one and all of whom, like myself, were leaving New Zealand for the first time. They shared my excitement at the prospect of the sea journey, and the more long term prospect of flying training in England. Of that gay company only two remain in the Air Force today, myself and Jack McKay who is now a Group Captain.

It was early on a September evening in 1937 that The New Zealand Shipping Company's SS *Rangitane* later to be sunk by a German raider in the Pacific – steamed out of Auckland where I was born. Three weeks passed before we sighted land in the shape of the Isthmus of Panama, a welcome sight after endless days spent mostly on deck wrapped up in rugs and gazing despondently out on to a seemingly endless expanse of water. A feeling of homesickness prevailed throughout the first few weeks but was soon to disappear under the warm skies of the South American Continent. The ship berthed at Panama City, at the Pacific entrance to the famous canal, for an overnight stop, and was scheduled to depart in the early hours of the morning. Permission had been granted for us to go ashore, but not before we had been lectured by the ship's Medical Officer on the dangers of associating with females in the more notorious districts of a city famed for its night life. He needn't have worried, we were certainly not going to jeopardize our final acceptance in England, having got so far towards achieving our life's ambition.

None of us had set foot on foreign soil before, and the activity and tempo of this gay city at midnight was therefore in vivid contrast to life in our own cities at the same hour. The thousands of dark-skinned Panamanians lounging and gossiping in the main square; the myriad of neon lights; the café bars crowded with people; and over and around everything the hum of a city fully awake.

The ship was due to sail at 5am which gave us only about six hours on shore, hardly enough to see and do all that we would have liked, but nevertheless they were hours in wonderland.

In twos and threes we drifted back to the ship, tired out but already feeling more knowledgeable and worldly, the memories of our former life already dimmed by the revelations of this new world. Most of us lost the battle to stay awake to see the wonders of the Panama Canal, with its intricate locks, its mechanical donkeys, the great gash of the Gaillard Cut, and the twin cities of Cristobal and Colon, between which the ship passes as it steams out into the Atlantic Ocean.

For two more weeks we ploughed across an ocean, unbroken by the sight of land, and the ship fought her way into the colder winter climate of the Northern Atlantic. At long last, England was in sight, its presence heralded by the twinkling lights of Weymouth and Portland, barely visible through the rain clouded night. Early morning found the ship anchored in the mouth of the Thames, awaiting the tide and a pilot.

Slowly she steamed up river with twelve excited New Zealanders running from one side of the ship to the other in an attempt to see all the famous landmarks about which so much had been heard and read. The busy upper reaches of the river, choked with craft of all types and sizes, presented a scene of absorbing interest. There were the heavily loaded barges, low in the water and battling their way upstream; the passenger ships gliding downstream, their decks lined with waving people; and an assortment of coasters, black and smoke-grimed, making their purposeful way down river to the wave-tossed Channel beyond and recalling to mind those vivid and oft quoted lines of John Masefield:

Dirty British coaster with a salt-caked smoke stack,
Butting through the Channel in the mad March days,
With a cargo of Tyne coal,
Road-rail, pig-lead,
Firewood, iron-ware and cheap tin trays.

This was the Pool of London, the centre of the world's maritime commerce.

Busy little tugs now appeared and manoeuvred the ship into the lock which gave entrance to the inner harbour of Tilbury Docks, and the end of our journey. The business of customs, immigration and the thousand and one formalities connected with a port of arrival concluded, we boarded the boat train for London. The cold discomfort of the railway carriage and the flat, treeless acres of Southern Essex, soaked in the drizzle which had persisted since our arrival, were depressing reminders of the warmth and sunshine of far-off New Zealand still very much in the forefront of our thoughts. Had I been able to see into the future, it would have caused me to look to the north as the train sped through Upminster for a glimpse of the hangars of Hornchurch airfield which in three short years was to be the scene of many stirring events recounted in later pages of this story.

We stared in amazement at the grim rows of East End houses, pouring their smoke into the clouded atmosphere, and were appalled by the bustle and grime of Liverpool Street Station, so different from the luxurious gateway to London of our dreams. But the size and complexity of London, its famous streets and buildings, its taxis, and its general air of purpose, made us feel that till now we had lived only on the brink of this great world of ours. There were wonderful things to see, and great achievements possible in this vast city; the hub of the British Empire of which we were proud members.

On the morning following our arrival, we reported to New Zealand House where we were greeted by the New Zealand High Commissioner, Mr W J Jordan, who wished us success in our venture and an assurance that we would always be welcome visitors to New Zealand House whose staff were only too willing to advise and assist whenever possible. During the war years I got to know Mr Jordan – or 'Old Bill' as he was affectionately known to the thousands of New Zealand troops in England – and we became firm friends. He was a wonderful ambassador for his country in war torn London.

The de Havilland Civil School of Flying at White Waltham near Maidenhead was to be our home for the next three months while we underwent an *ab initio* flying course before being finally accepted into the Royal Air Force as suitable for pilot training. A house called 'Altmore,' whose postal address of Cherry Garden Lane never ceased to intrigue me, served as a mess for the pilot trainees, and it was here we arrived that same evening. Our ship had been late and the start of the course had been delayed two days to enable us to be there on the opening day. This may have been the cause of the awkward silence which greeted us as we entered the ante-room to be met by the enquiring gaze of those who were to be our companions for the next three months. The looks we got suggested that it was all our fault, and what queer looking fish we were anyhow. I wondered if they expected us to be black. After all, our national rugby side was known as the All Blacks and an English schoolboy was reputed to have written to his parents, after watching the All Blacks training on Eastbourne College grounds, that they seemed very nice and were almost white! Whatever the cause, there was not the enthusiastic reception which we had expected, as would have been the case in our own country under similar circumstances. Besides, and this rankled, the wretches had taken all the good rooms and left the only big room for us, to be used as a dormitory.

It was some weeks before what I now know to be the natural reserve of all Englishmen gave way to a more friendly approach, and this was speeded up by, of all things, a game of rugger. On a particularly foggy day when flying was impossible and we had had more than enough of ground work, a game of rugger was suggested and it was decided that the New Zealanders would take on the rest. Among us we had some first-class rugger players, but so too did the opposition, three of whom played for London clubs. The fact that we won by a colossal score, long since forgotten in detail, seemed to convince the Englishmen that we wouldn't be such bad chaps after all and that, perhaps, under our rough exteriors there existed people like themselves. Anyhow, from that time onwards we were accepted into the family and, in the later stages of our service, became firm friends. Few of that grand bunch of Englishmen survived the war.

It was to be some two weeks before I commenced flying. On my arrival, a pre-flying medical revealed that I had slight blood pressure and I was packed off to Halton for observation, much to my chagrin. Repeated assurances that I felt one hundred per cent, had never had blood pressure in my life and that it was probably due to excitement, did not release me from kicking my heels around the Halton wards while my friends got on with their flying, some even going solo in that time. Eventually, sanity prevailed and I returned to White Waltham, determined to make good the ground I had lost.

It was heartening to find that I had an instructor who fully understood how I felt and, as a result, made every effort to give me extra flying whenever possible, so that in the end I made up the lost ground. It was particularly unfortunate therefore that I should have angered this self-same instructor by disobeying instructions on my first solo, even though it was only through over-keeness. Having done the customary dual circuit prior to being sent solo, Flying Officer Dixon taxied the Tiger Moth to the downwind side of the airfield where he got out to give me final instructions before letting me take the aircraft solo for the first time.

"Remember your height and turning points on the circuit and make sure you are nicely settled down on the final glide in before choosing your spot to land. If you are in doubt don't be afraid to go around again and have no hesitation in doing so if you bounce badly on touch down. I only want you to do ten minutes and in that time you should be able to get in two landings."

I was really straining at the leash by the time he had delivered these homilies and thinking he had finished, banged the throttle open – he always said I gave it a straight left – and so into the air, solo at last. One, two, three landings, around again and again I went the ten minute limit completely forgotten in the thrill and excitement of this momentous occasion. Finally, having convinced myself I was just about the best pupil that had ever flown a Tiger Moth, I taxied back to the airfield boundary, purring with pleasure.

"I thought I told you to make only two landings and not to take longer than ten minutes," an infuriated instructor, his rather large moustache waxed solid with the cold, greeted me on my return. Somewhat deflated, I answered:

"Sorry, sir, I thought I was to go on until I was satisfied that the landing was perfect."

"If that was the case, you would be up there for a week," was the sarcastic reply. "Not only did you disobey my instructions, you didn't even have the decency to wait until I had finished speaking, before opening the throttle and bloody nearly blowing me out of the field with the slipstream."

Not a happy first solo. However, Flying Officer Dixon was not the one to nurse a grievance and, in fact, never mentioned the incident again. This says a lot for his patience, because it wasn't the only occasion on which I put his powers of self-control to the test.

I had always determined to be a fighter pilot and put this down as my preference when towards the end of our three months, we were asked to make a choice, despite the conviction of my fellow students that bombers offered the best future. Whenever there was an occasion to do so, I reiterated my desire to be a fighter pilot on the principle that in the end someone was bound to take notice. And so it proved. At the end of our service training period, some nine months later, I was one of only four to go direct to a fighter squadron.

The next step on the ladder was a two weeks' officer training course at RAF Station Uxbridge where we were fitted for our uniform before proceeding to the real business of flying Service aircraft at No. 6 Flying Training School, Netheravon. The airfield at Netheravon formed a natural part of the rolling Wiltshire Downs and was one of the very early flying fields, its mess and living accommodation being witness to this fact. Nonetheless, it was a most comfortable station and I thoroughly enjoyed my time there. It was a wonderful life; lots of flying, good companionship and every opportunity for sport. I wouldn't have changed my lot for anyone; for flying and sport, my two ruling passions, to be available under such pleasant circumstances, was all that I asked.

In the junior term we flew Hawker Harts, an obsolete but wonderful old bi-plane, and I made good progress. But one incident nearly put paid to my career in the RAF I was not feeling too well after a rugger celebration the night before, when my instructor, rather a quick-tempered individual, set me the exercise of 'Spins under the hood recovering on instruments on a set heading.' To spin the aircraft first one way and then the other, under a hood which blotted out all but my instrument panel, and to recover from the spin with the aircraft pointing in a pre-determined direction was difficult at any time but impossible for me that day. The instructor's exasperated voice came over the inter-communication:

"If you think you will ever be a pilot let alone a fighter pilot, you are very much mistaken. I've had enough of your futile attempts on this trip, and there is no point in carrying on with the exercise."

Till this day I don't know what made me see red, perhaps my own futility combined with the hangover, but see red I did and promptly shouted back, "I'm damn well fed up too, why don't you get in this seat and have a go yourself?"

There was no reply, and I don't think I expected one. About five minutes later we landed back at base and taxied to dispersal where the instructor said, "You can come out of there now, Deere. Report to me in the flight commander's office in five minutes."

"This," I thought, "is where Acting Pilot Officer Alan Deere says good-bye to a career as a pilot in the Royal Air Force." My conduct was inexcusable, and I knew it. I really felt miserable and roundly cursed myself for letting my outspokenness, a trait no doubt inherited from my Irish ancestors, get out of hand.

"Deere, you have been a stupid young fool and I don't quite know what to do about it," said my flight commander before whom I stood rigidly at attention.

"I am sorry, sir. I apologize, and assure you it won't happen again."

"All right. You will have another chance. It is only because the Royal Air Force has already spent so much money on your training that I am persuaded to be so lenient. Remember though, there will be no second chance and on the next occasion, should there be one, you will be up before the Chief Flying Instructor who will be much more severe. You can go, and don't let it happen again."

A very chastened young New Zealander left that office full of good resolutions which, I am pleased to record, were not broken.

One morning shortly after our arrival at Netheravon, the Station Adjutant informed me that the Secretary of The Royal Air Force Boxing Association had phoned to ask me to box for an officers' team against London University, and would I be interested? Although keen on boxing at school, when I had boxed in the New Zealand Amateur Championships, I had not done any for some years and wasn't really keen on starting again. However, the Adjutant persuaded me it would be a good thing for my career, and so I accepted. This was the first of a number of occasions on which I boxed, and won, for the Air Force in my first year of service, finally giving it up shortly after I joined a squadron. On the first occasion of entering, I won the middleweight division in the RAF Individual Championships, and successfully defended my title the following year before hanging up my gloves for good. As a result of my success in the first year I was chosen as a member of the Royal Air Force team to tour South Africa in the summer of 1938. I was withdrawn from the team at the very last moment because the appropriate authority at Air Ministry considered it more important for me to finish my flying training course, on which I had just reached Wings standard. It was, of course, the right decision and a very lucky one for me. An aircraft carrying half the team, including Pilot Officer Moseby who replaced me, crashed near Bulawayo and all aboard were killed.

At the end of the first term at Flying Training School, the ceremony of presenting pilots' Wings was held. This involves a full ceremonial parade at which the Commander-in-Chief of Flying Training Command pins the much coveted Royal Air Force Wings on the tunics of the successful candidates. It is a momentous occasion in the life of a Royal Air Force pilot and well I recall the thrill of achievement and pride of service as I stepped forward to receive the famous emblem of a qualified pilot. It is an event in my service career second only to that when some two years later I was decorated in the field with the Distinguished Flying Cross by His Late Majesty King George VI.

Regulations were not so stringent in the senior term and I decided to buy a motor-car to save walking from the Mess to Flights four times a day. In the first term it was a rule that the pupils march to and from, more often than not, in gas masks. A relaxation on this rule therefore provided the senior term pupils with an opportunity to lord it over the first termers who enviously watched us sail by in our old crocks – they could hardly be called cars – while they marched the half-mile, nearly suffocating in their gas masks. I shared my first car, a 1934 open Austin Seven, for which I think we paid under £10, with Pilot Officer Steve Esson, about the craziest driver I could have chosen with whom to share the many exciting escapades which befell us in our nine months at Netheravon. Like the first aircraft allotted to me in an operational squadron, our little Austin still occupies a warm place in my heart for the many pleasant hours entertainment it afforded us.

In our senior term we flew Hawker Furies, still in use by front line squadrons at the time, and it was an enthralling experience and a taste of things to come. This single engined bi-plane fighter, powered by a Merlin, was a wonderful little aircraft and I shall always remember the first time I sat in the deep open cockpit, behind the small perspex windshield, and the thrill of pride at being at last behind a real fighter aircraft. It was a particularly nice aircraft for aerobatics, and I spent many hours struggling to master these manoeuvres, but never entirely succeeding in the time available at Flying School.

As the day of our passing-out drew closer, there was much speculation over the postings and not a little sadness at the thought of having to go our separate ways. It was known that there was a surplus of fighter pilots to fill current squadron vacancies and that a number of pilots were being held in a fighter pool somewhere in the North of

England. Those of us therefore who had elected to go on fighters, and had had our flying training directed to this end, were anxious as to our fate. On the night before the list was due out I had dreamt of going to Hornchurch, a station which, to the best of my knowledge, I had never even heard of. Imagine my surprise therefore when my name figured on the list as posted to 54 Squadron at Hornchurch. And they say dreams never come true!

CHAPTER THREE

Fighter Pilot

DESPITE the excitement of preparations for our departure to operational units I found it a little sad when at last the time came for parting. But the anticipation of life in an operational squadron more than offset any feelings of regret at this event. Pilot Officer Arthur Charrett, a Canadian, was posted to 54 Squadron with me, and we travelled to Hornchurch together. Art it was who christened me 'Al', a nickname or sort of halfname, which has stuck throughout my service career. It was thus he referred to me in our early days at Hornchurch, and my fellow officers there were not aware that it wasn't my full Christian name, and followed suit.

My first sight of Hornchurch, seen through the carriage windows as the train approached Elm Park, the nearest station to the airfield, was of three large hangars rising out of a sea of houses in the heavily built-up area which surrounded the small grass airfield of World War I vintage, when it was known as Sutton's Farm. It was a great disappointment to find on our arrival at Station Headquarters that 54 Squadron was on block leave and that the pilots were not due to return for another two weeks. To a suggestion that we take a few more days' leave, Art and I were not responsive, for reasons of finance. It was decided therefore that we would be temporarily attached to 74 Squadron which, with 65 Squadron, made an operational strength of three squadrons on the Station. I was sent to 'A' Flight commanded by 'Sailor' Malan, later to prove an outstanding pilot in the war and at that time leader of the flight which was to win the Sassoon Cup for flight attacks. 'Sailor,' who had been in the Merchant Navy, was older than most of his colleagues and a married man. He was most considerate towards me and although he couldn't give me much flying, because of the demands of his own pilots, he did allow me to get airborne in a Gloster Gauntlet fighter with which his squadron was equipped. We later became very firm friends and to this day exchange letters, 'Sailor' having now settled down to a farming existence in South Africa, the country of his birth.

By the time the squadron returned, I was comfortably settled in the mess and very proud of my room on the top floor in the west wing where I was most faithfully served by Fox, one of the old retainers on whom the smooth running of pre-war messes so safely depended. In my two and a half years at Hornchurch, Fox got to know my habits so well that he generally always acted before being asked, and whenever the occasion demanded, or he thought it did, was not averse to lecturing me on the observance of certain rules and regulations which I was prone to disregard.

54 Squadron was commanded by Squadron Leader Toby Pearson, who had not long been with the squadron, and my flight commander was Flight Lieutenant 'Bubbles' Love. There were eight pilots in each flight, three of whom were Sergeant Pilots. The squadron was equipped with Gloster Gladiators, a bi-plane with enclosed cockpit and four Browning guns, and later famous for its work in Malta and Norway.

The first week in the squadron was spent reading orders, learning about the aircraft, and generally doing all the dogsbody jobs such as officer-in-charge of clothing and pay parades, tasks which fell to the lot of all new pilots. I was also saddled with the Navigation Inventory, again something which was normally foisted on to new arrivals. In the course of doing a check on this inventory I found that one item was deficient – an Oxometer. This deficiency worried me quite a lot – as it had done many new Pilot Officers and would do many more – and, at last, I asked the flight commander what it was, not having wanted to do so sooner and thus display my ignorance. All he would say was that it was a very important piece of navigational equipment and that I had better find it or I would be required to report the loss to the Station Commander personally. A most frightening thought to a very junior officer on his first operational station. It was some days before I realized that no such item of equipment existed and that it was a trick played on all new pilots and one in which everyone, from the Station Commander downwards, participated.

My immediate successor to the Navigation Inventory was a young, and most serious, Pilot Officer who got so worked up about the missing Oxometer that it was decided to carry the joke a little further. With the co-operation of the station workshops an impressive looking gadget was constructed and fitted on to the pitot head tube of an aircraft. The worried inventory holder was informed that the Oxometer had been found and that it was across at 74 Squadron's hangar. When the officer arrived there to collect it a pilot was already seated in the cockpit of a Gauntlet aircraft and the Oxometer was fitted on the end of the pitot tube (from which the air speed is measured).

"You might as well let me test this equipment before you take it away," said the pilot to a now smiling inventory holder. "Will you just blow into the mouthpiece of the instrument and I will check that it registers on the air-speed indicator in the cockpit, as it should do. You know, of course, that an Oxometer is an instrument for measuring speed?"

Our hero needed no second bidding; with gusto, he blew into the mouthpiece only to be covered with a fine spray of soot which had been placed inside the gadget and now issued under pressure from tiny holes just above the mouthpiece. Squadron pilots, concealed in various spots around the hangar, witnessed and enjoyed this amazing experiment.

I was allotted Gladiator 7927 as my particular squadron aircraft, and the fitter and rigger who were also assigned to this aircraft became, from that day onwards, a part of my daily existence in the squadron. If I put up a good show at formation, gunnery or any other aspect of training they rejoiced in my success and were proud to point me out as their pilot. If, on the other hand, I was observed to be the one that bounced during a squadron landing, or was out of position when the squadron crossed the airfield, I was greeted on my return to the squadron lines by unuttered rebuke. Thus a feeling of pride was built up at pilot, ground crew, and flight level until an end result, *esprit de corps* at squadron level, was assured. It was to pay dividends beyond all measure in the summer of 1940. It is a great pity that the system was not possible in the rapid war expansion which followed.

On my third trip in a Gladiator, and my first away from the airfield, I was unfortunate enough to have engine failure, a rare event in the squadron and particularly on Gladiators. I was on a sector reconnaissance at the time, and doing a little cloud flying for good measure, when the airscrew stopped without warning. Forced landings were an essential part of our training, but I hadn't yet practised one on a Gladiator and it was with a feeling of uneasiness that I faced up to the prospect. My height was barely 1,500ft, leaving little room for mistakes, but I managed to land the aircraft undamaged in a field from which it was later flown out by the flight commander. A pat on the back from the Commanding Officer for a successful forced landing was a nice beginning to my flying days in 54 Squadron.

Gleaming white overalls were the order of the day for 54 Squadron fighter pilots and on the pocket the squadron badge was proudly displayed, but only after a pilot had served his three months qualifying period in the squadron at the end of which time he was tested by the squadron commander in formation, aerobatics and general flying ability. It was a proud day when I submitted my Flying Log Book to have the following endorsement signed on the first page, used for certificates of qualification: "...Certified that Pilot Officer A C Deere has qualified as first pilot on fighter landplanes WEF 1-1-39."

The majority of our training in a pre-war fighter squadron was directed at achieving perfection in formation with a view to ensuring the success of the flight and squadron attacks we so assiduously practised. These were known as Fighting Area

Attacks – Fighter Command was originally known as Fighting Area – and consisted of a series of five different types of formation attack. The order to attack was always preceded by the flight commander designating the number of the attack, viz. "FAA Attack No. 5 – Go." These attacks provided wonderful training for formation drill, but were worthless when related to effective shooting. There was never sufficient time to get one's sights on the target, the business of keeping station being the prime requirement. I know it is easy to be wise after the event, but looking back now on my peaceful days in a squadron I can see how dreadfully we neglected gunnery practice, live or by means of cine-films, and what an important part it plays in the make-up of a successful fighter pilot. The Air Ministry was, of course, fighting a constant battle to get suitable ranges – as it is today – and the monetary allowance for practice ammunition was cut to a minimum in an expanding Air Force which needed all the cash it could squeeze out of the Treasury to provide new pilots and aircraft to meet the number of squadrons required by the various Defence Budgets. Squadron morale carried us safely through the early fighter battles of the war, not ability to shoot straight.

They were happy days and I soon came to love the Gladiator, a docile and gentlemanly fighter and a wonderful aircraft for flight aerobatics. This latter mode of flying was a speciality in 54 Squadron whose team, under the able leadership of Flight Lieutenant P E Warcup, won the competition held in 1939 before a gathering of Members of Parliament at Northolt. Later on when the squadron was equipped with Spitfires I became a member of the team, and in the latter part of my stay with the squadron led my own flight on this most difficult of all flying thrills. Gladiator night flying over a brilliantly lit, pre-war London was also wonderful fun. By virtue of its slow speed and robust qualities, it was possible to dive the Gladiator almost vertically at the ground delaying the pull out until the very last moment. This manoeuvre was one which we had great delight in performing when on night flying detail with the searchlights. The idea was to dive straight down their beams, delaying our pull out until the very last moment so as to frighten the searchlight crews who, under the impression that they were blinding us, invariably doused their lights.

At the time of the Munich crisis 54 Squadron, like most other squadrons in Fighter Command, was still equipped with Gladiators. This fact, however, did not dampen the enthusiasm of its pilots for war. Visions of great air battles floated before us as, with brush and paint tin, we laboured to assist our ground crews to camouflage the beautifully kept and shining silver Gladiators. Squadron markings, colours and individual commanders' flags all fell foul of the hastily prepared, and generously applied, concoction which had been mixed from the station's dope and paint supplies. In many ways it was a heartrending operation having to desecrate one's beautiful Gladiator, but thoughts of aerial combat made the task a bearable one. It is callous and wrong to say it, but when "peace in our time" was agreed, I was horribly disappointed. In later years, the scars of combat on me, I often thought what would have been our fate if we had gone to war with the German Air Force in September 1938. There is only one answer; we would have been swept from the skies in our Gladiators and Gauntlets and the rest of our outmoded machinery. Courage would not have been enough against the then Messerschmitt-equipped Luftwaffe. Neville Chamberlain has since been sneered at, but the year of grace afforded by his visit to Munich enabled the Air Force to meet the onslaught, when it did come, on an equal footing at least in terms of quality of fighter aircraft.

Early in 1939 I joined Rosslyn Park Rugby Club, and played in some wonderful games, particularly those in which I played as inside centre to the famous Prince Obolensky. One day Squadron Leader George Beamish, the famous Irish International, asked me if I would like a game for his old club, Leicester Tigers, as a guest player. As he was then principal RAF selector I of course agreed. It wasn't until I walked on to the field at Leicester that I found I was facing my own club. It was a most embarassing situation, especially as I scored a try, and Leicester won by nine points to three; luckily my clubmates treated the whole thing as a huge joke.

On March 6th, 1939, I flew my first Spitfire, an aircraft very little different from the later Marks with which the RAF finished the war. In many respects, however, it was a nicer aircraft and certainly much lighter than subsequent Marks which became over-powered and over-weighted with armour plating and cannons. The transition from slow bi-planes to the faster monoplanes was effected without fuss, and in a matter of weeks we were nearly as competent on Spitfires as we had been on Gladiators. When one hundred per cent established with Spitfires, 54 Squadron flew its Gladiators up to Turnhouse to be handed over to 603 Auxiliary Squadron, the week-enders from Edinburgh. On the way up the squadron landed at Driffield to refuel and I was able to meet up again with Jack McKay who was thoroughly enjoying himself as a now fully established bomber pilot on Whitley aircraft, our front line bomber of the period. It was grand seeing him again – and 'Spud' Miller also, a great friend who had come over with us – and to hear that they, too, had never for one single moment regretted the decision to join the Royal Air Force.

Two days after my first flight in a Spitfire, I was sent down to Eastleigh airfield near Southampton to collect a new aircraft from the Supermarine Works where the Spitfire was produced.

The weather was pretty bad for the trip and I had the greatest difficulty finding Hornchurch. Such was my relief when I did find the airfield that I couldn't resist a quick beat-up, very much frowned on in those days. I noticed as I taxied towards the squadron hangar after landing that there was more than the normal complement of pilots to greet me. I was soon to learn why. Not only had I committed the sin of beating up the airfield, I had neglected to change from fine to coarse pitch after take-off from Eastleigh with the result that there was a great deal more noise than normal on my quite small beat-up and, worse still, the brand new Spitfire was smothered in oil thrown out by the over-revving engine. A very red-faced Pilot Officer faced an irate 'Bubbles' Love, my flight commander, who was decent enough to let the matter rest at a good "ticking-off."

Training on Spitfires followed the same pattern as on Gladiators, except that we did a little more cine-gun work to get practice on the new reflector sight with which the aircraft was fitted.

One unsatisfactory piece of equipment was the small transmitter which emitted a regular squadron identification signal to enable Operations to fix the position of aircraft. Unfortunately whenever the instrument (known to pilots as 'Pip-Squeak') was transmitting its signal, the pilot was unable to hear or be heard, and thus he missed many messages. Also the transmitters tended to get out of phase and aircraft were often wrongly identified as a result. This short-coming was demonstrated on one famous occasion when a flight from 74 Squadron, led by Flight Lieutenant Paddy Treacy, was being homed on fixes taken from the transmission of a 54 Squadron aircraft. Finally, Paddy when out of R/T range and short of fuel, let down below cloud to find himself over France where his flight force-landed, with a certain amount of damage to aircraft. Voice fixing, whereby the pilot merely pressed his R/T switch for a short period, eventually replaced this most unreliable system.

I had my first really frightening incident in an aircraft in May 1939, when I was overcome by anoxia during a height climb in a Spitfire. The oxygen system then in use required the pilot to regulate the flow with increasing height, usually at every 5,000ft. On the particular trip in question I had entered cloud at about 2,000ft and was still in it at 27,000ft. I was so busy flying on instruments that I had forgotten to turn up the oxygen flow as my height increased and although I was getting a small amount, having set it to 5,000ft before take-off, it was insufficient to avoid the effects of lack of oxygen which overcame me. I had just broken cloud, and was aware of the dazzling sun and blue sky, when I passed out. When I came to I was still, as I thought momentarily, pointing at the blue sky above. In fact, as I very quickly realized, I was diving at the sea in a patch of sky completely clear of cloud, and at a tremendous speed. I throttled back immediately I realized this, and pulled hard back on the control column. I managed to get the aircraft out of the dive but it was a near thing, and I was very much shaken and in great pain from what turned out to be a burst ear-drum. This little incident put me off flying for three months and ever since my right ear, with its resultant scar, has been suspect by the various medical officers who have examined me from time to time in the course of annual medical examinations in the Royal Air Force. In fact, it has given no trouble since, other than being difficult to clear when coming down quickly from heights.

The excitement and preparation for war was on us again as, in those fateful weeks before Hitler attacked Poland, units were brought on to a war footing. Aircraft were dispersed away from the hangars and along the far side of the airfield, and tents hastily erected for air and ground crews. The long hours of readiness, when pilots were required to be near their aircraft, dressed and ready to get off at a moment's notice, now began and continued until 1943, when the weakened Luftwaffe no longer offered any daylight threat to this country. Next, blast protection bays were built for our Spitfires. Flying was severely restricted because of the necessity to conserve aircraft hours, and the day was usually spent at dispersal filling and humping sand bags to build dispersal pens, one for each operational aircraft. We worked stripped to the waist, alongside civilians who were being paid a very generous hourly rate to do the same job.

On the very first Sunday of the war, a lone aircraft returning from patrol in the Channel was plotted as hostile and a squadron was scrambled to investigate. This squadron became split and sections from it were in turn plotted as hostile, and more aircraft sent off to investigate until eventually the operations room tables, on which were plotted the raids, were cluttered with suspect plots. For about an hour chaos reigned, and in this time nearly all the squadrons based to the East of London had been scrambled. I had trouble starting my aircraft and was late getting off and in the hour I was airborne I spent the whole time trying to join up with my squadron which was receiving so many vectors that it was impossible to follow them. When I did eventually join up, the squadron was near Chatham where the anti-aircraft guns heralded our presence by some lusty salvoes, at which we hastily altered course despite the controller still insisting that we investigate in the area. Not all the incidents connected with the first abortive attempt of the war were amusing – one had fatal consequences. 74 Squadron led by 'Sailor' Malan had also been sent off and their rear section of three encountered a pair of Hurricanes from nearby North Weald which, in mistake for enemy and in the excitement of this glorious muddle, they attacked and shot down, killing one of the pilots.

This truly amazing shambles – known to those pilots who participated as the 'Battle of Barking Creek' – was just what was needed to iron out some of the many snags which existed in our control and reporting system and to convince those who were responsible that a great deal of training of controllers, plotters and radar operators, all of whom had been hastily drafted in on the first emergency call-up, was still required before the system could be considered in any way reliable. It is significant to note that on five out of my next six training flights I was engaged on tactical exercises in co-operation with the control and reporting organization.

I had expected a sudden intake of new pilots into the squadron when war was declared but there was the barest trickle in the months that followed, and these were pilots who had been in the pipe line when war was declared with, perhaps, their final training period slightly shortened. One of the first to arrive was Pilot Officer Colin Gray who, on one of his first trips in a Spitfire, had the misfortune on landing to remove the aircraft's undercarriage on one of the sand-bag blast shelters which now ringed the airfield. The shelters reduced the airfield's effective landing area considerably, and this had caused Colin to make a low motoring approach. Although he was not aware of their presence, Colin was being watched by the Commander-in-Chief and the Station Commander; the former was paying a routine visit to the station. When the Commander-in-Chief saw the aircraft ploughing along the airfield on its belly, he turned to the Station Commander and said, "I could have sworn that the pilot had his wheels down!"

The Station Commander was not at all pleased with this exhibition of how not to do it in front of the great man himself and Colin, now sporting two beautiful black eyes, was marched into his presence. It was all the squadron commander could do to dissuade him from having the culprit posted to a drogue-towing outfit as punishment. What a fortunate day for 54 Squadron, and Fighter Command, that Colin was at Hornchurch when so sorely needed a few short months later.

The weary hours of readiness, occasional scrambles, some training flying, and boring convoy patrols were our lot throughout the winter of 1939–40. Such enforced activity provided plenty of scope for the practical joker; one such being Vincent Byrne, in 74 Squadron, who delighted in taking the 'micky' out of a fellow Irishman in the squadron – Flight Lieutenant Paddy Treacy. On one particular occasion Paddy was acting in the capacity of Commanding Officer and received a telephone call from the Guard Room to say that the Station Commander accompanied by the Air Officer Commanding was on the way down to the squadron dispersal and wished to have a word with the pilots. Ten minutes later, when the Station

Commander's car appeared, Paddy had all the pilots lined up in front of their aircraft and was himself standing stiffly at attention to greet the 'old man' as his car drew up in front of the dispersal site. As the car slowed down in front of him Paddy saluted smartly to be greeted by a smiling and familiar face, surmounted by a concocted 'brass' hat, at the window of the car and a voice which said, "You can stand at ease now, Treacle." A very very angry and humiliated Paddy, shook his fist at the departing Flying Officer Byrne. From that day onwards Paddy Treacy became 'Treacle' Treacy.

Night readiness was a thing we most hated and, to be truthful, feared. Very few of us had any experience of night flying on Spitfires, and that had been strictly limited to circuits and landings or short sorties away from the airfields and always under the most favourable weather conditions. It was a grim prospect therefore to be shot off into the black night with an indifferent radio and limited homing aids. It always amazed me that more pilots were not killed in this period before the specialist night fighters were introduced. I recall two occasions when fatal casualties might have resulted from night details, and I was concerned in both. Together with Don Ross, a Canadian, as my number two, I had volunteered to do an extra patrol over an important channel convoy off Harwich, which entailed returning in the darkness. We were well out of R/T range when we eventually left the convoy, and it wasn't until I had been flying for about five minutes on an approximate heading for home that I heard the controller at Hornchurch. On contact, I was given a series of vectors for base, which I followed religiously. It was now pitch black and completely horizontal and, with Don tucked in close and our navigation lights burning, I was flying almost solely on instruments. I knew from the sudden stabbing of searchlights which began to play around our aircraft that I must be now crossing the coast. This was confirmed in the most unexpected manner.

"Look out, Red Leader, there's a balloon straight ahead of us," shouted Don over the R/T.

There was barely time to glance up from the instrument panel before we were on top of the balloons. Instinctively I pulled back on the stick and miraculously passed over the barrage, with literally inches to spare and Don still tucked in beside me. In no uncertain terms I cursed the fool controller who had vectored us into the middle of the Harwich balloons. Unhappily, I forgot that my R/T was in automatic transmit, and everything I said was heard in the Operations Room at Hornchurch. No doubt it caused the controllers to smile – to say nothing of blushing WAAF plotters – but unfortunately for me the Station Commander was present on the Controller's dais: to him, it wasn't amusing.

Back at base the weather had fogged in, but we were forced to have a go at landing as neither of us had sufficient fuel for a diversion. I sent Don in first, and he landed safely. But in the few minutes that it had taken him to make his approach and landing the fog had thickened considerably so that when I lined up on the final approach, it was solid up to about 500ft. From 1,000ft the "goose-neck" flares were clearly visible but at a few hundred feet lower they were completely blanked out by the fog. When this blanketing occurred on the final approach I concentrated solely on my instruments, said a quick prayer, and hoped for the best. In fact, I touched down on the wrong side of the Chance Light (put at the landing end of the flare-path to light the touchdown area, but not used on this occasion) and bounced a considerable height – some onlookers said over the 12ft high Chance Light – to finally finish up entangled in the back fence, but in one piece.

Having volunteered for the patrol, and having got down reasonably intact under such trying circumstances, it was a little annoying, on return to dispersal, to be reprimanded for using bad language over the R/T.

A similar experience befell me on a later occasion when as

leader of one of two sections which were in the air on another unpleasant night, I was again caught by the fog coming down unexpectedly, as it was wont to do at Hornchurch. I managed to land undamaged at Hornchurch but my number three crashed on landing, not seriously, and the number two was diverted to Rochford where he landed almost out of fuel. One aircraft from the other section also crashed.

That very cold winter of 1939-40 was spent at Rochford airfield to which the squadron had moved some few weeks earlier. It was during our stay there that we were visited by Godfrey Winn who wrote an article on 'What is a Fighter Pilot?', or some such title, as a result of a day spent chatting to the 54 Squadron pilots. I recall him leaning over my shoulder in the mess, and asking me what I was reading. It was a shinybacked novel I had found lying in a locker in the building which served as a temporary officers' mess, and I was reading it to fill in time as much as anything. I was amused therefore to read in his article, which appeared later in the *Sunday Express*, that, "among other things he may read *No Orchids for Miss Blandish*." I wonder if the resultant popularity of that book had anything to do with his article.

The arrival of better weather in the spring of 1940, and the offensive on the Western Front which followed it, raised us from the lethargy of a winter of boredom to hopeful activity and thoughts of 'Action at last'. The frustrating hours on readiness, the many pointless scrambles and the fruitless convoy patrols were soon to be replaced by the real thing. The long waiting period, which had been invaluable in sorting out the many teething troubles in the control and reporting system, and in eliminating the chinks in Fighter Command's armour, was now at an end.

CHAPTER FOUR

Rescue at Calais/Marck

I T came as no great surprise to us when on the afternoon of the 15th May we learned that there was to be a briefing that evening for offensive operations the following day over the French and Belgian coasts in support of the British Army's withdrawal. This was the moment we had trained for and dreamed about. Excitement ran high in the squadron and on the faces of the ever-faithful ground crew there was an expression of purposeful endeavour for the first time in months.

That evening the pilots of 54 Squadron assembled in the officers' mess billiard room for a briefing by the Station Commander. The billiard room may seem a strange place for an operational briefing but at that stage of the war fighter briefing rooms were unknown. There was no need for any; our operations were purely defensive and aircraft were usually launched into the air at a moment's notice, the pilots having only the vaguest idea of what to expect. As I gazed around me, I studied the faces of my fellow pilots and wondered what each was thinking and how many would be here tomorrow night and the nights that were to follow the active phase we were now entering.

One group in particular attracted my attention. In it were most of my contemporaries in the squadron, including the two flight commanders. The central figure was, as always, Pilot Officer George Gribble. Very English, very good looking and bubbling over with the enthusiasm of his twenty years, he epitomized the product of the public school; young yet mature, carefree yet serious when the situation required and above all possessing a courageous gaiety which he was later to display in abundance. Next to him stood his great friend Pilot Officer 'Wonky' Way whose tall, angular frame had earned him such an unusual nickname. 'Wonky' was a product of Cranwell where he had won the Groves Memorial prize for the best all-round pilot on his course. He was an amusing and most likeable officer who was to fall early in the Battle of Britain when the contest was hottest and the odds greatest. In contrast to 'Wonky' there was Pilot Officer Colin Gray; short and wiry, he was a fellow New Zealander, and a fairly recent arrival in the squadron. His twin brother Ken had already won a DFC for piloting a crippled bomber back to base, and Colin was shortly to be similarly decorated and to emerge from the Battle of Britain as one of the highest-scoring fighter pilots. Then there were the two flight commanders Max Pearson and 'Prof' Leathart whose nickname stemmed from his academic ability at all things algebraical. Max's dark face was lit with a beaming smile of anticipation; he loved flying and couldn't wait to come to grips with the real thing. 'Prof', on the other hand, was plucking his cheek with nervous fingers, a gesture of his when tension was high, and gazing into space as if summing up the odds we were likely to meet. Last but by no means least, as he was to prove, was Pilot Officer Johnny Allen. A quiet and religious type, he seemed out of place in the bloodthirsty atmosphere prevailing in the room. He too was to fall early in the Battle of Britain but not before he had established himself as a courageous and determined fighter. Thus they stood, each in his own peculiar way different from the other yet all with a common purpose and a single aim, the aim of all fighter pilots, – 'seek and destroy.'

At the sound of approaching footsteps the hum of voices dropped to a whisper and then to silence as, brisk and businesslike, the Station Commander, Wing Commander 'Boy' Bouchier (better known to the Hornchurch pilots as 'Daddy') entered the room. Quietly he informed us that things were very serious in France and that certain British withdrawals were planned in the direction of Dunkirk and Calais. The Commander-in-Chief Fighter Command had been directed to provide as much air cover as possible for these planned withdrawals and Spitfire squadrons, operating from home bases, were to be used for this task. There was no hint of a full scale withdrawal; it was as the daily papers said, "a withdrawal according to plan." 54 Squadron was to take off as soon as possible after first light tomorrow to patrol about 10 miles inland from Calais-Dunkirk to engage any enemy aircraft operating in the area. Then followed a few generalities and a final, "Good luck, good shooting and show 'em what 54 can do."

So it came about that at 0800 hours on Wednesday, 16th May, twelve Spitfires bounced across the grassy surface of Hornchurch airfield and becoming airborne headed eastwards for the French coast. I was one of the twelve, confidently piloting my *Kiwi I*, as I had named my Spitfire, towards the Channel, and action. Pride of place on this memorable flight had been given to the twelve most experienced pilots, to the annoyance of the five left on the ground. Their turn was to come, and for some but once.

Steadily we climbed to 15,000ft where we levelled out and throttled back to an economical cruising speed. Our instructions were to stay in the area as long as possible and it was important therefore to conserve fuel for the combat zone. Slowly the broken coastline of Kent was left behind to be replaced by the sand-fringed shores of Northern France and Belgium now gradually taking shape ahead. In a matter of minutes the formation was crossing in over Calais. As it did so there was a hum in the earphones as the R/T was switched on and the CO's voice crackled over the air, "Hornet squadron battle formation, battle formation, GO." Symmetrically, like the fingers of an opening hand, the sections spread outwards. As my eyes scanned the empty skies I was conscious of a feeling of exhilaration and tenseness akin to that experienced before an important sporting event. There was no feeling of fear; how could there be? Like the child who plays with fire my fingers had not yet been burned by the flames of combat. All was still below us and no movement disturbed the peaceful French countryside which presented a panorama of changing patterns stretching into the distance finally to merge with the distant horizon.

For thirty minutes we cruised up and down our patrol line and, as each succeeding minute ticked by and there was no sign of the enemy, expectation gave way to doubt, doubt to uncertainty and uncertainty to a final bitter disappointment as the formation finally turned homewards. Back at base the ground crews concealed their disappointment in the feverish activity of refuelling, while the pilots walked dejectedly towards the dispersal hut. On entering the hut we were confronted with eager questions from those who has been left behind.

"What did it feel like, Al, knowing that at any moment a Hun might pop up and take a pot at you?" asked Colin Gray.

"Well," I answered, "At first I was tingling all over with excitement but when after a time nothing happened, I was damn bored."

"To my way of thinking," piped up George Gribble, "it was a waste of time flying so high and only along the coast. Why the hell didn't we go inland a bit, that way we might have stirred up some trouble?"

"Now, George," said the squadron commander who had overheard this remark, "I know how you feel, but orders are orders; perhaps next time we may have a bit more freedom of action. After all, it is a bit too soon to expect the Luftwaffe to be about in any numbers. It will take a bit before their newly acquired airfields can be put to use. When that happens we'll probably see more than enough of the Luftwaffe."

A general discussion now followed on the tactics to be used on the next show, and it was agreed that despite the necessity to conserve fuel for the patrol area, we should fly a little faster on the way out. As 'Wonky' so aptly put it, "We were going so slowly that I felt as if I was resting my bottom on the section below me."

Although this trip marked the commencement of what was

to be an intensive period of offensive operations, the nearness of the newly acquired Hun air bases put a greater emphasis than ever on the air defence of our own shores. This meant maintaining a high state of readiness by those squadrons not operating over Northern France with the result that as soon as we landed and refuelled we reverted to the now boring task of keeping pilots in cockpits ready for immediate take-off.

For the next seven days the squadron alternated between long periods of readiness both by night and day, and patrols in the Calais/Dunkirk area. On each successive trip we penetrated a little further inland and as our confidence grew we flew longer and lower in the hope that the Huns would see us and give battle. But to no avail; I first saw the famous black cross on a defensive patrol off the North Foreland, and then only fleetingly. As number two in a section of three, I spotted a Heinkel III skimming along at cloud top height some 5,000ft below us. Diving full throttle I was unable to get within firing range before being spotted by the pilot who quickly sought the comforting cover of the nearby cloud from which he never reappeared.

Johnny Allen was the first member of the squadron to fire a shot in anger. On the morning of the 21st May he had been ordered off to investigate a doubtful plot in the Channel. The word doubtful was an understatement, the plot turned out to be twenty Junkers 88s in close formation. Despite the fact that he was alone, his number two having returned with engine trouble, and regardless of the odds Johnny sailed into attack. Pressing home his attack despite heavy cross fire, he managed to destroy one of the enemy to record 54 Squadron's first confirmed victory.

May 23rd was destined to be the beginning of the shooting war so far as 54 Squadron was concerned, myself in particular. We did our usual patrol at dawn – the squadron's 12th for the week just ended – and returned once again with guns unfired. 74 Squadron had followed us on patrol, and it was they who drew first blood. When their section returned to land it was noticeable that the leading edges of the wings of many of the aircraft were black with burnt cordite denoting that the guns had been fired. Seeing this I lost no time in driving around to their dispersal to talk to the pilots as they landed. The first to land was 'Sailor' Malan, who on seeing me said: "Hello, Al, I might have known you would be sniffing around to find out the form. I always said that the 'Tigers' (as 74 Squadron was known) would be the first to get among them; aren't you envious?"

"You bet I am, 'Sailor', tell me more."

"Sorry, haven't got time. All I can say is that we were jumped, and all because some bloody fool would keep nattering on the R/T with the result that when Paddy Treacy gave a sighting report only one or two of the chaps heard it. On top of that the CO had engine trouble, and all in all it was a confusing and frustrating engagement. I think he finally made Calais/Marck airfield where he landed successfully."

There seemed little point in hanging around 74 Squadron dispersal so I took myself off to the mess for a long-delayed breakfast prior to going on readiness at 9 o'clock. While breakfasting with 'Wonky' I was called to the telephone to speak to 'Prof' Leathart, the flight commander.

"Al," he said, "will you collect Johnny Allen and get down here right away for immediate take-off. The Station Commander has suggested to Group that we fly the Master (a two-seater training type aircraft) over to Calais/Marck to pick up the CO of 74 Squadron. The AOC has agreed and we have been given the job; I'll fly the Master and you and Johnny can act as escort in a couple of Spitfires. I understand that there is a lot of enemy activity over there now and I think we stand more chance of getting away with it if just the three of us go. We can nip across at sea level and should avoid being spotted by Hun fighters as the airfield is right on the coast."

The trip to dispersal in my old barouche was made in record time. The plan was for the Master to land at Calais/Marck, pick up the squadron commander, if he was still on the airfield, and take-off again immediately without stopping the engine. Johnny and I were to remain orbitting the airfield to protect the Master whilst landing and taking off. It sounded a piece of cake. The trip out was uneventful and the Master landed without incident. There was broken cloud over the area which meant there was a likelihood of being surprised from above. I decided therefore to send Johnny above cloud, at about 8,000ft, while I remained below circling the airfield. I watched the Master taxi towards a small hangar, and was wondering if his passenger was about, when an excited yell from the usually placid Johnny pierced my ear-drums.

"Al, they're here. Huns! about a dozen just below me and making towards the airfield. I'm going in to have a go at them."

"OK, Johnny, for God's sake keep me informed. I must remain in sight of the airfield to try and warn 'Prof' and stop him taking off."

To warn the Master was not going to be easy. It carried no R/T and at best I could dive down towards where it stood on the airfield and waggle my wings hoping that 'Prof' would interpret this as a danger signal. With these thoughts in mind I wheeled my Spitfire around only to see the Master taxi-ing out for take-off. At the very moment I turned, a Messerschmitt 109 came hurtling through the clouds straight for the defenceless Master which by now was just becoming airborne. By the grace of God the hun flew right across my line of flight and I was able to give him a quick burst of fire which I knew had little hope of hitting him but which, I hoped, would divert his attention from the Master. It did, but not before a stream of tracer spouted from his guns and disappeared, it seemed, into the fuselage of the trainer. By this time my throttle was fully open and with the stick hard back to turn inside the Me 109 I was in range to fire. Just as I did so I heard Johnny screaming on the R/T.

"Red One – I'm surrounded, can you help me?"

"Try and hang on, Johnny, till I kill this bastard in front of me, and I'll be right up."

In a last desperate attempt to avoid my fire, the Hun pilot straightened from his turn and pulled vertically upwards, thus writing his own death warrant, he presented me with a perfect no-deflection shot from dead below and I made no mistake. Smoke began to pour from his engine as the aircraft, now at the top of its climb, heeled slowly over in an uncontrolled stall and plunged vertically into the water's edge from about 3,000ft. Immediately I broke back towards the airfield thankful to observe the Master parked safely by the perimeter fence apparently unharmed. Now to help Johnny.

"Hello, Red Two, how goes it?" I called over the R/T. "I'm coming up now."

Zooming up through the cloud I found myself crossing the path of two Me 109s which were diving inland. They must have seen me at the same moment because immediately the leader went into a steep turn. Again I found no difficulty in keeping inside the turn and was soon in range to fire. A long burst at the number two caused bits to fly off his aircraft which rolled on to its back and careered earthwards. Whether or not he was *hors de combat* I couldn't be sure but the leader was still there and must be dealt with. Reversing his turn very skilfully he too dived towards the ground. Momentarily I lost distance, but I had got in range again before he flattened out above the tree tops and headed homewards. A quick burst caused him to whip into another turn and from this point onwards he did everything possible to shake me off. After a second burst I ran out of ammunition but determined to stay behind him for as long as possible, if for no other reason than the fact that I didn't know quite how to break off the engagement. I had the feeling that he must know I was out of ammunition and was just waiting for me to turn for home. Fortunately for me his next manoeuvre was to straighten out and determinedly head eastwards at which I pulled hard back on the stick and looped through the broken cloud before rolling out and diving full throttle towards the coast.

I now called Johnny on the R/T and was relieved to hear his cheerful but somewhat breathless voice answer.

"I'm just crossing out North of Calais but am rather worried about my aircraft. I can't see any holes but felt hits and she doesn't seem to be flying quite right. I'll make for the North Foreland at my present height of 8,000ft. See if you can join up."

We managed to join up in mid-Channel and sure enough his aircraft had been holed. However, it didn't seem too bad and on my advice he decided to continue back to Hornchurch rather than land forward at Manston. He accomplished a safe landing to the accompaniment of a victory roll from me.

Excited pilots and ground crew clustered around us on the ground and our stories had to be recounted in detail. Johnny's only comment was that he hoped next time he encountered the Huns there would be fewer of them and he would not be alone; after all odds of 20 to 1 and 12 to 1 in consecutive engagements were too much for one's nerves.

Shortly afterwards 'Prof' arrived in the Master with his passenger, both none the worse for wear. From the safety of a ditch, into which he had dived on scrambling out of his aircraft, he had observed the air battle and was able to give his account of the affray. His story is best related by quoting verbatim from the official intelligence report he later made:

"…The moment I left the ground I saw from the activities of Red one that something was amiss. Almost at once a Me 109 appeared ahead of me and commenced firing. I pulled around in a tight turn observing as I did so the Messerschmitt shoot past me. I literally banged the aircraft on to the ground and evacuated the cockpit with all possible speed, diving into the safety of a ditch which ran along the airfield perimeter. Just as I did so I saw a Me 109 come hurtling out of the clouds to crash with a tremendous explosion a few hundred yards away. Almost simultaneously another Me 109 exploded as it hit the sea to my left.

From the comparative safety of the ditch my passenger and I caught momentary glimpses of the dog-fight as first Me 109 and then Spitfire came hurtling through the cloud banks only to scream upwards again. It was all over in a matter of about ten minutes but not before we observed a third enemy aircraft crash in flames. We waited about ten minutes after the fight ended, and when it seemed safe made a hasty take-off and a rather frightened trip back to England and safety."

As a result of my prolonged fight with the last Me 109, it was possible to assess the relative performance of the two aircraft. In the early engagements between the British Hurricanes in France and the 109s the speed and climb of the latter had become legendary and were claimed by many to be far superior to that of the Spitfire. I was able to refute this contention and indeed was confident that, except in a dive, the Spitfire was superior in most other fields and, like the Hurricane, vastly more manoeuvrable. The superior rate of climb was, however, due mostly to the type of Spitfire with which my squadron was equipped. Aircraft of 54 Squadron were fitted with the Rotol constant speed airscrew on which we had been doing trials when the fighting started. Other Spitfires were, at that stage, using a two speed airscrew (ie. either fully fine pitch or fully coarse) which meant that they lost performance in a sustained climb. There was a great deal of scepticism about my claim that the Spitfire was superior to the Messerschmitt 109; there were those who frankly disbelieved me, saying that it was contrary to published performance figures. Later events, however, proved me to be right.

In the mess at lunch I ran into Bob Tuck who had flown in that morning with 92 Squadron which he had joined earlier in the year from 65 Squadron at Hornchurch. He was with his CO, Roger Bushell, to whom he introduced me. What a nice chap Roger was and what a courageous officer he was later to prove when, as a prisoner-of-war, he was one of the leaders in the now famous mass escape from Stalag Luft 3, an undertaking for which he was shot by the Germans. Roger and Bob were on their way down to dispersal to prepare for their squadron's first patrol over France. It turned out to be the first and last for Roger, who was shot down and last seen standing near his crashed Spitfire waving the gaily coloured scarf he always wore in such a manner as to imply, "Don't worry, I'll be back." Unfortunately he never made it.

While at dispersal preparing for the next patrol, the CO handed me a signal from the Air Officer Commanding No. 11 Group, Air Vice-Marshal Keith Park, saying as he did so, "You can add my congratulations to those in the signal, Al, I'm very proud of yours and Johnny's effort this morning." The signal, which is still in my possession today, reads:

> "Air Officer Commanding sends congratulations to 54 Squadron on the magnificent fight put up by Flying Officers Deere and Allen who so severely punished superior numbers this morning."

At 1430 hours the squadron was once again airborne and *en route* for the by now familiar coastline of Northern France, under orders to patrol inland of Dunkirk/Calais. I was flying as number two in red section which led by the 'Prof' had Johnny Allen as number three. This was our tenth offensive patrol as a section since the emergency began and was to prove the first of many successful engagements, the Master episode excluded, in which we figured together as a team. On this patrol all of us had the feeling that something would happen. Prior to take-off, we learned that two other Hornchurch squadrons had been engaged and that there was considerable enemy activity over the area. The squadron had not been on patrol very long before Max Pearson's voice screeched over the R/T, "Tallyho, tallyho, enemy aircraft above and ahead." About 3,000ft above us and clearly silhouetted against a blue sky, a large formation of German bombers ploughed westwards towards Dunkirk unmolested and apparently unprotected. "Sitting ducks," I thought.

"Hornet squadron, full throttle, climbing to attack," came the order from 'Prof' who was leading the squadron.

It seemed an age before we made the extra 3,000ft in height and even longer before we closed the gap to firing range.

"Hornet squadron, No. 5 attack, No. 5 attack, GO."

Simultaneously the sections fanned out into the various echelons necessary for this type of attack and as they did so individual pilots selected a particular bomber target. So far, all very nice and exactly according to the book. But we had reckoned without interference from fighter escort; after all no consideration had been given to it in designing this type of attack and our peacetime training had not envisaged interference from escort fighters. Experience is dearly bought.

"Christ, Messerschmitts – BREAK, BREAK."

There was no need for a second warning. At the word "break" and with one accord, the squadron split in all directions, all thoughts of blazing enemy bombers momentarily ousted by the desire to survive. Messerschmitts hurtled through the formation. As I pulled back violently on the stick into a steep turn, one fairly singed my eyebrows as it screamed past my port wing, the pilot endeavouring unsuccessfully to haul his aircraft around to attack me. Coming out of the turn, when it seemed safe to do so, I spotted a Me 109 diving away below me and gave chase immediately. He saw me almost at once and half-rolled for the deck with me after him. Down we went throttles fully open, engines roaring and each determined to get the last ounce out of his straining aircraft. From 17,000ft down to ground level I hung to his tail losing distance slightly in the dive, finishing up about 700 yards astern as he levelled out and set course inland. Inexplicably he began to climb again from which I assumed he was not aware of my presence behind and below. He climbed, steadily but at full throttle, judging from the black smoke pouring from his exhausts, and I continued to close range until at about 15,000ft I judged that I was now near enough to open fire. A long burst produced immediate results. Bits flew off his aircraft which rolled slowly on to its back and dived, apparently out of control, towards the scudding clouds below. I was taking no chances. I followed him down and continued firing until flames spouted from his engine. By this time, I had reached such a speed that my Spitfire was extremely difficult to control and the ground was uncomfortably close. As I eased out of the dive I was able to watch the Me 109 hit the ground just near the town of St. Omer and explode with a blinding flash.

On arrival back at Hornchurch, the last to do so, I found that the squadron had destroyed nine enemy aircraft without loss: unfortunately none were bombers. A most successful first engagement. George Gribble, who had destroyed a Me 109 was, strangely enough, not babbling about how he did it but was cursing the fact that we had been jumped by fighters.

"Begging your pardon, 'Prof'," he said, "but No. 5 attack, I ask you! Didn't we agree that those stupid set piece attacks were all right in peace but unlikely to prove any bloody good in war. Everybody was so damn busy making certain he got into the right position in the formation that we were very nearly all shot down for our pains. If it hadn't been for Max we might have been. You ask Colin over there – have you seen the hole in his aircraft?"

"Sorry, George, thought we would have one go with the Fighting Area Attacks. After all we've spent most of our fighter training practising them. Anyhow, so far as I could see there was no fighter escort. Where the hell did they come from?"

"From behind me, I felt them," said Colin sarcastically, still rather shaken with the effects of being turned upside down by a cannon exploding in his fuselage. "In future," he went on, "I've no intention of offering myself as a target for Hun fighters while the rest of the squadron disappears in all directions other than that in which some unfortunate, like me, is getting hell beaten out of him."

"Well, there's one thing certain," said 'Prof', "from this time onwards there will be no more FA attacks carried out by 54 Squadron while I am leading."

"Hurrah," was the unanimous response.

And so it was that in the squadron's first engagement the type of formation attack which had been practised so assiduously by fighter squadrons since the 1914-18 war died at the birth of a new war. Unknown to us the same assessment of the feasibility of these peacetime attacks was being made by pilots all over Fighter Command as actual combat revealed the antiquity of the tactics on which they were based. To the best of my knowledge FA attacks were never again used throughout the war.

A quick refuel and the squadron was off again, this time to patrol Boulogne from which we understood a large civilian evacuation was taking place. No enemy aircraft were encountered and we returned to base to land in the dark. Thus passed the first day of real war for the pilots of 54 Squadron. That evening I was so tired I could hardly keep myself awake long enough to eat supper before rolling into bed utterly exhausted, with excitement as much as anything. What a day; up at 3.30am, four patrols involving seven and a half hours flying, two engagements and three enemy aircraft to my credit.

This memorable day set the pattern for those that followed. The next morning we were airborne again soon after dawn and when the sun set over Hornchurch that same evening the squadron had flown another three patrols destroying six more enemy aircraft, but not without loss. Two of our most experienced section leaders had been lost and a number of Spitfires damaged. The story from the other three squadrons on the station was the same. In 74 Squadron, Flight Lieutenant Paddy Treacy had gone down, Bob Tuck from 92 Squadron had been wounded in the leg and many others were missing as well as a number of Spitfires badly damaged. But the Hun had suffered, too, as the following signal received that evening will testify:

> "By shooting down thirty-seven enemy aircraft today the four Spitfire squadrons at Hornchurch set up a magnificent record that is especially creditable with such small losses. The Air Officer Commanding sends his sincere congratulations and hopes that most of the missing pilots will turn up again shortly. Immediately the critical military situation in France has passed squadrons will be given a well earned rest."

And so it went on. Day followed day, patrol followed patrol, and still the Spitfires flew off from Hornchurch but with waning strength as the losses in pilots and aircraft mounted. On the 26th May, 54 Squadron was reduced to eight aircraft and twelve very tired pilots. On the first patrol that morning we were heavily engaged by Messerschmitt 110s (twin-engined fighters) for the first time, a formation of Me 109s joining in the fight for good measure. It was in this engagement, while gloating over the fate of a Me 110 which was gliding towards the sea ablaze from stem to stern – it was my second that day – that I first experienced the frightening noise of cannon shells striking my aircraft. A Me 109 had jumped me from above and with his first burst hit the starboard wing with a cannon shell. My Spitfire flicked on to its back – I think rather fortunately because the Hun pilot veered off no doubt satisfied that he had done his work – and it took me a few thousand feet to recover. Having done so, I set course for home with no more thoughts of combat. I managed to land safely despite a punctured tyre and a gaping hole in my wing which had made the aircraft difficult to fly. George Gribble and Johnny Allen did not return from this trip leaving the squadron with ten pilots and five serviceable aircraft.

That same evening 'Prof' learned that he had been appointed to command the squadron and that I was to command 'A' Flight. Celebration was out of the question, there was neither the will nor the time. Nevertheless, we were both delighted and wished only that Johnny Allen, with whom we had shared so much and who would have become my deputy, could be there to share the good news. Imagine our joy when later that evening he appeared in the mess dressed in the uniform of a Naval Lieutenant. Apparently he had managed to bale out in the vicinity of a corvette which had put him ashore at Dover.

The ground crew, for whom no praise, however much, is too great, had by next morning managed to get eight Spitfires serviceable. On the first patrol that day a gruesome sight met us on arrival over the French coast. Dunkirk was aflame. Twisting spirals of black smoke climbed upwards from the burning oil tanks near the harbour and mixing with the grey clouds above shrouded the whole town in a curtain of gloom. It was a forbidding sight and one remembered, no doubt, by the many thousands of British soldiers who eventually struggled wearily towards the beaches and evacuation. It was into this black pall of smoke that Max Pearson disappeared on the tail of a Junkers 88, never to be seen or heard of again.

On my return from this patrol, I noticed that the two dispersal areas normally used by 65 and 74 Squadrons were occupied by Spitfires bearing strange markings. Two new squadrons had moved in and 65 and 74 Squadrons had gone to an airfield in 12 Group for a rest and refit. "Lucky devils," I thought, "we could sure do with a rest." It was not to be, however; the intention was to blood the two new squadrons before moving out 54 and 92 Squadrons. One pilot in the newly arrived 222 Squadron was to become world famous as a fighter pilot in World War II. I first met Douglas Bader, then a Flight Lieutenant, later that evening. He was desperately keen to get to grips with the enemy and although he had done one or two patrols had not, so far, been successful. He plied 'Prof' and me with questions and as I recall the occasion now I wondered if I was one of those pilots at whom, to quote from the book *Reach for the Sky,* he "gazed in mild derision" on his arrival at Hornchurch. Perhaps so. In any event, his very next trip he was in combat and was soon to learn that "the beard stubble," which he alleged we wore, was no 'line-shoot'.

A pleasant surprise awaited me when I walked into the mess on the way to supper. In the hall stood George Gribble with, of all things, the radio set from his aircraft under his arm.

"Do you mean to say that you carted that thing all the way back with you?" I asked, clasping him warmly by the hand.

"Seemed the sensible thing to do, old boy. So far as I know these particular sets are still on the 'secret' list and we don't want the Huns to get free copyright," he answered.

This was typical of George. He must have gone to no end of bother to carry such an awkward and fairly heavy piece of equipment back with him. Apparently the captain of the ship that brought him home had tried to dissuade him for, as he pointed out, space was at a premium, and it must be men before material. Once having made up his mind, nothing would deter George.

The intensity of operations continued on the 28th and the new squadrons were blooded only too realistically. By now, the surviving pilots in 54 Squadron were literally on their last legs and it was a great relief to learn that evening that we were to move north the following day. 41 Squadron from Catterick was to replace us and was expected to arrive mid-morning in time to get ready for operations in the afternoon. 54 Squadron was scheduled for its last patrol at dawn; a sort of swan song. It proved to be just that for me.

CHAPTER FIVE

Escape from Dunkirk

AT 3.30am my batman, the ever cheerful Roach, roused me from exhausted sleep with his by now famous words: "Lovely day, sir, sun will soon be shining." This despite the fact that it was pitch black outside and a tell tale drip, drip on the windowsill signified rain. Roach's belief in his own ability to forecast the weather was indestructible. He perhaps thought that the pilots wanted to be told that the weather would be fine. Two weeks ago he would have been correct. Now, however, those pilots who had been in the battle from the outset were physically exhausted to the point of not caring a damn what the weather was like; if only they could be allowed to sleep on.

A cold, wet, grey day was just breaking over slumbering Essex as 54 Squadron, with its eight remaining serviceable Spitfires, set course on the squadron's last patrol over Dunkirk. On this particular patrol we formed a wing of three squadrons from the station with the intention of matching the size of the ever increasing German threat over the battle area. The weather was extremely poor and flying at 1,000ft in rain and mist I found it was impossible to keep station on the other two squadrons; 'Prof' had remained behind to make arrangements for the move north, and I was in command. The cloud base was a little higher over the Channel and the visibility moderately good, but I could see no sign of the other two squadrons.

We crossed in over Gravelines and turning north-east commenced our patrol. No sooner had we done so than a Dornier 17 nosed out of the cloud about 1,000 yards on our beam and slightly out to sea. The pilot was obviously looking for likely shipping targets. Ordering the rest of the squadron to continue the patrol, I gave chase with my flight of four aircraft. The Hun pilot couldn't have seen us because he continued letting down towards the sea and away from the protective cloud cover which is a lone bomber's best haven of refuge. When we had closed to about 500 yards his rear gunner awoke with obvious fright, and began spraying bullets wildly in our general direction, the pilot at the same time banking steeply towards land. The initial fright over, the rear gunner's aim became much steadier and streams of tracer began to pass below my wings. When at approximately 300 yards I opened fire, the first burst from my eight Brownings producing a flash of flame from the Dornier's port engine. Steadying my aircraft for another burst, I was just about to fire again when bullets began to thud into my engine and almost immediately I was enveloped in a fine spray of glycol from a punctured header tank. The fine spray quickly turned to thick white smoke which completely obscured my forward vision. With a punctured coolant system there was no hope of reaching England, so I should either have to ditch her or land on the beach, now faintly visible on my right. The latter course seemed the best as there appeared to be no ships in the immediate vicinity to rescue a ditched pilot. Calling to the rest of my flight to finish off the Hun, I steered towards the coast pulling back my hood as I did so, only to be met by clouds of black smoke pouring from a punctured oil tank. I switched off the engine immediately and commenced side-slipping towards the nearest strip of sand. There was no time to choose a particular stretch of coastline; all I could hope for was that the stretch in front of me was free of obstacles, such as a sea wall. Luck was on my side. Just as the aircraft was about to strike the ground I picked up the wing, and coming out of the side-slip, pulled the stick back and hoped for the best. The aircraft struck the beach at the water's edge, throwing a jet of sand and water into my face as she ploughed through the wet sand on her belly. I pitched violently forward on to my straps and struck my forehead a sharp blow on the edge of the windscreen. I knew no more, for me, operations were temporarily suspended.

As consciousness gradually returned and the danger of my position in the now hissing and burning machine penetrated my bemused mind, I hastily undid my harness and scrambled from the cockpit, sinking sick and exhausted on a patch of sand well clear of the aircraft. Blood was pouring from a deep gash over my left eye, and oil mixed with wet sand covered my face and neck. I sat for some minutes in the drizzling rain before staggering to my feet. As I did so, I was confronted by a tall fearsome looking soldier in strange uniform who, pointing a rifle at me, said, "*Anglais*." What a relief when, in response to my halting "*Oui*," he lowered his rifle and beckoned me to follow him. By now my Spitfire was engulfed in flame, and turning to take one last look at it I could just discern the outlines of my 'Kiwi' emblem on the side near the cockpit. "That ends," I thought to myself, "the life of *Kiwi* number one."

Thus it was that I found myself at 5am on the morning of May 29th in the small Belgian town of Oost-Dunkerke, about three miles west of Nieuport and midway between Dunkirk and Ostend.

The wound over my eye was throbbing painfully but was eased somewhat by the skilful attention of a Belgian girl who had taken over from my escort and was bathing it with warm water. The wound having been dressed and myself washed, it was time to make my way back to England. Where to make for? That was the question. At this stage of my story it must be related that the RAF pilots operating over France and Belgium to assist in what we had been told was a planned withdrawal had no idea that a full-scale evacuation was under way, and that Dunkirk was the principal port from which this was being carried out. Had I known this, Dunkirk would have been the obvious place to make for, as by my reckoning it was no further than Ostend which was suggested to me by the Belgians as the best place from which to get a ship back to England. Indeed, the Belgian girl who attended to my wound gave me a letter to an uncle of hers who was some person of authority at the port of Ostend and whom she assured me would organize a passage for me.

At the very moment that we discussed this problem, unknown to us, the Germans were entering Ostend and the British front line had contracted to such a degree that its eastern flank was but five miles away. In fact, the Germans had reached a point about twenty miles from Dunkirk and the BEF was now confined to a sector enclosed in a triangle with its apex at Poperinghe and its base a line running from Nieuport to Dunkirk. The Germans had reached the coast on either side of these two towns.

The confusion of my Belgian friends was understandable. They had only just learned of their King's capitulation, were completely cut off by telephone and had had no contact with anybody in authority for the past few days. To me Ostend looked as good a bet as any and accordingly I set off on foot with the letter of introduction safely tucked in my pocket; a small gathering of well-wishers waved me good-bye, the girl in their centre and proudly wearing my bright yellow 'Mae West' life jacket with the name Flying Officer Deere painted in bold red letters down the front.

When I reached the main road the refugee traffic was so heavy in the opposite direction to Ostend that there was little choice but to follow the drift westwards. Besides, after one or two tentative enquiries about the possibility of reaching Ostend it was apparent that utter confusion existed in that direction. A loaded civilian bus squeezing its way along the crowded road seemed to offer an ideal method of transport, certainly preferable to my two feet. No one objected as I jumped aboard and pushed my way into its crammed interior where I remained until the bus was halted by a traffic jam some few miles further on. A bicycle, surreptitiously borrowed from beside a store, was my next mode of transport. This means of conveyance took me to a small town on the outskirts of Dunkirk – which I had by now decided to make for – where I caught my first glimpse of British khaki. Outside a small café stood a British army truck, obviously the property of three soldiers whom I espied taking refreshments inside. "This," I thought, "is where I get rescued. At last I'll be able to get in touch with somebody in authority."

"Hello there," I greeted the RASC Corporal the senior of the three, "Can you tell me where I can get in touch with the nearest military authority. I am an RAF pilot and I've just come from up the way there (pointing in the general direction of my crashed aircraft). I am anxious to get back to England to my unit."

"As far as I know, chum," he answered, "there isn't anybody in authority at the moment. Me and my mates here are the only members of our company who have got back this far; where the hell the rest of them are, and for that matter the rest of the British Army, I haven't a clue. We've been driving for two days and are making for Dunkirk because that is where we understand there is transport back to England. You can ride with us if you like."

To say that I was amazed at this revelation is an understatement. My belief in the newspaper stories that the British Army was "retreating according to plan," was shattered. "Hell, things must be in a mess; the sooner I get out of here the better," I thought.

We were forced to abandon the truck on the outskirts of Dunkirk as further passage, other than on foot, was an impossibility. The streets of the town were blocked by falling masonry and dangling telephone wires, and the entrances choked with abandoned transport of all descriptions, mostly British Army vehicles. Ahead and in the direction of the port, the burning oil tanks, which I had seen so often from the air, continued to pour out volumes of black smoke which, fanned by the wind and compressed by the cloud, hung over the town like a sentinel of death. The sight that greeted me on arrival at the beach, I shall never forget. My outstanding impression was one of discipline and control despite the obvious exhaustion and desperation of the thousands of troops who, arranged in snake-like columns, stretched from the sand dunes down to the water's edge. This was the British Army in defeat and, by jove, they were still able to appreciate that, no matter how desperate the situation, their chance of rescue were dependent on order and discipline. The spirit of the Tommy may have been dampened but it was not dead, as proved by the soldier who, having secured an unlimited supply of Craven A cigarettes from an unknown source, was careering in a truck up and down the lines of troops tossing cartons to all and sundry shouting as he did so "Here we are lads, all free and with the compliments of the NAAFI. Take your pick."

In the midst of all this, a machine-gun away to my right and half-hidden in the sand dunes, began firing. Looking up I saw a damaged Spitfire, with flames and smoke pouring from its engine, gliding inland. I ran like a demon towards the gunners bellowing as I went, "Can't you see he is friendly – stop shooting." The noise of the gun drowned my voice and the gun crew, intent on their prey, failed to see my frantic signals. Before I reached them they had ceased firing, and it was quite obvious from the looks on their faces that they had realized their mistake. Angry words boiled up in my throat but common sense prevailed, and I turned away without a word, muttering under my breath, "I can't blame them; after two weeks of constant air attack, they are bound to treat all aircraft as hostile."

While all this had been going on I was wondering how best to go about getting back to England. In the distance I caught sight of a Naval uniform and made for the wearer, a lieutenant, who promised to put me in touch with the beach Commander as soon as he finished his present task of shepherding troops through the waves to the mass of small boats riding the swell as near the shore as they dare venture. To my suggestion that perhaps I could get aboard one he answered, "No, far better to wait for the next destroyer in. It will get you back more quickly, and more comfortably."

It was many hours before a destroyer finally appeared, and

in the meantime a steady drizzle had set in. This had a depressing effect on the troops who huddled together under their coats, and stoically awaited their turn to be embarked. The weather did have the advantage of keeping away enemy aircraft, and for a time all was peace on the beach, but as the sky began to clear, so the Hun bombers reappeared in increasing numbers. Before long, Junkers and Dorniers, using the cloud cover to advantage, re-commenced attacks, dropping their bombs with uncanny accuracy despite defiant machine-guns and small arms fire from the troops. Above cloud, the chattering of machine-guns heralded the presence of RAF fighters, unfortunately not visible to the men they were endeavouring to protect.

After a prolonged and nerve-racking wait a destroyer finally appeared, making her way from out of the misty grey background over the sea towards the east mole where the loading was taking place.

"Come on," said the beach Commander with whom I had finally sought shelter, "this is where you say good-bye to Dunkirk."

We set off at once for the causeway leading to the mole, weaving our way through the long lines of troops who still maintained some semblance of order despite the constant attention of Hun aircraft. Just as we reached the causeway a formation of three Junkers bombers appeared overhead, hotly pursued by a single Spitfire. There was a mad scramble for cover, available only to those near the sand dunes or to those, of which I was one, who could shelter behind the rock causeway. Mostly the troops just dived into the water, re-emerging at neck level to fire their rifles in desperation and defiance in the general direction of the attacking bombers. From the comparative safety of the causeway I watched the Spitfire as it closed to attack only to see white smoke begin to pour from its engine as the pilot, obviously badly hit, turned away and glided inland. Silently, I wished him luck. A crescendo of bombs, accompanied by machine-gun fire from the rear gunners of the aircraft, descended on the beach. In a few seconds it was all over; a number of British soldiers would not now be requiring transport back to England.

In the mad rush to find shelter I had lost contact with my escort, so I decided to make my own way to the destroyer which had now docked safely beside the mole. Jumping to my feet I dashed towards the narrow causeway along either side of which were clustered groups of soldiers awaiting their turn to join the queue on the mole. It was quite obvious to me that the troops had been marshalled along the sides of the causeway to give cover from air attack, and that they were not allowed to walk along the top. Nevertheless, it was the quickest way of getting to the waiting destroyer, and I was not under orders. I therefore chose this course until halted by an angry voice.

"Where the hell do you think you're going. Get down from there and wait your turn." So saying an irate Army major jumped up in front of me.

"I am an RAF officer," I said, realizing that he could have no idea who I was. I had thrown a discarded army ground sheet over my uniform, and was dirty and unshaven, a bloody bandage around my head completing the picture.

"I don't give a damn who you are, get down off here and fall in line with the rest."

"All I am trying to do is get back as quickly as possible in order to rejoin my squadron which is operating over here," I said. I really meant this, realizing by now how desperately serious was the plight of the BEF and the necessity to get as many RAF fighters as possible over Dunkirk to cover the evacuation.

"For all the good you chaps seem to be doing over here you might just as well stay on the ground," he countered belligerently.

This was too much to stomach, and I retorted angrily, "You have absolutely no say over what I do, and can go to hell."

He was distinctly shaken by this rejoinder, and stepping past him I strode off down the causeway feeling a damned sight more uncomfortable than my stiff-backed walk suggested. Unfortunately, this small delay caused me to miss the destroyer which, crammed with troops, moved away from the mole before I could get aboard.

About four months after Dunkirk, my picture appeared in the daily papers in connection with the Battle of Britain and was seen by an army sergeant who had been one of the troops sheltering beside the causeway. He remembered my face and wrote me a letter in which he said that he had witnessed the incident and how pleased he and his mates were that I had got the better of the interfering major. That letter made me feel a little easier in my mind about pushing ahead; at least the troops, or some of them, had appreciated my point of view.

Having reached the mole, I thought it wise to join the queue. It wasn't long before another destroyer arrived, and I was soon aboard. My identity established, I was escorted below decks to the tiny wardroom, already crowded with Army officers. A stony silence greeted the announcement that I was an RAF officer. This caused me to ask of a young gunner lieutenant nearby, "Why so friendly, what have the RAF done?"

"That's just it," he replied, "What have they done? You are about as popular in this company as a cat in the prize canary's cage."

So that was it. For two weeks non-stop I had flown my guts out, and this was all the thanks I got. What was the use of trying to explain that the RAF had patrolled further inland, often above cloud, with the insuperable task of covering adequately a patrol line from Ostend to Boulogne? Why explain that the pilots of Fighter Command had no idea that the position was so serious and only knew, and believed, what they had read in the newspapers: that the British Army was retreating according to plan? To us, Dunkirk was just another French port with no more importance than Calais, Boulogne or Ostend all of which we had, at one time or another, been ordered to patrol. These thoughts and more flashed through my mind as I wearily sank into the nearest chair, past caring what the Army thought.

The strained relations between the Army and the Royal Air Force subsequent to the campaign in France are now past history. There was genuine bitterness which lasted until the now famous victories in the Middle East when Montgomery and Tedder paved the way for the mutual understanding and trust of each other's service which was to prove so valuable in the testing battles ahead and which was to reach fruition over the assault beaches in Normandy. The wound opened in those early days in France has, I think, closed for ever.

The destroyer had been under way for about ten minutes when the sudden bang, bang of pom-poms announced the presence of enemy aircraft. It was an eerie and frightening feeling being closeted below decks while the battle raged unseen overhead. With the opening of the gunfire, silence descended on the wardroom. The white strained faces, tense with expectancy, reflected the feelings of men whose nerves had already been strained to near breaking point. Silently they stood while the destroyer bucked and rolled to the accompaniment of her barking guns as she violently manoeuvred in her efforts to elude the attacking aircraft. Then the bombs began to fall, their whistling note plainly discernible above the noise of the guns. One, two, three; I counted the explosions, each louder than the last as the stick of bombs approached us. There was a mighty bang as the fourth bomb exploded perilously near the ship which, shaking from stem to stern, heeled over violently, tossing men and coffee cups in an undignified heap into the corner of the wardroom. Immediately we were plunged into darkness. For what seemed an eternity the destroyer had a heavy list to port but eventually she returned to an even keel, much to our relief. For the time being, all was then quiet.

Our respite was short-lived. Hardly had we regained our composure after the first attack than the ship began to vibrate as, full speed ahead, she twisted and turned in a desperate endeavour to evade more attackers. As before, we waited in tense silence but this time there was no whine of falling bombs; the attack petered out almost before it had commenced and once again we settled down, in the now silent darkness. There were audible sighs of relief as the lights flashed on again denoting 'all well,' and from me in particular, for at that moment a naval officer put his head into the wardroom and said: "Will the RAF officer please come up on deck to assist in aircraft identification? We think the last chap we've just had a go at was a Blenheim." I needed no second bidding.

From then onwards the journey back was uneventful but the destroyer continued to zigzag and alter course frequently, no doubt to make it difficult for tracking aircraft and possibly as an insurance against submarine attack. After three hours sailing we sighted the white cliffs of Dover; a most heartening sight. Before long we were nosing alongside the pier, the moment to set foot on British soil near at hand. Disembarkation was not to be a speedy affair. A single gangway only was run out which meant a long wait for the hundreds of troops on the lower decks. Soon there were vociferous protests followed shortly by positive action on the part of the more adventurous soldiers who began scaling the ropes which secured the destroyer to the pier. Feeble attempts were made to dissuade and stop them as the numbers choosing this avenue of escape steadily mounted, but to no avail. This escape route certainly speeded up the unloading which, to my way of thinking, was much more important than discipline at this juncture.

On shore, the troops were being directed to canteens and reception centres, but I decided to dodge this part of the proceedings. Sliding away unnoticed I made for the railway station, determined to catch the first train to London. The question of purchasing a ticket never entered my head. I had no money or means of identification – RAF pilots flew without either – but reasoned that I had earned the right to a free train ride back to my unit. Having found an empty first-class carriage on the London train (nothing but the best) I sank into a corner and was soon fast asleep. An insistent "tickets please" finally roused me from slumber to be confronted by the guard who was at that moment clipping the ticket of a senior army officer sitting opposite me. I explained my position to the guard who said in reply, "Sorry, but you will have to get off the train at the next station." Before I could reply the army officer, a Brigadier, intervened.

"It's obvious the boy is telling the truth, guard. Can't you see he's all in, and genuinely anxious to get back to his unit. How do you suggest he does it, walk?"

This did the trick. Shrugging his shoulders the guard walked out. I smiled my thanks at the Brigadier, who obviously hadn't heard about the RAF at Dunkirk!

It was fortunate that the Dover train ran to Charing Cross where I caught a tube train to Elm Park, the nearest station to Hornchurch airfield. There was no trouble with the ticket collector at Elm Park: he waved me through before I had half finished my explanation. At 11.15pm I walked into the officers' mess which I had left just nineteen hours previously. It was deserted except for three officers chatting in front of the fire in the reading-room. When I put my head around the door there was an amazed, "Good gracious, you've made it, I said you would," from 'Daddy' Bouchier who leapt to his feet. "Sit down and tell us all about it. But first you had better let the Doctor here," turning to Squadron Leader Derek Coltart the SMO who sat next to him, "have a look at that head of yours and replace that filthy bandage."

As Derek disappeared in search of the first aid kit, I proceeded to tell my story to the Station Commander and Robert Lea, a Squadron Leader controller, who made up the party. Derek returned shortly and proceeded to remove the dirty bandage while I carried on with my story.

"It's quite a nasty gash," said Derek. "But I think it will knit without stitching. I'll clean it up now, and have a good look in the morning. I expect you want some sleep so I suggest you pop off to bed and finish your tale tomorrow." This I was only too glad to do.

There is a sequel to this part of my story. Some twelve years later, when I was commanding RAF Station North Weald, I again met Derek Coltart, now a doctor in civilian life but serving as an auxiliary with 604 Squadron. He came up to me and said, "Hello, Al, I've got something for you." So saying, he produced a cleanly laundered bandage, "Yours, I think – remember it?"

"Only too well," I replied.

Next day, I learned that 54 Squadron had moved north as planned, having left early the previous afternoon. Two of the unserviceable Spitfires which they had left behind were now ready for air test after which, if there were no snags, they were to be flown up to Catterick. Having air tested them, I arranged to fly up that afternoon accompanied by a new pilot who had arrived that morning. The new officer, Pilot Officer Eric Edsall, was to figure with me in a miraculous escape in the Battle of Britain but a few few weeks later.

At lunch I met some of the 41 Squadron pilots who had taken our place. Already some of them had chalked up their first victories which they were excitedly relating to all who would listen. Many of them – Flight Lieutenant Norman Ryder, Pilot Offficer Tony Lovell, Pilot Officer 'Mac' McKenzie, to name but a few – I was to meet again on many a similar occasion when the two squadrons changed over at Hornchurch after an intensive period of operations; the outgoing squadron on its way to Catterick for a rest.

*   *   *

Five days after my return from Dunkirk, operation 'Dynamo', the Navy codeword by which the evacuation was known, came to an end. Thanks to their courage and discipline, as much as any other single factor, a third of a million troops were brought out from Dunkirk despite all the efforts of the strongest army and air force in the world at that date to stop it. History has since recognized the operation as "A classic example of co-operation by the three Services."* At that time, however, subjected to an utterly exhausting and terrifying experience, our soldiers and sailors returned home with a single question on their lips – "Where was the Royal Air Force?"

In spite of any contemporary opinion to the contrary, the RAF was there. I like to think their efforts are best summed up by quoting from a review of German air force operations over Dunkirk by General of the Air Force Werner Kreipe in the book *The Fatal Decisions*. Referring to the operations of the 3rd Wing of Bomber Group 2, he said:

> "The Wing set off next morning with its full complement of 27 aircraft to bomb Dunkirk. But before the Dorniers could unload their bombs...Spitfires, the first these German airmen had seen, hurled themselves upon the bomber Wing. Despite the heavy defensive fire of the German air-gunners the British attacked again and again, and succeeded in driving the Dorniers away from their target. As soon as the Wing landed it received orders to take off again...The moment the Dorniers appeared the tireless British fighters attacked. But on this occasion there was German fighter support, and though the British forced home their attacks time and time again, the German bombers managed to get through to their target. Our losses were not inconsiderable...
>
> Thus, on this one day, out of twenty-seven planes in one Wing eleven were put out of action. The days of easy victory were over. We had met the Royal Air Force head on."

It is not generally realized that air operations over Dunkirk were among the toughest undertaken by the pilots of Fighter Command throughout the war. When it is remembered that

*The War in France and Flanders, 1939-40

our pilots, hitherto untried in battle, grappled with an experienced and victory flushed Luftwaffe over territory greatly to the latter's advantage, there can be little doubt that the odds were heavily stacked against them. Admittedly the fight was brief. But its brevity was more than offset by the intensity of operations. In the battle, Fighter Command lost 229 aircraft, or approximately fifty per cent of its front line strength at the time, and 128 pilots. These losses were a serious set-back to the Command expansion then under way. On the one hand the loss of trained pilots – and the majority were flight and section leaders – made it difficult to find leaders for the new squadrons forming without seriously affecting the efficiency of those in being. On the other hand, the number of replacement aircraft required by the participating squadrons meant that there were none immediately available for the new squadrons.

In the light of the subsequent delay before the opening of the Battle of Britain, these losses were not so serious as at first thought. Indeed, the experience gained by those pilots who survived Dunkirk was to prove invaluable in the critical phase ahead. However, had the Germans carried the air war into England on the heels of the evacuating British, thus sterilizing the expansion of Fighter Command, the situation would indeed have been serious and the Battle of Britain might well have been lost.

CHAPTER SIX

Calm Before the Storm

THE next morning I presented myself at sick quarters where the Senior Medical Officer examined my wound.

"It's a clean cut," he said, "and I don't think stitching is necessary. It should have been done, had it been possible, immediately after the accident. Now, however, it is best left alone. I'll just remove the rest of this half-shaven eyebrow and put some sticking plaster on the wound to keep it from reopening. One thing is certain, you'll have a nice scar to remind you of the incident."

"Is it OK for me to fly?" I enquired.

"Yes," he answered, "but I should take it easy for a few days. Presumably you are going up to Catterick to join your squadron?"

"That's the idea. I want to fly up there this afternoon."

"OK, go ahead. Enjoy yourself and get fit for the next round."

When I arrived at Catterick airfield that evening the sun was just setting, its mellow rays embracing a compact cluster of hangars and domestic buildings nestling on the north side of a small grass airfield. "So this is Catterick," I thought, "looks a nice place; ideal for a few days' rest." And so it proved.

'Prof' was there to greet me. He had driven down to dispersal with the Station Commander, Wing Commander Carter. I felt most flattered being met personally by the Station Commander. When I got to know him later I realised that it was typical of his warm and friendly nature. Guy Carter was one of those men whom one instinctively likes. I have never met a nicer man. He possessed a gay charm and buoyancy of spirit which endeared him to all ranks on this very happy station. It was a sad day for the Royal Air Force when he was killed about two years later in the Middle East.

"Deere," he said, "I'm delighted to meet you. I've heard so much about you from 'Prof' here and the other boys. Throw your kit into the back of my car; I'll run you up to the mess."

"Could you just wait one moment, sir, I see the Flight Sergeant hanging around in the background. I think he wants some instructions about these two aircraft which Edsall and I brought up."

"Flight," I said, turning to the NCO "both these aircraft are OK. Both the Forms 700 (an aircraft's record of serviceability) are in the map pockets of my aircraft. I should like to keep the one I flew up for myself. Would you get your expert to paint my Kiwi emblem on the fuselage. The same place and size as before, but you had better get him to put a 'II' after it. Let's hope there won't be a third!"

In the mess, the round of handshaking over, I asked Flying Officer Desmond McMullen, who had been my sub-section leader on the last ill-fated trip, what had happened to the Dornier we attacked. Before he could reply, George Gribble broke in:

"Al, I always said that you 'line-shooters' in 'A' Flight couldn't shoot straight, now I have proof of it. It took no less than four of you to bring down that Dornier. From the bullet holes I saw in the other three aircraft and the look of that plaster over your eye, those Huns gave a little more than they got."

"Oh go to hell, George," broke in Desmond, "we did at least shoot him down. I must hand it to that rear gunner though, he was a damn fine shot."

"Come on, Desmond, let's have the story," I broke in.

"Well, as George so rudely put it, three of us had a go after you broke off the attack. He was then pouring smoke from his starboard engine, and obviously having difficulty in maintaining height. I gave him a couple of longish bursts when I too was hit. The same story goes for the other two. In the end, I think sheer weight of lead forced him down, and even then he managed to make a forced landing. In fact, he came down not far from where you bit the dust. Did you see anything of the crew?"

"No, and I am pleased that I didn't. I had enough bother looking after myself without having to worry about an antagonistic crew of Germans."

"To sum it all up," broke in George again, "you can give yourself one enemy aircraft destroyed, shared between four of you. A fourth each, how's that, Al?"

"It all goes to prove my point," chipped in Colin Gray. "It's absolutely useless having our guns harmonized to produce a rectangular cone of fire at 450 yards as at present. All this guarantee is a few hits by the indifferent shot; the good shot, on the other hand, is penalized. It just makes it impossible for those who are prepared to get in close, and can kill when they get there. I've always understood concentration of fire was a principle of war. Perhaps the slide rule expert who worked out our present harmonization pattern hasn't heard of it. We must get point harmonization at 250 yards or even less if the Spitfire guns can be brought to bear at that range. We'll get results then and a damn sight less ammunition will be used to achieve them."

At this point the Station Adjutant entered the room to say that a signal had just been received from Fighter Command announcing that 'Prof', Johnny, and Sergeant Phillips had been awarded the DSO, DFC, and DFM, respectively. Whoops of delight followed this announcement, accompanied by a chorus of "fetch Johnny."

"I'll find him, he's probably in his room reading the Bible," said Colin. So saying he disappeared in the direction of Johnny's room to break the good news and to drag him into the celebrations. A few moments later he reappeared with an embarrassed Johnny looking, if possible, far younger than his 20 years in his red-faced embarrassment at being the centre of so much hilarity. 'Prof' too was somewhat taken aback but rose manfully to the occasion by ordering champagne all round.

It was indeed an historic moment for the squadron; three pilots being honoured in the first round of the second world war, and all thoroughly deserved. A move was now afoot to include Sergeant Phillips in the celebrations and the Station Commander's permission was sought for the officers to visit the Sergeants' Mess where the news had already been conveyed to Phillips. At this juncture I judged it opportune to make my escape. I had been without a decent night's sleep almost from the outset of the Dunkirk operations, and the events of the past two days were beginning to tell. I was desperately tired. Before therefore I could be persuaded to join the party now moving off to the Sergeants' Mess, I received a whispered "OK" from 'Prof' and slid quietly off to bed.

The few days spent at Catterick were indeed a rest. The squadron was required to keep only a relaxed state of readiness and flying was limited to air tests and familiarization flights for new pilots. All our efforts were concentrated on getting maximum serviceability before returning to Hornchurch.

On the afternoon of the 4th of June, the squadron headed south. To those of us whose operational roots were sown there, it was just like returning to one's home. Much as we enjoyed Catterick as a station, and the rest it afforded, there was a feeling of warmth in our hearts as once again we circled the familiar grass which was Hornchurch airfield. 41 Squadron pilots were at dispersal when we taxied in, ready to take off to return to Catterick. In the few days the squadron had operated over Dunkirk opposition had been intense. Although their casualties had been relatively light the numbers were sufficient to make an impression on those who survived. To them, war was no longer a delightful game; Dunkirk had been the grim reminder.

The other two squadron members of the Hornchurch sector, namely numbers 65 and 74, had already returned from their rest stations in the north. It was good to see old friends again, all keen and ready to fight the next round when it came. The first shock of combat losses had been absorbed to be replaced by a purposeful air of determination, at least on the part of the older hands. The short rest afforded the operationally tired pilots was invaluable. Speaking from personal experience, and there must have been dozens like me, I was too tired to be effective on the last two or three days over Dunkirk. Although not yet frightened of operations to the extent of dreading the next patrol, a symptom I was to experience at a later stage in the war, I was yet sufficiently tired mentally for my judgement to be impaired. There is a very fine balance between over-tiredness and fear; the latter often results from the former. In the case of squadrons kept in the line for too long a period, morale among the leaders tends to suffer and this can, and does, engender fear in the less experienced pilots. When this occurs, it is the responsibility of higher commanders to take appropriate action. In the case of individual tiredness, the squadron commander must act.

The handling of the squadrons operation over Dunkirk by Commander-in-Chief, Fighter Command was a perfect example of balanced employment. As in the case of 54, squadrons were taken out of the line as soon as their leaders began to show signs of excessive fatigue, and new squadrons were brought in. The case of individuals within those squadrons hardly arose over such a short period, but it was to be of increasing importance as the war progressed and pilots returned for second and third tours on operations.

All three squadrons now had their establishment of sixteen aircraft per squadron. In addition, the pilot strength of each squadron had been raised to about twenty, or three more than 54 Squadron had had at the outbreak of Dunkirk. A few weeks in which to work up the new pilots, and give the newly appointed section leaders an opportunity to get experience in their new role, was essential. Fortunately, there was a lull in intensive operations of from four to five weeks. In this time the task was accomplished; Hornchurch squadrons were ready when the fighting was renewed.

The controversial question of gun harmonization was again raised with higher authority. 'Sailor' Malan, perhaps the best shot in Fighter Command, was adamant in his decision to harmonize guns in his aircraft on a point at 250 yards, regardless. The weight of pilot opinion in favour of adopting this course eventually won the day. Command issued instructions that point harmonization at 250 yards was to be standard for all day fighter aircraft.

At the same time as this harmonization was agreed, a new type of incendiary ammunition was introduced into the Command in limited supply. It was known to the pilots as 'De Wilde' ammunition, a name with a faintly foreign, and therefore mysterious, ring. In fact, we were given to understand that it was a Belgian invention which had been brought to England on the fall of that country. Production was not fully under way, hence the limited supplies. 'De Wilde,' unlike the standard incendiary ammunition in use, was without any flame or smoke trace. Its greatest value lay in the fact that it produced a small flash on impact thus providing confirmation to the attacking fighter pilot that his aim was good. In the official* despatch on the Battle of Britain Air Marshal Dowding said: "…'De Wilde' ammunition became available in increasing quantities…and it is extremely popular with the pilots, who attributed to it almost magical properties…" With all due respect to Lord Dowding, this was not strictly true. As I have said, its great value lay in the fact that, for the first time pilots were able to confirm their aim; a most important consideration in the conservation of ammunition and the delivery of the *coup de gràce*.

It was not until some three years after the war that I learned the true story of this ammunition. Far from being a foreign invention, the 'De Wilde' incendiary bullet was the design of Brigadier Dixon, a Ministry of Supply expert. Why the introduction of this ammunition was shrouded in secrecy

*Supplement to the *London Gazette,* 10th September 1941

to the extent of giving it a foreign sounding name is a mystery, even to the designer who was eventually rewarded by the Royal Commission of Awards in recognition of his achievement. I am pleased to record that I was one of the many pilots who supported his claim.

As there seemed little likelihood of a renewal of fighting in the immediate future 'Prof' decided that it was an opportune time for his flight and section leaders to get in a few days' leave. Accordingly I was summarily dismissed for seven days with the words "Al, you get to hell off the station for a week. You need a break. I don't care where you go so long as I don't see your face around here in that time. The same applies to George."

George and I decided to spend the first couple of nights in London doing the night clubs before going our separate ways for the remainder of the leave. There could have been no gayer companion than George with whom to spend a couple of nights in London, an undertaking not new to either of us. He was the source of entertainment wherever he went, so I was assured of an amusing time. We had an amusing time, as one could in a London not yet subjected to night bombing. On the Sunday morning, having awakened with a ghastly hangover, I determined to take myself off to the country to stay with friends. No amount of pressure on the part of George could persuade me to spend another night in town. Accordingly I set off after lunch for Buckinghamshire. Mr and Mrs Raymond Dumas, with whom I was to stay, had befriended me before the war as a lonely New Zealander. From then onwards, I was accepted as one of the family. Their lovely home, Little Missenden House, was to me a home away from home and a haven of retreat in the quiet of the English countryside. This was to be the first of many wartime visits to Little Missenden, or to their cottage in Cornwall, where I spent many delightful rest periods throughout the war. To a New Zealander with no family or relatives in England, it was always a great comfort to me to know that I would be welcome at their home at any time, no matter how short the warning. I owe them both a great deal, and their friendship means much to me.

After five days of riding, swimming and just lazing I returned to Hornchurch very much refreshed and genuinely keen to get at the Hun again. The day after my return, instructions were received that we were to begin reconnaissances in squadron strength over Northern France and Belgium with the aim of keeping a watch on enemy activity, both air and ground, and to report on any unusual build-up of forces. The first two trips undertaken by 54 Squadron were uneventful, except for some very accurate anti-aircraft fire in the vicinity of St. Omer. At least the enemy was getting his defences organized. On the third trip a few days later 'Prof' suggested that Johnny and I make up Red Section with him leading. He said that there was likely to be little opportunity for us to fly together as a section when the battle was rejoined. There were so many new pilots in the squadron that when things got hot it would be essential for flight and section leaders to be leading, not following. This was to be a sort of farewell to a most successful partnership.

The squadron task was to recce airfields in the Amiens area. When over the Channel *en route* to Amiens the R/T silence, always maintained on these trips, was broken by the sonorous voice of Squadron Leader Ronald Adam, the Controller at Hornchurch, passing instructions to investigate an unidentified radar plot in the Boulogne area.

"Hornet Red Leader from Control; do you read me?"

"Red Leader to Control, loud and clear. Pass your message."

"Control to Red Leader. Investigate unidentified plot off Boulogne travelling north-west at 3,000ft."

"Red Leader to Control; your message received and understood. Will investigate, out."

"Hornet Blue Leader from Red Leader. Will you take over the lead. I am going to take Red section to investigate. Please carry on as briefed. Red section will rejoin you later, if possible."

"Blue Leader to Red Leader, message received and understood."

"This is a bit of luck," I thought to myself. "It looks as if 'Prof' had a premonition when he suggested that Johnny and I should make up his section for a last trip together."

Further courses to steer were received from the Controller until eventually the section was over Boulogne. I could just discern the harbour through a break in the clouds and was peering hopefully in that area when Johnny broke through on the R/T. "Enemy aircraft behind and below, passing through that break in the clouds at 4 o'clock." (This is a reference to the clock code used by pilots for reporting the position of enemy aircraft in relation to the heading of their own formation which is always assumed to be pointing at 12 o'clock.)

"Understood, Red Three, you take over and lead us to them. I can't pick them up for the moment," radioed 'Prof'.

Slipping into the lead Johnny wheeled the section to the left and dived at great speed in the direction he had indicated. Into the grey haze below cloud we hurtled in search of our prey. Luck was with us. As we levelled out at 4,000ft Johnny re-established contact with the enemy aircraft which he identified as three Junkers 88s flying in loose formation. They were probably in search of shipping targets.

"OK, Red Two, I see them," came 'Prof's' voice over the radio. "Red Two, you take the one on the port side, Red Three, the one on the starboard side and I'll take the leader. Make your attacks individually."

We were now closing fast but before we could get within range the enemy spotted us and immediately broke formation, each pilot making for the nearest cloud cover. Before, however, my target could disappear I had him in my sights. The first burst was on target, the 'De Wilde' confirming my aim as it burst in yellow splotches along the starboard wing. Almost immediately fire appeared in this engine but before I could repeat the dose the Junkers entered cloud. I followed, peering eagerly into the opaque dampness which now enveloped my aircraft. I had little hope of picking him up in cloud, indeed the necessity to concentrate on my blind flying instruments made searching almost impossible. As suddenly as I had entered cloud I burst through into the blinding sun and an empty sky. Down again into the clammy hide-out and out at the bottom. But there was no sign of my target nor for that matter of any other aircraft. There seemed no point in hanging around so I set course for home, somewhat disgruntled. An unescorted bomber was such a juicy target that I cursed the clouds around me for making it possible for the Hun to escape.

'Prof' and Johnny followed me in to land in quick succession. It was obvious from the blackened edges of their wings that they too had fired their guns. 'Prof's' story was similar to mine. Johnny's more conclusive. He had, to use his own words, "set the Junkers alight from stem to stern." Apparently two of the crew members managed to bale out successfully and, as they were but a few miles off the French coast, he thought their chances of being picked up were very good.

As it turned out, and as 'Prof' had prophesied, this was to be the last trip that we three did together as a section. It was therefore a most fortunate finale – one destroyed and two damaged. The confirmed victory by Johnny brought the total of enemy aircraft destroyed by us three, operating as a section, to eighteen. In the process we had lost two Spitfires, mine and Johnny's during Dunkirk, with a further three suffering damage of varying category. A handsome profit on the balance sheet. A record, in fact, which I believe to have been unequalled in the Royal Air Force at any time in the war, at least in the European theatre of operations.

My cup of success was filled to overflowing when that afternoon I learned that I had been awarded the Distinguished Flying Cross. News travels fast. Less than an hour later the dispersal telephone rang for me. It was 'Sailor' Malan calling from Rochford, our forward base near Southend from which 74 Squadron was then operating.

"Hello, Al. Congratulations on your award and that goes for all of us here. I've just been speaking to the Controller who tells me that you had some joy this morning." He went on to ask what I thought about point harmonization, and also the 'De Wilde' ammunition.

"As a matter of fact 'Sailor'," I answered, "I only managed to get in a short burst. Johnny was more successful, and he firmly believes that point harmonization coupled with 'De Wilde' was the difference between destroying the aircraft and only damaging it. Personally I found it most satisfying to find that my aim was good: 'De Wilde' bursting on the wings was proof of this. Undoubtedly it is a big improvement; one supplements the other and our kill rate is bound to go up accordingly. Incidentally, 'Prof' agrees with me on this."

'Sailor' thanked me and said that this was most interesting. Now that we had got the point harmonization recognized we must obviously push the 'De Wilde' matter more strongly. There was still a shortage, probably because the Command armament staff was lukewarm.

"Ask 'Prof' to include a strong recommendation for its use when he makes out his report on the operation," he said. "That should help."

As a result of our recommendation we received a visit a few days later from the Command Armament Officer, who hinted that we were making an unnecessary fuss about the importance of the new incendiary ammunition. Trials, he said, had shown that 'De Wilde' was no better than the normal incendiary bullet. A chorus of disapproval from the pilots soon put him right on this point. We contended that it was better and, as we were the users, our views were more important than synthetic tests. I rather think that Lord Dowding's reference to pilots and the magical properties of 'De Wilde', as previously quoted, stemmed from a report made to him by this officer. Nevertheless, action was taken because supplies steadily increased as the battle progressed.

The reconnaissance in force in the vicinity of airfields in enemy-occupied territories continued without producing any worthwhile information. The pilots disliked the job and considered it to be a waste of effort, especially at a time when training of new pilots was of paramount importance. The flak was getting more accurate and more concentrated with consequent damage to aircraft, thus forcing the squadrons to fly higher and higher and at a height which was useless for accurate ground observation. In the ten or so trips I did I can honestly say that, apart from the fortuitous interception off Boulogne, nothing useful was achieved.

Throughout this period of inactivity by day the Luftwaffe was busy at night. Increasing numbers of enemy bombers penetrated the east coast defences and, in some cases, flew well inland. Searchlights and anti-aircraft guns were active on most nights. Certainly the heavy battery sited adjacent to Hornchurch could always be guaranteed to go into action just when we were dozing off after a particularly long day of boring readiness and frustrating armed reconnaissances.

On one particular evening, or to be exact in the early hours of the morning, I was ordered off during a period of night readiness and directed to the Clacton area where large numbers of enemy aircraft were reported to be operating. I floated around for nearly an hour spending most of my time chasing crossed searchlight beams, the sign that an enemy aircraft was being tracked there, but failed to make any contacts. 'Sailor,' who was airborne at about the same time, destroyed two enemy bombers. He was the first fighter pilot in the war to do so at night; a magnificent feat by a great fighter pilot.

June 25th found the squadron installed at Rochford. We liked operating from this base despite the comparatively primitive accommodation available there. We were an independent unit there and there was little interference, or visits from 'brass'. The very isolation of the place in relation to any permanent type base seemed to produce an inter-dependence among sections of the squadron not always so apparent when working under more civilized conditions. 54 Squadron had been the first squadron to use this airfield on the outbreak of war and were soon to be the first to fight the Battle of Britain from there. The routine at Rochford followed that observed at Hornchurch; long periods of readiness, occasional flight or squadron reconnaissance patrols over occupied territory and training flying whenever possible. One day when I returned from a training flight I was met by Johnny Allen with the news that we two were required at Hornchurch, together with 'Prof' who had already gone on ahead.

"What for?" I queried.

"All the Adjutant would say on the telephone was that a VIP was visiting the station and we were required to be there to meet him," answered Johnny.

"How do we get there?"

"In the Magister, (a two-seater training aircraft) and we are to be there as soon as possible."

On arrival at Hornchurch we found the station buzzing with excitement. The distinguished visitor was none other than His Majesty the King. A small parade was to be held at which we three, 'Sailor' Malan and Bob Tuck were to be presented with our decorations. The ceremony was carried out with a minimum of fuss, the normal activities of a station at war carrying on undisturbed. The parade was held on a small square of tarmac between two hangars and, appropriately, adjacent to the parked Spitfires of 65 and 74 Squadrons. For me it was a memorable occasion. As a New Zealander brought up to admire the Mother country and respect the King as her head, it was the honour of a lifetime, an ultimate milestone of my flying ambitions – the Distinguished Flying Cross presented by the King, in the field of action.

After the ceremony the decorated pilots joined the King for

sherry in the Officers' Mess. I had the opportunity to chat with His Majesty and found him charmingly informal, and very well versed on the Royal Air Force. He was particularly interested to hear the pilots' views on the Spitfire compared with the Messerschmitt 109s, our chief adversary in the battle ahead. He smiled understandingly over our confidence in the outcome, and said that he thought the Hurricane, too, would give a good account of itself, as indeed it had done in France.

CHAPTER SEVEN

The Battle Begins

WHEN did the Battle of Britain begin? The History of The Royal Air Force says mid-August;* other publications say July; some even as late as September when the assault on London was at its peak. The German General Kreipe† says, and I quote, "The date that I should ascribe to the opening of The Battle of Britain is May 1940." It is difficult to be precise on the exact date but Dunkirk was certainly the overture. From a fighter pilot's point of view, I put it at July 3rd when enemy bombers, operating singly and taking advantage of extensive cloud cover, made repeated attacks on Channel shipping. Throughout this day the fighter squadrons in No. 11 Group were constantly alerted, ordered off and engaged in combat, and from then onwards there was to be little respite for the pilots defending our Channel shipping. Indeed, one or two slack periods apart, July 1940 was to be a particularly intensive phase of what we now know as the Battle of Britain.

German documents captured since the war confirm July 3rd as the date intended for the re-opening of the air offensive. On July 2nd the German Armed Forces Supreme Command issued its first operational instructions to the Luftwaffe for the campaign against the United Kingdom which was intended to culminate in the invasion of the British Isles. There were two basic tasks assigned to the Luftwaffe:

(1) The interdiction of the Channel to merchant shipping, by means of attacks on convoys, and the destruction of harbour facilities.

(2) The destruction of the Royal Air Force.

*The Fight at Odds – HMSO
†Werner Kreipe, Chief of Operations, Third Air Fleet (The Fatal Decisions)

Between the date that this order was issued and the 10th July bad weather conditions over the Channel precluded the mounting of large scale bomber operations. It was not therefore until this latter date that operations in force were undertaken by the Luftwaffe when bomber formations, with heavy fighter escort, attacked two convoys in the Dover-Dungeness area. This operation was to be repeated many times in the weeks that followed, and with increasing effort particularly in fighter support. Phase I of the Battle of Britain had begun.

No story of the Battle of Britain is complete, at whatever level it is written, without a brief survey of the opposing air forces. Only by doing this is it possible to bring home to the reader the immensity of the task faced by the fighter pilots of the Royal Air Force. Furthermore, the extreme fatigue reached by the squadron, flight and section leaders can be more readily appreciated when the odds against Fighter Command are related to the acute shortage of pilots, and in particular leaders, at the time.

At the end of the Dunkirk operations, Fighter Command could muster only 300 serviceable Spitfires and Hurricanes. This figure improved to about 500 by July and was further increased until there were about 600 Spitfires and Hurricanes in the battle by mid-August. It is interesting to note that this latter figure represented just half that considered by the Air Staff to be necessary for the defence of the United Kingdom, when they reviewed the strategical consequences of the fall of France. The pilot situation was more unfavourable. Despite the invaluable intake into the Command of fifty-two pilots on loan from the Fleet Air Arm – and what good pilots they were too – the squadrons were still under strength and embarrassingly short of experienced leaders.

What of the opposition? The lull between the end of the French campaign and July had enabled the Luftwaffe to regroup its forces which were now disposed on captured and rebuilt airfields throughout the occupied territories. On July

3rd, when the Armed Forces Supreme Command directive was issued, their forces amounted to some 3,000 aircraft of which no less than 1,480 were fighters. As for their pilots, I again quote the erstwhile General Kreipe who, referring to this period, said of the Luftwaffe:

"The power of the Air Force was now at a zenith which it was never again to achieve during the long years of war...The pilots were highly skilled...Their morale was very high and they were confident of victory..."

The outcome of the battle was to the Germans a foregone conclusion. "It will take," reported General Stapf of German Intelligence to General Halder (German General Staff) on 11th July, "between a fortnight and a month to smash the enemy air force."

It was against this background that the Luftwaffe re-opened operations in July. The first few incursions made it quite clear that the pick-up range of our RDF chain (as Radar was originally known) was insufficient to enable defensive fighters to achieve effective interception on enemy raids whose objectives were shipping or coastal targets. It was therefore decided that a flight of aircraft from each Sector Station would operate, on a daily basis, from the most forward airfield in that particular sector. Manston was chosen for the Hornchurch squadrons, and it was to this airfield that I moved with my flight on July 4th. The only other aircraft based there at the time belonged to 600 Auxiliary Squadron, equipped with Blenheims and operating in the night fighter role. This squadron had moved to Hornchurch on the outbreak of war but had deployed to Manston for operations against the German night bombers now active over the countryside. When, during the airfield bombing phase in August, conditions at Manston became almost untenable, the pilots of 600 Squadron set a splendid example to the ground crews by assisting in the refuelling and rearming of the day

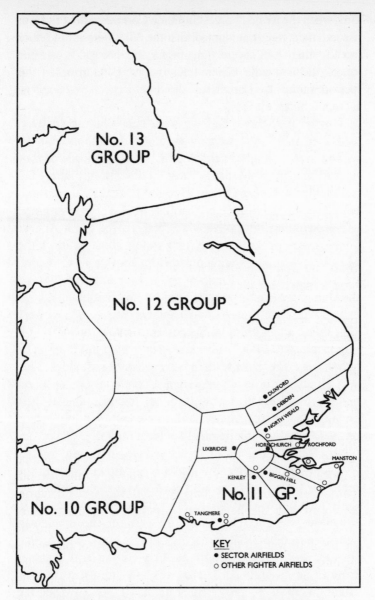

Map of England Showing Groups and 11 Group sector boundaries

squadrons. More often than not this was done under fire from the enemy and despite the fact that the 600 pilots should have been resting from the previous night's operations. It was due largely to them that we were able to continue to operate from Manston long after the airfield should have been evacuated as tactically unacceptable.

For the next three days we were busy chasing sporadic raids, but indifferent weather favoured the enemy and the results were usually inconclusive. On the fourth day of operations from Manston, my sub-section, under the leadership of Flying Officer Desmond McMullen, ran into trouble in tackling a formation of twin-engined Messerschmitt 110 fighters which had crossed the coast near Dungeness. The section of three was just about to attack the Me 110s when they were jumped from above by a formation of escorting Me 109s. This was a classic example of "beware the Hun in the sun." The Spitfire pilots, to put it bluntly, were caught with their trousers down and two of our aircraft were shot down and a third damaged. Fortunately, apart from a minor injury to Pilot Officer Coleman which put him out of action for a few weeks, there were no pilot casualties. This was a most unfortunate first engagement over our own soil and it proved that the Luftwaffe pilots had lost none of their cunning and aggressiveness and, worse still, that the lessons of the Dunkirk air fighting had not been fully digested by our pilots. This was one lesson re-learned at heavy cost.

Enemy activity was now increasing, particularly with the return of better flying weather, and it was decided that the daily deployment to Manston was to be increased to squadron strength. The procedure was for the nominated squadron to take-off at first light from its home base for the forward airfield and return at dusk, or later if weather conditions permitted. There was no hardship in this commitment in the early part of the battle. As, however, the intensity of operations increased and enemy bombing destroyed the facilities at the forward airfields, take-offs and landings were generally made under hostile enemy surveillance, a nerve-racking experience for the pilots and the ground crews assisting in take-off preliminaries.

For the time being, the squadron continued to operate in flight or section strength, one section always being in position over a convoy when it was within the Hornchurch area of responsibility while the other section was at standby or readiness on the ground as a reinforcement, the actual state depending on the weather conditions prevailing at the time. If an important convoy was in the area the patrol was usually increased to a flight and the remaining aircraft on the ground brought to standby. It was *en route* to relieve my flight on patrol that 'Wonky' had the good fortune to be diverted to intercept a suspect plot south of Dover. It turned out to be three Me 109s presumably on reconnaissance, two of which were destroyed – the pilots baling out over England – and one severely damaged. George Gribble was exultant and was waiting to break the news to me when I landed from a period of convoy work.

"Well, Al, it took 'B' Flight to redress the balance of your flight's losses the other day, and with the added pleasure of providing two prisoners for interrogation. Valuable birds at this stage, I should think."

'Wonky', who was standing nearby, beamed at me and said, "They didn't even get a chance to put up a fight, at least the two we shot down, and I'm sure the Hun pilots must still be wondering what hit them."

July 11th was particularly hectic, and both flights flew continuous convoy patrols throughout the day. 'B' Flight were engaged on two occasions, with losses on both sides. On the fourth trip of the day I ran into trouble while leading my flight to investigate what was reported as unidentified activity five miles east of Deal. We had just crossed the coast at a height of 1,500ft when I spotted an aircraft flying at wave top height. It was a seaplane painted silver, and from a distance there appeared to be civilian registration letters painted on the upper surface of the wing. I was wondering what to do about this unexpected discovery when Johnny burst through on the R/T.

"Red Leader there are about a dozen 109s flying in loose formation, well behind and slightly above the seaplane."

"Thanks, Johnny," I replied, "that makes the seaplane enemy so far as I am concerned."

The camouflaged 109s were difficult to pick up against the grey background of the sea and it was a moment or two before I could locate them.

"OK, Yellow Leader, I see them. You take your section and go for the seaplane. We'll try and distract the escort; they don't appear to have seen us as yet."

I ordered red section to follow me and banking around to get behind the enemy fighters, dived into the attack. The Huns soon spotted us, or perhaps Johnny's section diving towards the seaplane, for as we levelled out behind them the leader split his formation in two. One half broke upwards and to the right in a steep turn while the other half performed a similar manoeuvre, but to the left. "No fool this leader," I thought to myself. "That's a smart move." I remembered this manoeuvre later on when the RAF was on the offensive, and used it with telling effect against defending German fighters.

The Hun leader had timed his break perfectly and he had certainly put us at a disadvantage by splitting his force. There was only one thing to do; break formation and have a go, each pilot for himself. We were outnumbered by about six to one and were more likely to confuse the Hun in this way thus diverting attention from Johnny who had just given the order for his section to attack the seaplane.

Fastening on to the tail of a yellow nosed Messerschmitt I fought to bring my guns to bear as the range rapidly decreased, and when the wingspan of the enemy aircraft fitted snugly into the range scale bars of my reflector sight, I pressed the firing button. There was an immediate response from my eight Brownings which, to the accompaniment of a slight bucketing from my aircraft, spat a stream of lethal lead targetwards. "Got you," I muttered to myself as the small dancing yellow flames of exploding 'De Wilde' bullets spattered along the Messerschmitt's fuselage. My exultation was short-lived. Before I could fire another burst two 109s wheeled in behind me. I broke hard into the attack pulling my Spitfire into a climbing, spiralling turn as I did so; a manoeuvre I had discovered in previous combats with 109s to be particularly effective. And it was no less effective now; the Messerschmitts literally "fell out of the sky" as they stalled in an attempt to follow me.

I soon found another target. About 3,000 yards directly ahead of me, and at the same level, a Hun was just completing a turn preparatory to re-entering the fray. He saw me almost immediately and rolled out of his turn towards me so that a head-on attack became inevitable. Using both hands on the control column to steady the aircraft and thus keep my aim steady, I peered through the reflector sight at the rapidly closing enemy aircraft. We opened fire together, and immediately a hail of lead thudded into my Spitfire. One moment the Messerschmitt was a clearly defined shape, its wingspan nicely enclosed within the circle of my reflector sight, and the next it was on top of me, a terrifying blur which blotted out the sky ahead. Then we hit.

The force of the impact pitched me violently forward on to my cockpit harness, the straps of which bit viciously into my shoulders. At the same moment, the control column was snatched abruptly from my gripping fingers by a momentary, but powerful, reversal of elevator load. In a flash it was over; there was clear sky ahead of me, and I was still alive. But smoke and flame were pouring from the engine which began to vibrate, slowly at first but with increasing momentum causing the now regained control column to jump back and forwards in my hand. Hastily I closed the throttle and reached forward to flick off the ignition switches, but before I could do so the engine seized and the airscrew stopped abruptly. I saw with amazement that the blades had been bent almost double with the impact of the collision; the Messerschmitt must have been just that fraction above me as we hit.

With smoke now pouring into the cockpit I reached blindly forward for the hood release toggle and tugged at it violently. There was no welcoming and expected rush of air to denote that the hood had been jettisoned. Again and again I pulled at the toggle but there was no response. In desperation I turned to the normal release catch and exerting my full strength endeavoured to slide back the hood. It refused to budge; I was trapped. There was only one thing to do; try to keep the aircraft under control and head for the nearby coast. The speed had by now dropped off considerably, and with full backward pressure on the stick I was just able to keep a reasonable gliding altitude. If only I could be lucky enough to hit in open country where there was a small chance that I might get away with it.

Frantically I peered through the smoke and flame enveloping the engine, seeking with streaming eyes for what lay ahead. There could be no question of turning; I had no idea what damage had been done to the fuselage and tail of my aircraft, although the mainplanes appeared to be undamaged, and I daren't risk even a small turn at low level, even if I could have seen to turn.

Through a miasmatic cloud of flame and smoke the ground suddenly appeared ahead of me. The next moment a post flashed by my wingtip and then the aircraft struck the ground and ricocheted into the air again finally returning to earth with a jarring impact, and once again I was jerked forward on to my harness. Fortunately the straps held fast and continued to do so as the aircraft ploughed its way through a succession of splintering posts before finally coming to a halt on the edge of a cornfield. Half blinded by smoke and frantic with fear I tore at my harness release pin. And then with my bare hands wielding the strength of desperation, I battered at the perspex hood which entombed me. With a splintering crash it finally cracked open, thus enabling me to scramble from the cockpit to the safety of the surrounding field.

At a safe distance from the aircraft I sat down to observe the damage to person and property. My hands were cut and bleeding; my eyebrows were singed; both knees were badly bruised; and blood trickled into my mouth from a slightly cut lip. But I was alive! I learned later from the technical officer who examined the wreckage after the fire had been put out, that the seat had broken free from the lower retaining bar thus pivoting upwards, and so throwing my knees against the lower part of the dashboard.

The aircraft had ploughed a passage through three fields, studded with anti-invasion posts erected to prevent enemy gliders from landing, and bits of aircraft and posts were strewn along the 300 yards of its path. My Spitfire was now a blazing mass of metal from which a series of explosions denoted that the heat was igniting the unused ammunition, to the consternation of a knot of onlookers who had by now collected at the scene of the crash.

A woman, whom I had observed coming from a nearby farm-house, approached me and said:

"I have telephoned Manston airfield and they say that an ambulance and fire engine are already on the way. Won't you come in and have a cup of tea?"

"Thank you, I will, but I would prefer something stronger if you've got it."

"Yes, I think there is some whisky in the house. Will that do?"

"Yes thanks, just what the doctor would order. I'm sorry about messing up your fields; let's hope the fire engine gets here before the fire spreads to that field of corn. Incidentally, how far are we from Manston?"

"Oh not far, about five miles by road. Your people should be here soon."

Turning to a small cluster of the more curious onlookers,

who had crept closer to the wreckage, I said, "I advise you to stand well clear of the aircraft. There is plenty of high-octane fuel in the tanks and an explosion is a distinct possibility." This remark had an immediate effect and they hastily retreated to a safe distance.

Before long, an anxious MO arrived with the ambulance and examined me cursorily before conveying me back to Manston. The squadron had returned to Rochford by the time I arrived so I was forced to spend the night there. If the doctor had had his way I would have been bedded down in the station sick quarters, but after a certain amount of persuasive talk on my part he released me to return to the mess. The following morning saw me airborne in a Tiger Moth trainer, accompanied by Flying Officer Ben Bowring, a pre-war rugger compatriot, and headed for Rochford with thoughts of a couple of days off. There was to be no respite, however. 'Prof's' first words on seeing me were:

"Thank heavens you're back, Al. Are you fit to fly?"

"Reluctantly, yes," I answered. "A bit shaken I must admit. Why the urgent note in your voice?"

"Well, we are damned short of pilots. Perhaps you haven't been told yet, but we lost two of your chaps in that show yesterday, both presumed killed."

"I am not surprised, 'Prof,' those 109 pilots were smart boys. I knew that at least one of our chaps had been shot down; I heard Yellow two screaming for help over the R/T. He said he was on fire and needed assistance as there were four Huns on his tail. He sounded hysterical, poor blighter. There wasn't anything I could do about it; I was in a real pickle at the time. Who was the other one?"

"Tony Evershed."

"Hell! He was one of the brightest of the new boys. I had high hopes of him turning into a good section leader. Were there any claims, apart from the seaplane which I understand has been beached near Deal?"

"Yes, Johnny got a Me 109 probably destroyed, and

Sergeant Lawrence a 109 confirmed. What are you claiming?"

"I certainly damaged the first Me 109 I shot at, but as for the one with which I collided I just don't know. I can't see him getting back, but then it was a miracle that I got away with it; he might well have had the same luck. He had a damn sight further to go, of course."

"We'll leave Patrick (Flying Officer Patrick Shallard, the squadron Intelligence Officer) to sort out that particular claim. Now for the position of pilots and aircraft. In the last ten days we have had six pilots killed and two injured. That reduces us to twelve pilots and, while at the moment we are down to eight aircraft – thirteen have been lost or damaged since our return to operations – some replacements are expected to be ready for collection from Hornchurch this afternoon."

"It certainly isn't a bright outlook, 'Prof'." Frankly, I had hoped for a day or two off the station, perhaps a quick sortie to London. I was pretty sore, and a bit shaken but quite obviously I couldn't be spared.

"I'm sorry, Al, but I hope that the whole squadron will be given a short rest ere long. We must be just about due for another break. I could do with it, I'm bloody tired."

The long periods of readiness, interspersed with convoy patrols and days of action like yesterday, were beginning to tell. The shortage of leaders was worrying and it was chiefly for this reason that 'Prof' was anxious for the squadron to be taken out of the line for a bit. There was some tough fighting ahead and we could only hope that Command had the situation in hand.

"You had better go and sort out your flight, Al. With McMullen on the injured list, you'll be short of section leaders."

Down at dispersal Johnny greeted me with, "We are in quite a mess for aircraft. There are only four serviceable, so you needn't expect to fly this morning."

"I'm in no hurry," I answered. "What was that seaplane you attacked, Johnny?"

"A Heinkel 59. I only managed to get a short burst at it, my overtaking speed was too great, but apparently I hit the engine because the pilot landed on the water with a dead motor. I caught a glimpse of red crosses on the side of the fuselage as I whistled past, but there wasn't time to see much. The 109s were hot on our tails and they occupied my attention from then on. Patrick Shallard tells me that the crew have been taken prisoner; it will be interesting to hear their story – not that we ever shall."

"Red Cross markings eh! It seems queer to carry those and yet have such a heavy escort of fighters. Damned aggressive blighters too. Any black crosses or swastikas?"

"No, just civilian registration letters on the mainplane."

"I must say it is an intriguing affair. Let's go and rout out Patrick, perhaps he'll have some more 'gen' on it."

We found Patrick in his office surrounded, as always, with a host of combat reports which he was including in the squadron history, a labour of love for Patrick and a task which he undertook extremely well.

"Any more on the He 59?" I queried.

"As a matter of fact I have, Al. Air Ministry have been on the phone this morning wanting further details of this combat. Apparently the Government is considering issuing some form of warning to the Germans about these aircraft with Red Cross markings flying off our coast. By the way, the Intelligence Officer put in his report that you had run out of ammunition and deliberately rammed that Me 109. Is that true?"

"I may be a mad New Zealander, Patrick," I answered, "but not so mad that I would deliberately ram an enemy aircraft head-on. The truth is that it all happened so damn quickly, there just wasn't time to get out of the way. I'm sure that applied to the Hun pilot also. Incidentally, what are you claiming for me?"

"One damaged, which you claimed in your report at Manston, and a 'probably destroyed' for the one with which you collided. That suit you?"

"Yes, fine, but I'm damn curious to know what happened to the latter one. See if you can find out anything?"

About three weeks after this incident the Air Ministry issued a Communique on the subject of enemy aircraft using civil lettering and marked with the Red Cross. This read:

"It has come to the notice of His Majesty's Government in the United Kingdom that enemy aircraft bearing civil markings and marked with the Red Cross have recently flown over British ships at sea and in the vicinity of the British coast, and that they are being employed for purposes which His Majesty's Government cannot regard as being consistent with the privileges generally accorded to the Red Cross.

"His Majesty's Government desire to accord to ambulance aircraft reasonable facilities for the transportation of the sick and wounded, in accordance with the Red Cross Convention, and aircraft engaged in the direct evacuation of sick and wounded will be respected, provided that they comply with the relevant provisions of the Convention.

"His Majesty's Government are unable, however, to grant immunity to such aircraft flying over areas in which operations are in progress on land or at sea, or approaching British or Allied territory, or territory in British occupation, or British or Allied ships.

"Ambulance aircraft which do not comply with the above requirements will do so at their own risk and peril."*

Bad weather most fortunately arrived at this critical period for the squadron and afforded a most welcome respite to the tired pilots. Despite the fact that a high state of readiness was still necessary we were able, in this period, to do a certain amount of continuation training for the new pilots, and at the same time give practice to the newly promoted section leaders.

*AM Communique dated 29 July 1940 (20) (AM No 1254)

A sudden break in the weather was the signal for the opening of the next and final round in July. It was to be a short but furious encounter, and for 54 Squadron a sad one. The opening gambit by the enemy was a co-ordinated attack by two heavily escorted bomber formations; one against a convoy entering the Thames estuary, and the other against one off Dover. Our short, but welcome, respite was at an end. The squadron, with myself leading and Colin in charge of the second flight, was once again in action. At 8.15am on the morning of July 24th we were ordered off to intercept one of these two convoy raids. When midway between Dover and the North Foreland, and at a height of 20,000ft, I was informed by Control that two large enemy raids were approaching across the Channel. The one heading for the Thames estuary was to be our target. I acknowledged this order, but before I could turn about on to the new course to effect interception Colin's urgent voice cut in on the radio. "Tallyho, Red Leader, a large formation of enemy just south of Dover."

At this precise moment I spotted the second formation approaching the North Foreland. I therefore ordered Colin to ignore his original sighting and to follow me. The enemy formation, the largest I had seen up to that time, consisted of about 18 Dorniers protected by a considerable number of escort fighters weaving and criss-crossing above and behind the bombers. I reported the unpleasant facts to control and requested immediate assistance.

An attack against such numbers was a frightening prospect. The escort fighters, all Me 109s as far as I could see, were stepped up in layers to a considerable height above the bombers – the top aircraft being some 5,000ft or so above our height – and presented a formidable looking defence. Clearly visible below I could see the convoy sailing unsuspectingly towards the estuary, presenting an ideal target to the enemy bombers who must be very near the point from which to start their bombing run. It was vital to get among them quickly. "Blue Leader," I called over the R/T, "you cover with your flight while we try to get at the bombers." A most unexpected reply came back from Colin.

"What the hell do you mean, Red Leader? We are already stuck into the fighters," queried a puzzled Colin.

"You clot," I bellowed back, "you're after the wrong formation. I told you to follow me."

There was no reply, and this was no time for recriminations; I should have to take my flight alone.

"Red and Yellow sections, echelon starboard as I turn in, and do your damnedest to get a shot at the bombers before the 109s get at us." This was the signal for attack.

Taking advantage of our height above the enemy bombers to work up a high overtaking speed, thus making if difficult for the protecting fighters to interfere with our initial run in, we turned into the attack. A momentary buffeting as I hit the enemy bombers' slip-stream, a determined juggling with the control column and rudder, a brief wait for the range to close, and the right-hand bomber received the full impact of my eight Brownings. In a matter of seconds, in which time only a short burst was possible, I was forced to break off the attack for fear of collision. It was perhaps just as well: as the 109s were now all around us. In the next few minutes, a frenzy of twisting and turning, I managed quick bursts at three enemy fighters, as singly they passed fleetingly through my line of fire, but without conclusive results. Suddenly, the sky was clear and I was alone; one moment the air was a seething cauldron of Hun fighters, and the next it was empty. There were to be many occasions in later battles when a similar occurrence took place but on this, the first, it was a unique experience.

Away in the distance a dark blob was faintly discernible on the horizon; the enemy bombers making for France and safety. Below me the convoy sailed serenely on, apparently unharmed, while in its wake a line of light brown circles in the water, contrasting vividly with the dark grey around them, marked the points of impact of exploding bombs. I reported to Control that I was returning to base and was greeted in reply by Ronald Adam's voice, apologetically intoning his regret that he had been unable to get reinforcements airborne in time. It was cold comfort to me to learn that a squadron was now on its way to take up station over the convoy.

Sad news awaited my arrival back at Rochford. Johnny Allen had been killed. He had been hit by a 109 on the initial attack against the bombers. His number two stuck with him and was able to report the sequence of events leading up to his death. In the words of this pilot: "I followed him down as he glided towards the coast. Just as he crossed in his engine appeared to pick up again and he turned towards Manston hoping, no doubt, to get it down safely there. The next moment fire broke out in the engine and at once the aircraft flicked on to its back and dived into the ground on the outskirts of Foreness." So died a gallant officer. With eight enemy aircraft destroyed to his credit, and many others probably destroyed and damaged, Johnny had at last been struck down. A tragedy for the squadron and a sad day for his family and many friends. He was truly one of The Few.

There were two further engagements that day and for the next three days we operated at an average of four squadron sorties a day, almost all of which were directly connected with convoy protection. My log book records twelve trips in the period, and although not all of these represented engagements, the strain of combat was always present. Our losses in pilots mounted but we continued to give as good as we got, despite the vastly heavier fighter escorts now being employed by the enemy. On the fifth day of the re-opened fighting, tragedy again overtook us. 'Wonky' Way was killed. I was on convoy patrol at the time and heard the battle developing over the R/T. 'Wonky's' flight was patrolling a second convoy in our sector of operations when attacked by large numbers of 109s which were escorting a formation of Junkers 87 dive bombers. According to George, the flight had made one pass at the Junkers, during which 'Wonky' had shot one into the sea, and they were closing for the second attack when down came the 109s. At this juncture I recognized George's excited voice, "Watch out, Blue One, 109s coming in from above – hundreds of them." I immediately called control for permission to reinforce 'B' Flight but was refused, and ordered to stay over the convoy. Again I heard George, this time in urgency, "Break, 'Wonky,' BREAK." From the long silence that followed I had a premonition that the warning was too late. Again George's voice crackled in my earphones, this time in half-sobbing anger: "Damn and blast this bloody war, they've got 'Wonky'." So died another gallant airman; as with Johnny, not outfought but out-numbered.

The loss of six pilots in three days, including two of our most experienced leaders, coupled with the strain of long hours at readiness and repeated combats against overwhelming numbers, was having a depressing effect on the more inexperienced squadron pilots. Of the seventeen pilots in the squadron when the Dunkirk fighting opened, only five now remained. So long as the morale of these five held good the squadron could continue to operate, and with reasonable success, despite a preponderance of inexperience among pilots, and an acute shortage of section leaders. But the five Dunkirk survivors had reached the point of physical and mental tiredness beyond which lies the realm of fear, a symptom in a leader passed on to his immediate juniors who, in turn, transmit it to the younger pilots until, like a disease, it spreads through the squadron; even down to the ground crews whose keenness and efficiency can be directly related to the morale of the pilots.

A rest and refit was now vital if the squadron was to be an effective force in the more serious threat yet to be launched. Was the Station Commander aware of our predicament? If so, did the Air Officer Commanding the Group agree we should be rested? Would the Commander-in-Chief act?

These were questions we asked each other as that evening 'Prof', George and I reviewed our position. The big point at issue was: should 'Prof' have a word with the Station Commander? I held he should, he wasn't sure. And George, embittered by 'Wonky's' death, was all for going on, whatever the cost. In the event, no action was required for that evening orders were received for 54 Squadron to move to Catterick the following morning. The Commander-in-Chief had proved that he was controlling the battle with his finger on the pulse of operations.

Thus ended another phase of operations for 54 Squadron; a phase which the participating pilots truly claim was an integral part of the Battle of Britain. History shows that the Germans planned August 12th as their ADLER TAG (EAGLE DAY) but from early July the German Air Force was at full readiness and, as the events in these pages reveal, had been operating intensively throughout the month. Admittedly, the really full-scale air assault opened on August 13th – bad weather had precluded operations on Eagle Day – but to the Germans the air battles of July were a necessary preliminary to the intended knock-out blow.

While claiming August 12th as the beginning of the battle, the History of the Royal Air Force qualifies this statement when, in an earlier chapter, it says:

"...In the month (July) preceding the Battle of Britain...the flying effort forced on Fighter Command by the daylight attacks was very large, amounting to some 600 sorties per day; and since the fighter escorts with our ships were of necessity small, and the warning usually too short for further squadrons to reach convoys before they were attacked, most of the combats found our pilots at a grave disadvantage. Over and over again a mere handful of Spitfires and Hurricanes found themselves fighting desperately with formations of a hundred or more German aircraft..."

CHAPTER EIGHT

The Onslaught

THE process of rehabilitation at Catterick followed the same pattern as for our first visit; priority on regaining one hundred per cent aircraft serviceability, and familiarization flying by the new pilots. The squadron was required to maintain a readiness state but only on a flight basis which allowed a reasonable rotation of leaders and 'experienced' pilots, so called because they had survived the first round in July.

As was to be expected, our losses in July had not been spread evenly between the flights which were now unbalanced in experience and therefore required some adjustment, never a very popular move among those pilots who had been with a particular flight for a reasonable period of time. Thus it was that on the first morning after our arrival, George and I were summoned to 'Prof's' office to discuss these moves; each to argue his case for the retention of a particular pilot whom 'Prof' had provisionally decided should change flight allegiance.

"Before we sort out the pilots, sir, I should like to get a decision on Sergeant Dennis.* You remember; I spoke to you about him?" queried George.

"All right, George, go ahead, I'll be interested to hear Al's views," answered 'Prof'.

"To be blunt, he's 'yellow'. You remember I said I was suspicious of his actions and claims in that first scrap on our return south. On the next one, the show in which 'Wonky' was killed, he disappeared as soon as we had made the first attack. You know how it is after the first attack; just a wonderful mix-up and impossible to tell who's who and what's what. Anyhow, as I broke to re-position myself for

*The name is entirely fictitious

another attack on the Junkers 87s, I noticed a Spitfire diving away towards our coast. There wasn't time to find out who it was and just at that moment the 109s attacked. You know the rest of the story about the fight. One more Spitfire might have helped 'Wonky'."

"Did you tackle him on landing, George?"

"Yes, I did, sir, but not before I had made certain that it could only have been Dennis who dived away at that particular moment. He was quite frank about it and said that his engine had sounded funny on the way out and that it cut during the first attack and he thought the sensible thing to do was to get back before it finally packed up on him. To be fair, the 109s had not been spotted at the time he broke off the attack. When I landed I checked with the Flight Sergeant fitter on the engine; and he told me that a thorough test run had been made but that there was nothing that a couple of minutes at full revolutions wouldn't have cured. Oiled plugs, in fact. Dennis should have guessed this; after all, he's had a reasonable amount of experience on Spitfires."

"Well, George, we've got to be careful. One occasion such as you have described is hardly enough for me to act. What do you think, Al?"

"I agree with you, sir. While I sympathize with George I feel that Dennis should be given another chance."

"OK by me," said George, "but I am willing to bet any money that he will not come up to scratch."

The problem of Dennis solved, at least temporarily, we proceeded to allocate the remaining pilots to flights, together with those expected to arrive before the squadron returned south; the flights being built around George and Colin in 'B' Flight, and myself and Desmond in 'A' Flight – four survivors of Dunkirk, 'Prof' making the fifth.

The question 'when does a man lack the moral courage for battle?' poses a tricky problem and one that has never been satisfactorily solved. There are so many intangibles; if he funks it once, will he the next time? How many men in similar circumstances would react in exactly the same way? And so on. There can be no definite yardstick, each case must be judged on its merits as each set of circumstances will differ.

In the case of day fighter pilots, in particular, it presented squadron and flight commanders with a really difficult problem and one with which they were being continually faced. Up till the moment the air battle is joined, each pilot is a member of a team and should he be inclined to cowardice the presence of other aircraft serves as an antidote to his feelings, the more so when he knows that for the initial attack he is under the censorious eyes of the other pilots in the formation. It is immediately subsequent to this first attack that the opportunity occurs for the less courageous to make their get-away without seeming to avoid the issue. Against unescorted bombers, or perhaps small enemy formations, the opportunity doesn't normally occur, and in such cases there exists a natural feeling of superiority sufficient to convince the waverer that he is in a position to impose his terms. It is against overwhelming odds, as faced in the convoy battles of July, that the urge to run is uppermost in one's mind, and it is on these occasions that fear normally gets the upper hand. But, under just such circumstances is it most difficult to prove that a particular pilot has not pulled his weight. After the initial attack it is almost impossible to observe the actions of any one pilot, and unless a watch has been set on a suspect – it has been done – there can be no positive proof of cowardice. Lack of proof, however, doesn't rule out suspicion and, in some cases, a conviction that a suspect member of the team is, to use George's expression, 'yellow'.

I know only too well the almost overpowering urge to either break off an engagement, or participate in such a way as to ensure one's safety, when surrounded and outnumbered. On many an occasion in July I had to grit my teeth and overcome fear with determination in just such circumstances or, alternatively, when I became temporarily isolated from the main battle, to talk myself into going back. I refuse to believe that there are those among us who know no fear. Admittedly, there are those who show no fear and again others who are demonstratively more brave than their comrades in arms; but everyone in his innermost heart is afraid at some time.

As I said in an earlier chapter, the dangerous state is reached in battle when one is so tired mentally and physically that the ever present urge of self-preservation overrules the more normal urge to do one's duty. This latter state may well have been reached by Dennis who had been in action continuously since the last week of the Dunkirk operations. It was for this reason that I was in favour of giving him another chance despite the fact that there was a danger he would infect the younger pilots in his capacity of section leader. The short rest at Catterick would, I hoped, do the trick.

Ten days at Catterick had worked wonders. The squadron wore a new look in both aircraft and pilots of which there were now 22, the highest on record for our squadron but, as events were to prove, not enough. The squadron strength in pilots considered by the Commander-in-Chief to be the minimum was 29, and I think that had this figure been realized before the Battle opened – and assuming a proportionate increase in leaders – the truly desperate straits certain squadrons found themselves in towards the end of the Battle would have been avoided. The state of 54 Squadron at the end of August, as I shall show, was to be proof positive of the Commander-in-Chief's sound assessment of the numbers required.

The now familiar faces of the pilots who formed the hard core of 41 Squadron – they too had suffered fairly heavy casualties – headed by Flight Lieutenant Norman Ryder, greeted us on our return to Hornchurch. I was never sure whether, on these occasions, they were pleased to see us back or not. I do know, however, that we were pathetically pleased to welcome them into Hornchurch a month later. One person whom we knew would be pleased to see us back was the Station Commander. 'Daddy' Bouchier had commanded 54 Squadron at Hornchurch not long before the war and always looked on its pilots as his particular 'babies', or perhaps more aptly, 'chicks' as Winston Churchill referred to the Battle of Britain pilots when congratulating Air Marshal Dowding on their successes.

We were soon into the familiar routine of convoy patrols again, but for the first two days after our return there was very little enemy activity due, no doubt, to unfavourable weather over the Channel. The 11th August witnessed the resumption of the attacks on convoys and channel ports, and introduced a short-lived phase of enemy fighter attacks against the Dover barrage balloons. It always puzzled me why the Huns bothered to shoot down these balloons, unless it was to clear the way for dive-bombing attacks on the harbour by Junkers 87s. Even then it didn't make sense; these aircraft could pull out at a height which would enable them to clear the balloons, and yet bomb effectively. A bright clear August 11th witnessed three squadron engagements over or near Dover against large formations of enemy fighters acting as a diversion and forward escort to bombers attacking the harbour, and latterly a convoy off the south coast. I added to my personal score with another enemy aircraft destroyed and the squadron, although losing two pilots and with a further three Spitfires damaged, amassed a total of eleven confirmed victories. A good opening and an encouraging first day's combat for the new pilots.

Arriving back at Hornchurch that evening, having operated from Manston all day, we were greeted with the news that there was to be a show on the camp, featuring the famous Windmill girls. "A most delightful thought," muttered George in a tone of voice which made it clear that his thoughts were still at Catterick with his little WAAF.

"Well you needn't go," countered Colin. "All the more for us to choose from."

"My dear Colin, when I cease to be interested in the spectacle of partly clad females, and from what I hear luscious ones, you can ask to have me transferred to bombers because then I really will be a 'dead-beat'," retorted George.

The evening's performance certainly proved a most welcome and delightful interlude, and the party afterwards no less entertaining. I was agreeably surprised to find that the famous Windmill girls were so young and unspoilt. Furthermore, they were such gay companions and were, without exception, dedicated troupers working their way up through the ranks of the theatrical world. So far as we were concerned they could come again – and they did.

August 12th witnessed the opening of a new phase of operations; the attack on airfields and radar stations for which the Germans used all their bomber types, and always with very heavy fighter escort. We had just settled down to the inevitable game of cards in our dispersal hut at Manston (pontoon was the normal relaxation between operations) when the telephone shrilled warningly. How we hated the dispersal telephone; its very note was abnormal and the unexpectedness with which it rang had the immediate effect of producing an awful sick feeling in the pit of one's tummy. A pin could have been heard to drop as, with cards poised and eyes turned expectantly towards the orderly as he reached for the receiver, we strained to hear the message from the now faintly urgent voice which came over the wire.

"Hornet squadron scramble."

There was no need to hear more – the orderly would pass the full message to 'Prof' as he strapped himself in his cockpit – table, cards and money shot into the air as first one and then all the pilots dived headlong for the door.

High over Dover, and unfortunately well above us, we saw the enemy raid; about thirty Dorniers escorted by about three times that number of fighters.

"Hornet squadron from Red Leader – open out into loose formation and watch out for the escort fighters. We'll try and get to bomber height but I doubt if they will let us. Green Three, keep a sharp look out."

I must digress here to explain 'Prof's' specific reference to Green Three. At this stage in the Battle, squadrons introduced the tactics of operating an independent aircraft – usually the third and last aircraft in the fourth section – above and behind the rest of the squadron. This pilot's task was to combat surprise attack from above and behind, a form of attack to which the rigid type of squadron formation we then flew was very susceptible. While the squadron would fly a straight course, the independent aircraft would weave to and fro across the track. Often squadrons would return, unmolested as they thought, only to find that the 'weaver' – as this unfortunate pilot became known – had disappeared, and no one had seen him go. This costly and stupid practice – stupid because if the scheme was to succeed an experienced pilot should have been detailed as 'weaver,' not the most junior as was the practice – was eventually discontinued.

'Prof's' fear that the squadron was unlikely to get to bomber height was realized; the 109s had obviously seen us, and were now streaming down from above, their canopies winking in the sun and producing the illusion that their pilots had already opened fire. The squadron maintained station until the last possible moment when 'Prof' gave the order to break.

"Hornet squadron break and engage, BREAK – NOW."

This was the signal for the section leaders to turn their sections towards the attackers and for individual pilots to single out a particular enemy aircraft for attack. Soon the early morning sky over Dover, or 'Hell's Corner' as it was now known, was patterned with weaving and darting Spitfires and Me 109s while the bombers thrust on towards their target unmolested, as yet.

As always, and almost inevitably, the fight was over in a matter of minutes and the sky was clear of aircraft; at least that patch of sky in which I found myself, after having chased a 109 to destruction on the outskirts of Deal. Faintly, because I was flying low, I heard the Controller: "All Hornet aircraft to land at home base. I repeat, home base."

"What the hell's up now?" I thought to myself. The answer was soon forthcoming; just below and to my right lay Manston aerodrome, half hidden in mushrooms of smoke which drifted across its now bomb cratered surface. The first of the many attacks that were to be made on Manston had been launched.

All that day the German formations continued their onslaught. First Manston, then Hawkinge, then Lympne and further along the coast the radar stations. Manston was serviceable again in a matter of hours and 65 Squadron, which was airborne shortly after our return to Hornchurch, was diverted there to fill the gap caused by our withdrawal. They had barely refuelled before the second wave was plotted in mid-channel heading for Manston. The squadron managed to get airborne but only just in time to miss a stick of bombs that exploded behind them as they became airborne. Miraculously, none of the Spitfires was hit, but there were several casualties among the station personnel.

54 Squadron landed at Manston again later that afternoon, after a second engagement, to be met by a very shaken body of airmen and a no less frightened gathering of 600 squadron pilots. The airfield was a shambles of gutted hangars and smouldering dispersal buildings all of which were immersed in a thin film of white chalk dust which drifted across the airfield and settled on men, buildings and parked aircraft in the manner, and with the appearance, of a light snow storm. The rows of yellow flags, marking the safety lane for landing, and the chalk-coated men and materials were to become symbolic of Manston in the days that followed, and remain as a lasting impression with all those who worked and operated from there in August 1940.

The day's operations brought the problem of Sergeant Dennis to the fore again. I was called to 'Prof's' office shortly after landing from the last sortie of this most hectic of days, to be met by an angry George exclaiming heatedly:

"I tell you, sir, I don't want him in my flight. He's 'yellow' and there's no getting away from it – not just tired, 'yellow'."

"What's the story, sir," I broke in.

"It looks as if George was right, Al. Apparently Dennis'

number two, a new boy on his first trip, was overheard by Colin telling one of his contemporaries that he couldn't understand the tactics. He went on to say that as soon as an order was given to attack Sergeant Dennis dived into and through the enemy fighters and although he fired his guns in their general direction he just kept on going down, and made no further efforts to rejoin the battle. Collett, you know that new sergeant, was the number two and he looks a good type and promising material."

"There have been quite a few suspicious incidents connected with Dennis, as Colin will confirm, and I'm all for getting rid of him before it's too late," said George.

"I agree, sir. It will be damaging to morale to keep him if that's the case, and I must say George seems to have been fairly patient. I suggest he is posted as operationally tired, which he might well be."

"So long as he goes, that's all that matters," interjected George.

"All right, George, leave it to me. You can exclude him from tomorrow's detail and I'll fix it that he leaves the squadron with the minimum of fuss. Leave, pending posting is the answer," said Prof.

"That's taken a load off my mind," said a relieved George. "Come on, Al, let's go up to the mess and wash away the taste with a glass of beer."

In the mess we met Flight Lieutenant Gordon Olive, an Australian commanding a flight in 65 Squadron, who greeted us with a jovial accusation:

"Trust you chaps to arrange your scrambles so as to avoid landing back at Manston and so leave us to face the music: as you know, we were caught taking off. Bloody frightening it was too, but amusing in one respect. Did you hear about Jeffrey's experience?" (Jeffrey Quill, the well-known Supermarine test pilot, was on a short attachment to 65 Squadron at the time.)

"No, but go on, Gordon, and don't be so damned

dramatically Australian about it," said George impatiently.

"Well, Jeffrey wouldn't believe that any pilot could get airborne more quickly than he could from a scramble," said Gordon, going on to quote Jeffrey:

"'After all,' Jeffrey said, 'I have been test flying Spitfires now for the past four years doing a regular two or three trips a day, and the procedure of getting strapped in and started up is purely automatic; I can do it blindfolded. You young fighter pilots might think you're quick at it, but just wait till the next scramble and I'll show you.'"

"Unfortunately for Jeffrey," continued Gordon, "the next scramble was in the face of an imminent attack on the airfield, and this gave an extra spur to the pilots. Just as I got airborne as leader the bombs started falling and on looking back I could just see a single Spitfire appearing out of the bomb bursts. I learned later it was Jeffrey. He was damned lucky to get away without injury to himself or damage to his aircraft. He hasn't mentioned young fighter pilots since."

All next day the German assault on our coastal airfields continued with Manston once again the pivot of the attacks. At the end of the second day the airfield was in a sorry state. The power supply was cut; the telephone cable, over which came our orders, was severely damaged; the hangar area was a shambles; and there was extensive damage to administrative buildings – not that they mattered a great deal! In the words of one pilot of 600 Squadron, commenting on the regularity of the attacks, "When day dawns, like rabbits we return to our burrows to merge again only when night brings peace and quiet." However, 600 Squadron pilots enacted some sort of revenge when they brought down a Messerschmitt 110 one of nine which attacked the airfield that day. A second one was brought down by Bofors fire from the station defence; 600 Squadron's victim being picked off with a Lewis Gun mounted on the top of their dug-out.

For some time now the Germans had been waiting for a day on which the weather would prove favourable enough for them to launch a concentrated and simultaneous effort against our northern and southern fighter bases. It would thus be possible for them to determine to what extent our defences in the north had been stripped to supplement the hard pressed squadrons in the south. August 15th was the chosen day; a day which was to see the heaviest fighting of the whole Battle.

The first wave, consisting of about sixty Ju 87s escorted by an equal number of 109s and with Lympne as their target, was met by 54 Squadron as it crossed the coast between Dover and Dungeness. Against such odds it was impossible to prevent the bombers reaching the target. Nevertheless, we did manage to get among the Junkers 87s and to harass them throughout their attack, despite the presence of the 109s. It was an impressive yet frustrating sight as the dive bombers, in perfect echelon formation, swept towards the airfield and peeled off to attack. A mere handful of Spitfires altered the picture very little as, virtually lost in the maze of 109s, they strove to interfere.

With ammunition exhausted, and at least one Hun to my credit, I broke off the engagement to return to Manston, but not before I had observed a fresh Spitfire squadron join in the fray; 501 Squadron, I learned later.

On final approach, wheels and flaps down, I concentrated on the airfield ahead intent on landing safely between the lines of yellow flags marking the safety lane, outside of which half-filled craters and unexploded bombs constituted a grave danger to the unwary pilot. Bang, bang, rat-a-tat-tat, all round me the airfield defences sprang into life. "What the hell," I thought, this is no place for me in an unarmed Spitfire." Taking action to suit my thoughts I raised the undercarriage and flaps, eased the aircraft down to ground level, and headed off inland under the very nose of a Me 110 as it levelled out from a dive-bombing attack, closely followed by a second and surrounded by bursting Bofors shells.

Well away from the airfield, and hugging the tree tops to make the best of my camouflaged aircraft, I waited for silent guns at Manston to signify the all clear. When this occurred I did not return immediately – the 110s might still be in the vicinity and I had no wish to tangle with them unarmed – but waited a further five to ten minutes before sneaking back into the circuit. There was little apparent damage to the airfield surface and, apart from a small fire in 600 Squadron dispersal area, all seemed clear to land.

"Nearly got you that time, Al." Smilingly Flying Officer Norman Hayes of 600 Squadron greeted me on landing.

"Why the hell didn't you fire a red to warn me?"

"There wasn't time. And anyhow we didn't know you were there. Teach you to sneak in behind the hangars."

"The sensible and safe thing to do on this airfield is to sneak in, there are always too many 109s hanging about to come in in the normal manner. Tell me, Norman, why has 65 Squadron been moved over from Rochford? That means too damned many aircraft on the airfield for my liking and added encouragement to the Hun to return for another attack. You can bet your boots those Me 110 pilots will report it."

"65 pilots will agree with you after their little picnic taking off yesterday," interjected Flight Lieutenant David Clackson, a 600 Squadron flight commander who had joined us. These two officers were always on hand when we landed to give encouragement and invaluable assistance in the business of re-fuelling and re-arming, more particularly when the scale of attack against the airfield reached its peak towards the end of August. As with the majority of their fellow squadron pilots, they longed for an opportunity to get into the Battle but were destined to serve in the unrewarding role of night fighters flying slow, ill-equipped and badly armed Blenheims. A thankless task at the time, but the experience gained was to prove invaluable to both crews and controllers in building up the night fighter defence forces which more and more were to play a vital role in the defence of our shores.

"Come and see what we've got over here," said Norman pointing to a nearby smouldering heap of metal which was being liberally sprayed with foam by the ever vigilant station fire fighters.

"What is it?" I asked.

"The remains of a Me 110 which went in with its bomb still in. We shot it down with that little gun over there," said Norman proudly pointing to a Lewis mounted over the air raid shelter. "A second was shot down by the Bofors guns, that makes two out of nine. I reckon that will teach the Huns to leave us alone in future."

Manston was not attacked again that day, and continued to be the scene of intensive activity as relays of Spitfires took off and returned from repeated sorties against enemy formations attacking other airfields in the area. The first raid of the day had crossed the coast near Dover at 11.20am and the last enemy aircraft departed our shores at approximately 7.15pm, when a heavily mauled force of Me 110s, which had attacked Croydon airfield – an uncomfortable reminder to Londoners that the air battle was moving in on them – retreated to their lair in occupied territory. In that short period of time I had been airborne on six occasions. Some idea of the intensity of operations can be gauged from the fact that a normal sortie averaged forty minutes, and that on four occasions re-arming and refuelling was necessary.

So 15th August closed. The enemy had launched six major assaults – and many minor ones also in the south-east – against airfields as far apart as Acklington in Northumberland to Middle Wallop in Hampshire. In all, 2,000 enemy aircraft had been hurled against our shores in successive waves only to be met by a determined defence which, although penetrated on occasions, never failed to close the gaps.

In the north-east, the Germans were given conclusive proof that our defences in that part of the world were not wholly stripped to reinforce the south. Of the two raids launched – one in the Sunderland area and one against Driffield airfield –

neither was successful, and the aircraft of Luftflotte 5 from Norway suffered such severe casualties that throughout the remaining weeks of the Battle of Britain they never again attempted a daylight raid against the north-east.

Nightfall brought blessed relief to the weary pilots of the 11 Group squadrons who had once again borne the brunt of the attack. To me the reverse was true; I was shot down on the last sortie of the day and spent five agonizing hours in the back of an RAF ambulance which bounced and bumped its way through the blacked-out highways and byways of Kent in search of Kenley airfield, only to finish up at the Queen Victoria Hospital, East Grinstead.

CHAPTER NINE

Backs Against the Wall

"IF we are ordered off again before dusk the Controller says we are to land back at Hornchurch," said 'Prof' addressing a tired, but happy, assembly of 54 Squadron pilots lounging on the grass near their parked Spitfires.

"I've had enough today," said Colin. "I reckon the Huns have too. Perhaps they will let us return in peace to Hornchurch. I'm just dying for a beer, a good meal and bed."

His hopes were not to be realized. Hardly were the words uttered when the warning bell, the signal to the ground crews that a scramble had been ordered, was rung by the telephone orderly who could be seen running towards 'Prof' with instructions from the Controller. With one accord nine Spitfires, all that remained serviceable, roared into life and, with pilots impatiently waving the guiding airmen away from the wing tips, they taxied towards the take-off point soon to be airborne and lost to view as the formation climbed at full throttle towards Dover.

"Hornet Leader from Control. Make angels 20,000ft over Dover." Ronald Adam's voice floated over the R/T, unruffled and as precise as ever despite the hectic day the Controllers must have had in the Operations Room.

"Hornet Leader to Control; your message received. What's the form?"

"Seventy plus aircraft, now in mid-channel, should make landfall between Dungeness and Dover. You are to engage the escort fighters. Is this understood?"

"Hornet Leader to Control, understood."

"That's a new one," I thought. "The first time we have been given specific orders to engage the escort fighters; must enquire when I get down what it is all about."

Steadily the squadron climbed towards the south coast

until at 25,000ft we levelled out and turned south-east in the direction of the approaching enemy. Bitter experience of being jumped from above had taught us to add on at least 5,000ft to the inaccurate radar heights passed over the R/T. The wisdom of this was now apparent. As we swept in a wide arc from the south towards the now plainly visible enemy formation, it was clear that there would be little height advantage over the top escort which formed an unbroken chain down to the bombers tucked tightly together some 7,000ft below. "If we can manage to draw off some of these escort fighters," I thought, "some lucky chaps are going to have a wonderful picnic. Those are Me 110s acting as bombers." The Me 110 was a particularly vulnerable aircraft and a dream target when on a formation bombing mission, as they were then precluded from forming a defensive circle, their normal tactic when attacked and one against which there was no real answer.

'Prof's' manoeuvre to the south brought us in behind the enemy fighters which were completely taken by surprise. We were in among them before they took any action, and two 109s were destroyed in the first attack. Breaking upwards from this attack, I soon found myself another target; a 109 dived underneath me and headed eastwards towards France. I realized that if he spotted me the Hun pilot would immediately go into a steep dive, in which the Messerschmitt was superior to the Spitfire, and there would be little hope of catching him. My tactic was therefore to stay just below his height and in the blind spot formed by the tail unit of his aircraft to exploit to the maximum the bad rearwards visibility of the Messerschmitt. A long stern chase ensued and the shores of England were soon far behind us as the enemy pilot rapidly lost height towards home.

At about 5,000ft, and when I was almost in range to fire, the Messerschmitt entered a thin layer of cloud and was lost to view momentarily. So intent was I on the chase that I hadn't realized that we had crossed the Channel. It was only when I broke through the cloud behind the Hun that I saw with horror the coast of France was directly below. The Messerschmitt was still ahead – he obviously hadn't seen me – and now steepening his dive towards an airfield to our left. I dared not wait any longer to open fire and, although not quite in range, I pressed the firing button. The Hun's reaction was to stand his aircraft practically on its nose and dive vertically towards the airfield which I now recognized as Calais/Marck! An omen, alas, for I again met more enemy than I had bargained for; the circuit was infested with 109s two of which detached themselves and turned to cut me off as, with throttle wide open, I headed home at sea level, muttering to myself "You b_____ fool."

The 109s were winning the race, having the shorter distance to go, and I waited for the first attack to develop. A most unpleasant prospect, and the likelihood of more joining in made it more so; and me so far from our coast. At all costs, I reasoned, I must try and keep them both in view while at the same time making headway towards England. It wasn't going to be easy; the 109s had now split, one on either side of me. There was no point in just staying to fight, I was on the run and intended to keep it that way if I could.

Down came the first one to the attack; around went my Spitfire in a vicious turn in his direction causing him to break without firing. In came the number two; around the other way I went and he too broke without firing. And so it went on. I knew that before long they would bring their guns to bear as with each succeeding attack I became more tired, and they more skilful. At last one of them found his mark; bullets riddled my aircraft shattering the instrument panel and canopy. It was a miracle that I wasn't hit, the armour plate behind my seat no doubt deflecting a great number of bullets. Again and again they came at me; again and again I turned into the attack, but still the bullets, fortunately no cannon shells, found their target until eventually the now vibrating engine confirmed my worst fears. The oil tank had been punctured; a steady stream flowed over the cowlings and on to the windscreen, partly obscuring my vision ahead. How long would it keep going? I wondered. There was no longer any point in turning into each attack; I must get nearer to England and the only way to achieve this was head straight for the now faintly visible Dover cliffs, while at the same time presenting as difficult a target as possible. This I achieved by kicking violently on first one rudder and then on the other, alternatively shoving the stick from side to side to introduce a slipping effect into the violently yawing aircraft. Thus I offered a none too easy shot to the attackers.

At long last the beckoning white of the Dover cliffs lay just ahead, as welcome now as on that memorable return trip from Dunkirk. The nearness of the coastline spelled danger to the Hun pilots who disengaged and turned tail for home, displaying a discretion I would do well to observe in future.

In one backward movement of the control column I increased my height to about 1,500ft, using my forward speed to effect the manoeuvre, and throttling back I peered anxiously at my oil gauges. Both were shattered. As a precautionary measure I jettisoned my splintered hood. It was as well that I did for a matter of seconds later the engine burst into flames despite the fact that I had now throttled fully back, having decided to make a forced landing in the immediate vicinity.

I wasted no time in making a decision to abandon the aircraft, it was the only safe way of escape in the circumstances. I rolled the aircraft on to its back – as recommended by Johnny Allen who had successfully used this manoeuvre when he baled out during Dunkirk – having first released my Sutton harness, and pushed the control column hard forward. Immediately I shot out of my seat only to be caught by my parachute fouling some part of the cockpit when I was almost clear of the aircraft. Before I could get back into the cockpit, which I tried to do, the nose of the aircraft dropped alarmingly and it was then I realized that I hadn't put the actuating trimmer fully forward, a necessary precaution when attempting to bale out of an inverted aircraft as it tends to keep the nose up. Frantically I struggled to get free, but the increasing airflow over the cockpit was forcing me backwards against the fuselage. With the aircraft almost vertical, and the ground alarmingly close, I at last broke loose and was hurled backwards against the tail plane which struck my right wrist a crushing blow. The parachute responded immediately to the pull of the rip-cord, and a matter of seconds later I hit the ground not a hundred yards from where my burning *Kiwi* had exploded in a sheet of flame.

I suffered no further injury on landing and was in the process of disentangling myself from the parachute harness when two airmen appeared unexpectedly on the scene.

"Where did you two spring from?" I enquired.

"We are on our way to Kenley," answered one of the airmen. "I am an ambulance driver and he's (pointing to his companion) a nursing orderly. We saw the aircraft crash and were on our way to see what we could do when we saw you in this field. Can we do anything? The ambulance is just beyond that clump of trees over there."

"Yes, you can give me a lift. I'll come to Kenley with you. How long before you expect to reach there?"

"We are not far from Ashford at the moment and should make Kenley in about two to three hours."

"Good, let's get cracking then. This wrist looks as if it might be broken and the Medical Officer there can have a look at it."

"Excuse me, sir, but are you aware that your wrist watch has been broken?" asked the nearest airman, pointing to my left hand.

"Good heavens, so it is," I exclaimed. All that remained of my watch was the strap and the outer casing; the body had disappeared. Across the back of my hand was a red weal which seemed to indicate that a bullet had grazed it and removed the body of the watch, leaving only the outer casing. Whatever the cause, I had lost a perfectly good wristlet watch, and they were not service issue in those days. I duly claimed for the loss when I returned to my unit but it was some months before the Air Ministry finance experts agreed to pay, and only then through the intervention of 'Prof' who, by that time, was working at Air Ministry and followed up the claim on my behalf. The claim also included a uniform jacket lost at Dunkirk.

Refusing a front seat, I settled comfortably in the back of the ambulance on one of the stretchers, and resigned myself to sleep. Reaction from the day's operations had now set in; I was very very tired. I must have dozed off almost at once, because I remembered nothing of the journey until awakened by the sound of voices. It was pitch black in the back of the now stationary ambulance. I could hear the driver enquiring of a passer-by which fork would put him on the right road to Westerham, and then we started off again with a jolt. My wrist was throbbing unbearably and further sleep was out of the question. Shortly after restarting we stopped again, a further parley between the two airmen, and off into the night. This procedure went on for hour after agonizing hour until, nearly frantic with the pain, I banged on the cabin window for an audience.

"Where are we, and how long to go?" I asked the orderly who opened the door.

"We're not quite sure, sir. We've been lost quite a bit and think we are near East Grinstead. We are going to ask the next person we see. If it is East Grinstead, there's a hospital there and we can take you to it; RAF personnel from Kenley are admitted as patients."

"For God's sake get cracking, I must get something to deaden this pain."

The next town turned out to be East Grinstead. At long last I was able to bid farewell to my kindly, but frustrating, rescuers who ushered me into the presence of a solicitous night Sister.

"That wrist looks bad," she said examining my now

swollen and purple joint. I'll give you something to make you sleep and we will see to an X-ray first thing in the morning."

I was shown into a small ward in which two other air casualties dozed. One of them badly burned, judging from the bandages which swathed his face and neck; the other had a leg encased in plaster and swung from a sort of gantry above the bed. Whatever it was the Sister gave me, it did the trick. I had hardly settled myself in bed than I was asleep. I was awakened in the grey light of dawn by the early shift bustling around the ward.

"Do you know if the night Sister managed to get through to Hornchurch last night to tell the Duty Officer that I was safe and here in hospital?" I asked the nurse who came over to speak to me.

"No, she couldn't get through. She left a note to say that the telephone connections were hopeless and that she had to give it up."

"Oh well I don't suppose it matters too much; I asked the airmen who brought me here to phone from Kenley when they got back, so perhaps they have had more success over a service line. In any case I'll ring as soon as I get dressed, if that's all right." As it turned out the airmen had forgotten to phone and thus it was that on the following day my parents in far away New Zealand were notified that I was missing in action.

An X-ray of my injured wrist revealed that there were no bones broken but as a precaution, and at my request, it was encased in plaster so that I would be able to fly on my return to Hornchurch. After the plaster had been fixed, I was kept hanging around the ward so long awaiting an interview and final release by the Medical Superintendent that I made up my mind to sneak off to the railway station and catch the first train. An air raid alarm, which sounded a few minutes' later, caused a general upheaval in the wards with the moving of patients to shelters, and this enabled me to slip out unnoticed. Within minutes of my arrival at the station I caught a train and was back at Hornchurch shortly after midday.

Sir Archibald McIndoe, the famous surgeon at East Grinstead has recently told me the rather amusing background to my rapid departure.

"I deliberately held you up that morning," he said, "because I was trying to get through to your Station Commander on the telephone. You had a slight fracture in your wrist and you looked absolutely all in, so I asked if I could keep you in for a few days. The Station Commander said that he would be very grateful, as it was otherwise impossible for him to stop you flying. When I came out to tell you this – the bird had flown."

Pilot Officer Hopkin, or John Willie as he was affectionately known to his fellow pilots, greeted me on arrival at dispersal the news that the squadron was away at Manston but expected to return soon from a combat in which they were now engaged – or so the Controller told him – as Manston had again been put out of action temporarily. John Willie, with his slim figure, shy manner and boyish features looked hardly old enough to be out of school let alone be a seasoned fighter pilot as he now was, having joined the squadron at the tail end of Dunkirk and survived the convoy battles of July. He was, in fact, just nineteen.

The Medical Officer gave me the all clear to fly again with the proviso that the plaster remained on for at least two weeks. As I sat talking to John Willie I watched some Spitfires landing; could see from their markings that they were strangers to Hornchurch

"Who do they belong to?" I asked John Willie.

"They're the new squadron which arrived in this morning to replace 74 which has gone north for a rest."

"Good heavens, have 74 gone already."

'Yes they left a short time ago. As a matter of fact I overheard the Station Commander saying that 'Sailor' was surprised when he heard the order but nonetheless pleased to get a breather."

While awaiting the squadron's return, I took the

opportunity to pay a visit to the Operations Block to have a chat with the Controllers and to see if there were any raids in progress. The floor of the main Operations Room presented a scene of feverish activity and the plotting table was smothered in coloured plaques which indicated the various aircraft tracks in, or near, the Hornchurch Sector. One particular plaque indicated that an enemy raid of 150 strength was threatening the Sector and, in fact, as I entered the air raid warning 'red' was flashing on the raid indicator. This was a signal to the Operations Room Staff to don their steel helmets which the WAAF plotters proceeded to do with a sort of studied nonchalance, as if to defy the German bombers to frighten them away from their place of duty. Never once did they desert their posts, even when the airfield was under attack and then only to duck beneath the plotting table as the bombs were falling; more as a gesture of defiance than of fright.

The squadron had just done its fourth trip that day, and had been in combat on two occasions. It was no wonder that the pilots looked tired as they drifted into dispersal. 'Prof' looked really worn out.

"Glad to see you back again, Al. I thought you had had it this time when there was no news late last night. George said you would turn up all right, and added something about a bad penny. As you can see we are down on aircraft, we lost one on the ground at Manston today, but I expect some more will have been flown in during our absence. Replacement aircraft are flown in really quickly now. If only the pilots would come in at the same rate; I'm afraid we're not keeping abreast of our casualty rate. Although the proportion of fatals to injured is small, certainly compared with July, there are quite a crop of chaps out of action indefinitely, some for extended periods. You're OK to fly I hope?"

"Yes, I'll be on the starting grid first thing tomorrow. Did we lose any section leaders today?"

"Yes, Alan Campbell; he's gone off to hospital and I think we can count him out from now on. He had a most miraculous escape. A bullet hit his earphone, having first obviously flattened itself on the fuselage or hood and although partially stunned he managed to land his badly damaged aircraft safely. When he removed his helmet his ear was discovered to be terribly lacerated. The earphone was completely shattered and the sorbo-rubber pad surrounding it was filled with steel splinters; I'm sure it was the rubber which cushioned the blow and saved his life."

The cry for more pilots, give us more pilots, was being echoed by all squadron commanders at about this time. There was a desperate shortage throughout the Command. Not so fighter aircraft. The miracles worked by Lord Beaverbrook at the Ministry of Aircraft Production were being felt at squadron level where replacement aircraft arrived in on virtually the same day as the demand was sent. This achievement was due in no small measure to the sterling work of the Maintenance Unit which serviced the Spitfires allotted to operational units. On-the-spot repairs of damaged aircraft were carried out by our own ground crews, who were magnificent. All night long, lights burned in the shuttered hangars as the fitters, electricians, armourers and riggers worked unceasingly to put the maximum number on the line for the next day's operations. All day too they worked, not even ceasing when the airfield was threatened with attack. A grand body of men about whom too little has been written but without whose efforts victory would not have been possible.

The pilot picture was not so rosy. Not only was the replacement problem serious, but this growing strain on those who had been in action continuously, with only brief rests, was also beginning to tell. Small things which earlier would have been laughed off as irrelevant, now became points of bitter contention. At this stage of the Battle pilot losses far outstripped the replacements and it was only a question of time before the serious position became a grave one. Referring to this aspect of the Battle, the History of the

Royal Air Force says:

"The replacement of casualties* was the most serious aspect of the pilot problem, but it was not the only one. There was also the growing strain on those who survived...The long hours at dispersal, the constant flying at high altitudes, the repeated combats, the parachute descents, the forced landings – all took their toll, even where the harm was not at once apparent. The growing tiredness of those who had been most actively engaged was a factor which Dowding could neglect no more than his casualties. Fighter Command was still successfully resisting the enemy. Its own strength was being steadily sapped in the process."

The aircraft safely stowed away in their pens, and the readiness state for tomorrow ascertained from operations, we motored off to the mess where a late supper of bacon and eggs awaited the pilots.

"Hello, Sam, surprised to see you here at this late hour," said 'Prof' addressing our popular mess chef who ruled the pilots like a tyrannical housemaster. "I thought that when it came to bacon and eggs, you left it to your underlings to cope."

Drawing himself fully erect, his gleaming white chef's hat seemingly stiff with resentment, Sam answered in hurt pride "Sir, you know that I never go off duty until all my pilots have returned from operations and are properly fed." And how true it was; Sam would cheerfully work all night, so long as he knew that it was for the benefit of the pilots whom he affectionately addressed as 'me hearties'. A great character whose cheerful presence in the dining-room was a great tonic to the weary pilots lining up at the hot plate for their roast beef and brussels sprouts (where once it had been a choice of six to seven dishes), all carefully prepared by Sam.

"Got another Hun today, Al" said Colin exultantly as we

---

*154 pilots had been killed, missing or wounded in ten days' fighting and only 63 new fighter pilots were produced in the same period sat down to our supper. "I had the most wonderful scrap with a 109, from 20,000ft down to ground level. The Hun pilot tried everything he knew to shake me off his tail, but he wasn't losing this baby." (This was no idle boast; Colin was an exceptional pilot, experienced in combat and one of the best shots in Fighter Command, as his total of twenty-six enemy aircraft destroyed in the war testifies.)

"What happened in the end?" I asked.

"Well, as I said, he tried damned hard to get me off his tail, and this made him a damned difficult target. Eventually I put his engine out of action and he made a forced landing in a field, a good one too. I was amused to see that as soon as he got clear of his aircraft the first thing he did was to take off his helmet, throw it on the ground, and jump on it. He was obviously peeved at being shot down, and must have reckoned himself a bit of an ace. Wonder who he was?"

"Good for you, Colin. But, I say, just take a look at George."

Further along the table George had dropped off to sleep and, with his head nodding lower and lower, was gently swaying to and fro in his seat, his bacon and egg untouched in front of him. As we watched his face pitched forward into his eggs, much to the amusement of the assembled pilots.

"Hi, George, you are meant to eat those eggs, not put your face in them," shouted Colin across the table.

George sat erect with a start and looked around with hostility before departing in silence to his room. This action was most unlike George, but indicative of the state of fatigue reached by the over-worked leaders, and the effect of strain on even the most forbearing of chaps.

"Tell me, Colin," I said resuming our conversation. "What was the significance of that order yesterday about going for the escort fighters?"

"As a matter of fact it was the same again today. Apparently the AOC* has decided to draw off the escort fighters by detailing selected Spitfire squadrons to this specific task. The

*Air Vice-Marshal KR Park, Air Officer Commanding No. 11 Group

remaining Spitfire squadrons, and the Hurricanes, can then get a better crack at the bombers. From now on we can look forward to a lot of very high flying and some tough battles, especially as the strength of the escort is bound to be increased in order to combat our tactics. At least it might mean that we remain back at Hornchurch instead of going forward to Manston. I must say I just can't see the point in being stationed so far forward; in our new role height is absolutely essential and if we continue to operate from Manston it will mean climbing inland to get to a decent height before we can effect interception on the escort fighters. Still it's a damn good idea and should make the Germans scratch their heads. Incidentally, talking about Manston, it was badly hit again today. How those 600 pilots stick it, I don't know. The ground crews have certainly got the jitters; can you blame them?"

No one was sorry when the following day brought a lull in operations. The two previous days had evidently imposed a strain on the Germans no less than on Fighter Command, for although the weather was set fair, only a few sporadic raids were made, and then mostly on reconnaissance.

August 18th saw a return to operations in force, although not quite on the scale of August 15th. For the first time two vital sector stations, Kenley and Biggin Hill, were attacked, the former suffering considerable damage.

Four times 54 Squadron entangled with the enemy and four times returned without loss of pilots or aircraft. Operating at great altitudes under the new scheme of drawing off the escort, we destroyed or probably destroyed fourteen enemy fighters, an achievement which was to mark the peak of the squadron's efficiency in the Battle of Britain. From this day onwards our efficiency gradually deteriorated, as we grew more and more tired, until in the end we were but a token force in the air. The turning point had been reached. It was appropriate therefore that the day's successes merited a signal of recognition from the Chief of Air Staff:

"Well done 54 Squadron. In all your hard fighting

this is the way to deal with the enemy."

If only the squadron could have been moved out of the Battle then, and on such a happy note. But it was not to be.

Manston had once again been the scene of our operations and also of many German strafing attacks which resulted in two aircraft being destroyed on the ground. To make matters worse, a section of 54 Squadron was attacked while coming in to land, but luckily escaped unharmed. As a result of this incident 'Prof' decided that, whenever practicable, one section would remain airborne as cover to those landing. This was a wise precaution and on more than one occasion proved invaluable in fending off stray Hun fighter attacks against Spitfires about to land.

Time and again the squadron was ordered off with the specific task of engaging the escort fighters but, just as Colin had prophesied, we found it necessary to gain height inland before turning to intercept the enemy. Any other tactic would have meant climbing up underneath the escort with the added disadvantage of being jumped by the many stray 109s which hung around off our coasts hoping for just such a target.

Admittedly, it was important that we got among the escort fighters as soon as possible but Manston was just that little too far forward to enable a straight climb up to interception height. Somewhere between Hornchurch and Manston was the ideal distance, but Manston was, for some reason, considered a must for continued operations.

CHAPTER TEN

Undaunted by Odds

"The gratitude of every home in our Island, in our Empire, and indeed throughout the world, except in the abodes of the guilty, goes out to the British airmen, who, undaunted by odds, unwearied in their constant challenge and mortal danger are turning the tide of world war by their prowess and devotion. Never in the field of human conflict was so much owed by so many to so few."

I T was during a lull in the Battle that the Prime Minister spoke these now famous words in the House of Commons. August the 20th was the date. I remember clearly hearing the BBC announcer repeating them with commendable emphasis in a late news bulletin. I was listening with George Gribble who said, "It's nice to know that someone appreciates us, Al. I couldn't agree more that bit about mortal danger, but I dispute the unwearied."

Despite the flippancy of George's remarks such encouraging words from a most inspiring leader were a wonderful tonic to our flagging spirits. To me, and indeed I believe to all of us, this was the first real indication of the seriousness of the Battle, and the price we would have to pay for defeat. Before, there was courage; now, there was grim determination.

The main object of the enemy was still the destruction of the Royal Air Force, and especially Fighter Command. But so far the Luftwaffe had not succeeded in its first aim: the destruction of the RAF's fighter force. This was obviously worrying the Luftwaffe's corpulent commander who at Karinhall on 19th August was explicit on this point. "We have reached," he said, "the decisive period of the air war against England. The vital task is to turn all means at our disposal to the defeat of the enemy air force. Our first aim is the destruction of the enemy's fighter force. If they no longer take the air, we shall attack them on the ground, or force them into battle by directing bomber attacks against targets within range of our fighters."

The enemy had now altered his tactics, no doubt as a result of Goring's observations on the Battle. Clearly the attacks on coastal airfields and other 'fringe' targets had not decisively weakened Fighter Command. A new approach to the task was badly needed; the full fury of the attack was therefore switched to No. 11 Group's vital inner airfields from which the operations of the fighter forces were controlled; this would ensure that the British fighters were forced into battle, for once the control system was paralysed London and the invasion coast would soon lie at the mercy of the German hordes.

A further most welcome spell of indifferent weather delayed this new German plan, but in the weeks that followed it was well under way. In the meantime, 54 Squadron continued to operate forward from Manston, now a veritable shambles.

In the course of a squadron scramble from there and during an air raid alert on the airfield, 'Prof' had engine failure on take-off and finished up entangled with the perimeter fence, fortunately without injury to person. He returned on foot to dispersal where he found the Technical Officer marching up and down outside one of the air raid shelters exclaiming in a loud voice: "If they don't come out of there in two minutes, I'm going down to shoot the first man who refuses."

"What's up?" enquired 'Prof'.

"Those damned airmen down there won't come out, and there's work to be done."

"I should leave them there if I were you; after all, there is an air raid warning in force and they are much safer underground until the all clear is given. Remember, those boys are doing a damned fine job under most difficult conditions and I shouldn't antagonize them if I were you. They've had a hell of a time for the past few days." Fortunately, this advice was heeded; I hate to think what might have happened had not 'Prof' arrived on the scene so fortuitously.

When 'Prof' told me the story later, he was still a very angry Squadron Leader. "To think," he said, "that he hadn't the intelligence to see that those chaps had had about as much as they could take, and needed careful handling. I imagine the poor chap is at his wits' end, the strain is just too much for him. I shall have a word with 'Daddy' on our return to Hornchurch. Something must be done, the position here is getting beyond a joke."

On the day following this incident Manston was again heavily attacked but still not put out of action, much to the disgust of 54 and 65 Squadrons whose pilots had had more than enough of the place. On this day there was some trouble with the staff in the Officers' Mess – and who can blame them? – which meant that the pilots got their meals as and when they could. This, of course, was not unusual at Manston in the height of the Battle when meals were most uncertain affairs. Invariably, we would be awaiting confirmation from operations that a relaxed state of readiness had been agreed to enable us to get food when a scramble would be ordered. There were occasions when lunch was taken as late as 4 o'clock, and sometimes not at all.

I missed the cheerful faces of the 600 Squadron pilots when, later that evening, the squadron landed after the fourth engagement of the day. On enquiry, I learned that 600 Squadron had received orders to evacuate to Hornchurch and were expected to complete the move sometime tomorrow. "Not before time, perhaps whoever is responsible will wake up to the fact that we should have given this place up long ago," muttered George on hearing the news.

We returned to Hornchurch that evening full of hope for tomorrow and in the sincere belief that we had seen the last of Manston, only to be told on landing that 54 Squadron was scheduled to operate from there again tomorrow. Despondently I made out the detail for the morning – "The following pilots will proceed to Manston at first light...", avoiding as I did so the despairing looks on the faces of the unlucky. In the event, bad weather meant a comparatively quiet day but it also prevented us from returning to Hornchurch that evening. What a relief to learn next morning that the airfield was finally to be evacuated and that we were to return to Hornchurch right away. None of us needed a second bidding; we were airborne and away in record time.

And so after seven major attacks, and countless smaller ones, Manston was finally closed for operations. It has long been a mystery to me, as indeed it was at the time, why we continued to operate from there in the face of such difficulties. Certainly, once the convoy assaults had given way to attacks on airfields there seemed no tactical advantage in continuing to use an airfield so far forward, especially when it had such a damaging effect on the moral of the pilots and ground crews to say nothing of the aircraft lost on the ground. At the time it was generally believed by the pilots, who had the misfortune to operate from there, that it was because the evacuation of one of our major airfields was considered a moral victory to the enemy. If this was so, it is difficult to understand the reasoning behind it. Manston was not a Sector airfield and, in any event, a tactical withdrawal has never been accepted as a moral victory to the enemy.

Who made the decision to retain Manston for so long? Was it the Air Officer Commanding No. 11 Group; was it the Commander-in-Chief Fighter Command; was it the Air Council; or was it the Government in the person of the Prime Minister? War records give no answer!

It seemed as if the Germans knew that 54 Squadron had been moved back to Hornchurch permanently for on the very day of our return there the airfield was bombed for the first time. It suffered only minor damage, and we were able to land back there after engaging the enemy formation which attacked our base. North Weald, the adjoining Sector airfield to the north, was less fortunate and suffered very heavy damage.

Yellow flags now dotted our home airfield, a familiar sight to pilots who had been operating from Manston but not, alas, to the ferry pilot who arrived home shortly after the attack.

"Two to one that he lands the wrong side of the flags," said Pete Matthews to the watching squadron pilots. Needless to say there were no takers, as from the uncertainty of the pilot's behaviour it was obvious that a flag-dotted airfield was something new to him.

Two or three exploratory passes at the airfield were obviously enough to convince the pilot that amidst the flags was the place to land (it must be remembered that at that time there was no flying control tower, as we know it today, to pass landing instructions to the pilot, even if he had carried the correct R/T frequency in his aircraft). Down came the aircraft amidst the flags to touch down just short of a partially filled bomb crater into which it rolled and promptly stood unceremoniously on its nose, much to the amusement of the watching pilots. But the Flight Sergeant was not amused; he had discovered that the aircraft was a new squadron allotment.

"Well, that's one aircraft we won't be getting," said 'Prof' turning to me. "By the way, Al, did you know that the two new pilots due in today are both New Zealanders?"

"Good, we need some stuffing in the squadron," chipped in Colin who was standing nearby.

"Anyone would think our troubles will be solved by the arrival of two of your countrymen. If they lose as many aircraft as Al, we'll have nothing to fly at the end of the week." This from George, good humouredly.

"Well, you're going to have one in your flight, George, so you had better make sure that he doesn't" said 'Prof'.

Whatever the calibre and training of these two pilots they were more than welcome to bolster up our waning strength. Pilot Officer Mick Shand, who came to my flight, certainly looked promising until I learned the grim details of his flying experience. Mick was a rugged, aggressive looking New Zealander typical of the type one would expect to find in the second row of an 'All Black' pack. He had a most cheerful and easy going disposition and was a great favourite among his fellow officers; as I was to learn sometime later when we again served together. On this occasion there was to be little time in which to assess his value.

"Hello," I said greeting him at dispersal that afternoon. "I hear you're a fellow-countryman of mine."

"Too right, and glad to be here," was the cheerful rejoinder.

"What flying experience have you got?"

"I've got a total of 140 hours approximately, mostly on Wapitis.* I only managed to get twenty hours on Spitfires at OCU and it was hardly enough to get the feel of flying again after a two months' lay-off. As a matter of fact I know damned all about fighters, I was trained as a light bomber pilot."

"Have you fired the guns on the Spitfire yet?"

"No, I haven't; apart from a very little free gunnery from a rear cockpit, I've no idea of air firing."

"What about the reflector sight, do you understand it?"

"Haven't the remotest idea what it is, much less understand it."

"Good grief," I thought. "It does seem a shame to throw him into battle so soon." There was no alternative, and certainly no time or aircraft to fit in any further training.

"Get yourself kitted out, and when you are ready come and find me and I'll run over things with you. You will be required to fly later on today, if things warm up a bit." I said this as cheerfully as possible in order not to give him any hint of my thoughts.

This was typical of the replacement pilots arriving in the squadrons (although the circumstances were a little different for New Zealanders trained in their own country, because of the time taken to get to England); all desperately keen to get

*Outmoded bi-planes

cracking but all lacking in basic flying experience.

I took Mick Shand as my number two on his first trip, having first briefed him to stick close to my tail and not to attempt to get mixed up with the 109s until he had had an opportunity to see a little of what was going on. "There will be time enough," I urged.

At the end of the following day neither Mick nor his compatriot was with us. Both were in hospital somewhere on the south coast having fallen foul of 109s over the famous 'Hell's Corner'. So much for our New Zealand replacements, both of whom did very well later on in the war, though Mick became a prisoner-of-war and Charlie Stewart was unfortunately killed in action.

"I hear a Defiant squadron is expected in here, it will be interesting to see how they fare," said George addressing me in the mess that evening.

"Is that so?" said Colin, all ears as usual. "It's difficult enough in a Spitfire, I should hate to try in anything as slow and unmanoeuvrable as a Defiant. Still I must say they did damn well at Dunkirk. If I know the Hun pilots they'll have the answer to them by now, though."

264 Defiant Squadron, which did so well at Dunkirk, arrived at Hornchurch the very next day. Unfortunately for them, they arrived at the opening of a renewed German offensive which, one day excluded, involved an average of a thousand enemy aircraft a day from 24th August to 6th September, with a peak of nearly 2,000 aircraft on 30th August.

The story of this squadron is a sad one. The Defiant had no front guns, and was unable to fire directly forward with its turret guns, which meant that it was extremely vulnerable to head-on attacks, and it was this form of attack on which the Messerschmitt 109s concentrated. As Colin had prophesied they had decided on this tactic as a result of their experience in attacking the closely formating Defiants from astern on the occasions they met over Dunkirk. Gallantly as the Defiant crews strove to get at the bombers – and they had some success – they were incapable of combating the escorting fighters. In 10 days of combat, the squadron lost 14 aircrew killed, including their ex-squadron commander who was flying on his farewell sortie before handing over command on his promotion, and 11 aircraft were completely destroyed. In addition, other crew members were injured and a number of aircraft damaged. After only 14 days in the line 264 Squadron, with only two remaining aircraft, departed Hornchurch to rest and re-equip. Defiants were never again used in daylight operations.

By the evening of the 26th August and after a particularly intensive day of operations, 54 Squadron was down to seven serviceable aircraft. A quiet 27th August, however, enabled the ground crews to put twelve aircraft on the line, much to the satisfaction of the new squadron commander who had arrived the previous day to take command.

After three months of almost continuous operations 'Prof' had been rested. In that time he had not only commanded the squadron but had led it on almost every occasion. The strain of battle alone was bad enough; but when the responsibility of command was added to it, more particularly with such heavy losses, it was a miracle that 'Prof' hadn't cracked under the strain. Not that he had cracked now; a very wise Station Commander appreciated the need to rest him. He was to go, at least that's what we thought; events were to prove otherwise.

The new squadron commander was Donald Finlay, the famous Olympic hurdler, who had been a pilot in 54 Squadron before the war. He was, to quote him, "delighted to get away from a chair and specialization (he was an engineering specialist), and get back to a flying job."

"I would like you to lead the squadron on the first show, Al, I'll come as your number two and see what goes on," were his first instructions to me.

"Right-ho, sir. I suggest you stick fairly close. More than likely our task will be to get among the escort fighters, which means we shall be operating around 30,000ft. If once you fall behind at this height you'll find it most difficult to catch up, and probably find yourself a target for the Hun pilots. We usually find ourselves over Dover or in that area, so if you get separated make inland a bit, it's less dangerous there."

The telephone bell; orders to scramble; the usual mad rush to cockpits; a feverish pushing of starter buttons; a roar as twelve Merlins sprang into life; a jostling for places at the take-off end; and the squadron was airborne for another combat. Up and up we climbed; first Gravesend was left behind, then Chatham, then Canterbury, and finally Dover, plainly visible to twelve pairs of eyes which gazed down as it passed below the squadron, now at 33,000ft. This was the highest we had been and, in the jargon of the fighter pilot, "we were hanging on our airscrews." It was cold, extremely cold; my feet were like lumps of ice and tiny prickles of cold stabbed at my legs, just above the knees. "Why is it," I thought, "that in a Spitfire the cold always seems to get one just above the knees."

"Your target directly ahead of you, Hornet Leader," the Station Commander's voice came over the R/T, suddenly and without warning, causing me to jump uncomfortably in my seat. "You should see them any moment now."

See them; we couldn't avoid them. They covered the whole sky ahead, a solid mass of aircraft from about 15,000ft up to 32,000ft at which height a dozen or so 109s weaved along in the wake of the hundreds of escort fighters below.

"Tallyho," I gave the sighting call over the R/T for the benefit of control to whom it was a signal that no further assistance was required in vectoring the squadron on to its target.

"Hornet Leader to Hornet Squadron – we'll take those 109s just below us on our left. Pick out your own target as we go down."

I turned in for the attack and, as I did so, called to my number two, who had dropped behind, to keep up a bit. The battle was short-lived. Three 109s fell to the Spitfires' guns without loss; some of the escort had been effectively drawn off while the bombers and the remaining 109s swept on to meet the next attack.

A very shaken squadron commander returned to Hornchurch having been the target for the leading 109 which had got on to his tail soon after the attack developed, and as a result of lagging behind in the turn.

"I believe you wanted to get me shot down, Al, so that you could get the squadron," he accused me jokingly as he recounted the incident. "Seriously though, I certainly see the importance of keeping well up when formating at that height. I was at full throttle most of the time but just couldn't make up the lost ground once I realized I was lagging a bit."

One of the new pilots complained about misting on his windscreen as he followed a 109 down, only to be told by Colin that he could expect that to happen on almost every occasion when fighting at altitude in a Spitfire. This problem of misting windscreens and canopies was one which was never solved on British aircraft throughout the war. It was undoubtedly the cause of many an unfortunate pilot being shot down when, because of restricted vision through misting, he fell to the guns of an enemy pilot who had crept up on him unseen. My predecessor as wing commander at Biggin Hill, later on in the war, was an unfortunate victim in just this set of circumstances.

"I'm just about to make out the detail for the next trip, sir. Will you be leading, and which flight will you fly with?" I asked the squadron commander.

"I'll do another trip following, and go with 'B' Flight," he answered.

In the Flight Sergeant's office George and I checked on aircraft serviceability before entering pilots against aircraft in the Authorization Book. George had decided to stand down, and Colin was to lead 'B' Flight with Don Finlay following. With Desmond on stand-down I was a bit short of section leaders and decided to give Pilot Officer Jack

Coleman, who had been with the squadron since early July, a chance to prove himself. I was most surprised therefore when some five minutes later he came up to me and said "I would rather not fly again today, Al, I don't feel well."

My immediate reaction was one of annoyance. "He's lost his nerve," I thought, and aloud, "What do you mean, not well?

"You're probably just over-tired like the rest of us. I'm sorry, but you will have to fly, there's no one else capable of taking the second section."

"If you say so," answered Jack in a very abrupt tone of voice, turning and walking out of the dispersal hut. The subject did not arise again that day but I determined to keep an eye on him in case he turned out to be another Dennis on our hands.

On the very next trip, the new squadron commander was shot down. Colin reported seeing him come down, and afterwards saw him standing in a field waving, apparently unharmed. Such was not the case; he was badly injured and spent quite a few weeks in hospital before returning to command 41 Squadron, which by that time was again installed at Hornchurch.

This was the time when 54 Squadron should have been moved out of the line for a rest. Without a squadron commander, only four survivors with any experience of leading a flight, and no other pilot really up to the standard required to lead a section, the squadron was in an extremely bad way. It was a grim situation not made any easier to bear by the move out, on that very day, of 65 Squadron to a northern airfield for a rest. Once again 54 Squadron was to act as guinea pig for the blooding of the new squadrons being brought into the Battle.

In the twenty-one days since our return, I had not been off the airfield, except for the one unhappy night in hospital, nor had any of the four leaders on whom the squadron now depended. Indeed, the mess by daylight was an unfamiliar sight – when dawn broke we were already at dispersal, and it was after dark when we returned to the mess. The strain had almost reached breaking point. The usually good natured George was quiet and irritable; Colin, by nature thin-faced, was noticeably more hollow-cheeked; Desmond, inclined to be weighty, was reduced to manageable proportions; and I, although I had no way of knowing how I appeared to the others, was all on edge and practically jumped out of my skin when someone shouted unexpectedly over the R/T. But still we continued to operate – there was no alternative.

A few days before 65 Squadron left Rochford I had occasion to land there and was surprised to see a crashed Dornier on the airfield. On enquiry I learned that the squadron had disabled it in combat and the pilot was forced to make a crash landing on the airfield. It so happened that the Medical Officer from Hornchurch was paying a routine visit to Rochford and was on the airfield when the enemy aircraft came into land. He saw the Dornier in the circuit and thought at first it was going to attack the airfield, but then he noticed a Spitfire in attendance and realized that the bomber was going to land. This it did, with wheels retracted, and slithered to a stop not far from where the amazed MO stood. The rest of the story belongs to him, and I repeat it as told to me later that afternoon:

"I could see the pilot slumped over the controls, and obviously injured. I dashed across to the aircraft and after a struggle I managed to get him out of the cockpit and on to the grass beside the aircraft. I then looked around to see if there were any other crew members and to my horror I found myself looking into the muzzle of a machine gun pointed at me from the top turret, with the rear gunner gazing unflinchingly down the sights. I confess I felt goose pimples breaking out all over me, and I deliberately turned away to give aid to the injured pilot as proof of my good intentions. When I looked up again the gun was still pointed at me, so I made a quick dash for the shelter of the aircraft's wing. From there I made my way along the side of the fuselage to the turret. One look was enough to tell me that the gunner had fired his last shot."

In the late afternoon of August 28th I was airborne at the head of the squadron for the third time that day; the now familiar gaggles of 109s were our inevitable playmates. In the mêlée that followed the first attack, I was once again on the receiving end – but this time of a Spitfire's guns. I had fastened on to the tail of a Me 109, one of three in close line astern formation, and was trying to close to firing range, when a Spitfire dived in from above and pulled around behind me. I clearly saw the RAF roundels as, fully banked in a steep turn, the aircraft was silhouetted against the blue sky. "Good, he's coming in to give me a hand," I muttered into my mask.

Imagine my surprise to find that I, not the three 109s ahead of me, was the subject of his wrath. Before I could do anything about it, he had found his aim and I was riddled with a burst of fire which struck the fuselage and port wing, cutting my rudder control cables and seriously damaging the port elevator. One burst was all he allowed himself before breaking down and away underneath me. It was all over in a matter of seconds, but even in that time the 109s had made good their escape, no doubt encouraged by the support afforded them!

I throttled back immediately and, by so doing, was able to keep going straight and level, but at a very reduced speed. There was practically no elevator movement and, of course, I had no rudder control. What was I to do? Stick with the aircraft and try a landing or do the sensible thing and bale out. I decided on the latter course, influenced by the fact that my radio was dead, and I was above a considerable amount of cloud and therefore unable to position myself in relation to an airfield. Also, there was no way of really knowing how serious was the damage to my fuselage and whether or not I could maintain elevator control at the lower and more turbulent altitudes. Any misjudgement on the approach requiring the use of throttles would certainly make the aircraft uncontrollable.

There was to be no rolling on to my back this time. I

made up my mind to take a header over the side in the conventional way, having trimmed the aircraft as best I could to maintain an even course.

Thus it was that I found myself swaying in my parachute at 10,000ft over Kent, with my abandoned Spitfire diving away to destruction somewhere below me, and my thoughts wandering back over the years to my childhood.

There was a feeling of splendid isolation as, snugly held in my parachute harness, I swayed gently to and fro high above the cultivated acres of Kent which stretched out below me, here and there flooded with warmth as the slanting sun rays pierced the broken cloud from whose vaporous interior I had just emerged. To one side I could see the long straight stretch of highway from Canterbury to Gillingham – the Watling Street of earlier and happier days – and on the opposite side a dark broken line marked the edge of the North Downs along whose edge the early Pilgrims had trudged their devout way to worship at Canterbury. In the distance, Detling airfield was plainly visible, a cleared space in the wooded area which sat astride the roadway that ran from Maidstone to Sheerness.

The descent from 10,000ft took about 15 minutes and thus there was plenty of time in which to ruminate on the past. Also it afforded me an opportunity to practise side-slipping in my parachute. It was as well that I practised this manoeuvre for it enabled me to avoid a farm-house towards which I was blown on the last few feet of my descent. I missed it by inches and landed instead astraddle a plum tree in an adjoining orchard. Apart from a few scratches in unpleasant places, I was unhurt.

"Stay where you are, I've got you covered," an angry voice reached my ears. Startled, I peered through the plum-loaded branches and straight down the barrel of a shot-gun held in a businesslike manner by an irate farmer who occupied the key position at the foot of the tree. In amazement and not a little afraid, I gaped at him. Finding my tongue, I said in most precise English, "I'm British," hoping that he would not misinterpret my New Zealand accent as belonging to a German trying to pretend he was English. Fortunately he didn't.

"Oh, I thought you might be a German, and I wasn't going to take any chances. Did you have to choose my prize plum tree in which to land? I was saving that crop," he added surlily.

In the course of extricating myself and my spread-eagled silk canopy from the tree, a great deal more of his prize crop fell to earth, much to his annoyance. I feel sure that had I been a German, he would have let me have both barrels. As it was, he grudgingly allowed me to use his telephone to contact Detling airfield from which a car was sent out to pick me up.

Detling, a Coastal Command station, was still showing signs of recent heavy bombing. The domestic area was a shambles and damage to other buildings was considerable. The operations block in particular was badly hit, the roof having caved in and buried all inside. I wondered at the time if the Germans knew that it was not a fighter airfield.

Less than three hours after I had taken off, I was back at Hornchurch, having been flown there in an Anson from Detling, accompanied by Squadron Leader Desmond Garvin who was the CO of the ill-fated 264 Squadron and who had also come to earth by parachute. I arrived back at 54 Squadron dispersal just in time to hear Lord Trenchard address the pilots. It was the first time I had seen or heard this famous airman, and it was fitting that it should have been in the middle of such a momentous battle.

Tony Allen, Patrick Shallard's replacement as the Squadron Intelligence Officer, was concerned over what he should say in his report about my having been shot down by a Spitfire. "Put it in," I advised. "I'm going to say so in my combat report. After all, it was a mistake. The pilot quite obviously mistook me for a Messerschmitt and thought I was with the three 109s which I was about to attack. Anyhow I've no idea who it was; he'll probably claim a 109 and as there were dozens of Spitfires in the area about the time I was shot down, I don't suppose he'll ever be traced." Of course, I was mad at the time, but once safely on the ground, I was able to see the incident in its right perspective. It had happened before, and was to happen again many times before the war ended, fortunately not to me.

I recall a rather amusing story as told by a close friend of mine in a neighbouring Spitfire squadron who was repeatedly attacked by a fellow squadron pilot, a new boy in the squadron, in similar circumstances to mine. In desperation, and after swearing roundly at the offender over the R/T, he, to use his own words, "turned and let him have it." The new pilot returned to base with a most colourful account of a thrilling combat with a Me109 and how he had beaten off the attack. He was a rather red-faced pilot when the true facts were disclosed by my friend who landed shortly afterwards.

'Prof', I had noticed, was present at dispersal when Lord Trenchard arrived, and I was surprised to see him there; I thought he had left the station. At the first opportunity I asked him the reason.

"When it was learned that Don Finlay would be in hospital indefinitely and that you had not returned from the last sortie, I was sent for and asked to take up the reins again. Now that you are back the idea is for me to run the squadron on the ground and for you to lead it in the air." This arrangement just didn't make sense to me. There could be no question of 'Prof' being content to stand by and watch the squadron take off time and again without him. And, of course, he didn't. He was back in the thick of it again the next day and had the satisfaction of adding another Hun to his credit.

"By the way, Al, did you know that Jack Coleman is in hospital at Bromley and very ill with malaria?" asked 'Prof.'

"Good heavens; is he?" I answered feeling very guilty as I recalled my last conversation with Jack.

"According to the doctor, he's had it for at least a week and should have been off operations long ago."

So, I had been wrong about Jack; he really was ill and not just frightened as I had smugly imagined. What a damn fool I had been not to seek advice from 'Prof' or the medical officer. I hadn't told 'Prof' of the incident, and avoided doing so now. But could I really blame myself? I was not wholly responsible for my actions at this stage of the Battle and, even under the most favourable conditions, I could hardly be blamed for making such an ill-considered decision; after all, I was only just twenty-two; not exactly the age of wisdom.

I am pleased to be able to report that I visited Jack in hospital and duly made my apologies. He did not rejoin the squadron until after we had moved to Catterick but we later became firm friends. Sad to relate, he was killed before the year was out.

A further two trips on the following day and then forward to Rochford, in lieu of Manston, from where the squadron was airborne on two further occasions. After an inconclusive battle with the escort fighters on my third sortie of the day, I came across a lone Dornier 215 which had become separated from the main formation and was heading hell-bent for home. It was a wonderful piece of luck, and I took every advantage of it. After two prolonged bursts, the Dornier with both motors on fire was seen to land north of the Thames by Squadron Leader Lea, a Controller from Hornchurch, who was enjoying a few hours off duty and witnessed the engagement from the ground.

There was a surprise in store for us that evening when we returned to the mess, in the person of a Luftwaffe bomber pilot, who had crash-landed and was under escort in the writing-room. He had made a forced landing not far from the airfield and, together with a crew of three NCO's, had been brought to Hornchurch for safe custody. Full of curiosity to get a look at this specimen of Hitler's Aryan *élite* and, if nothing else, to poke faces at him, we hurried into the writing-room to be met by a rather small, dark and jack-booted officer who gave us a most haughty look as if to say, "You can stare, but my turn will come." Through the medium of Pilot Officer Howe, a squadron pilot who spoke German, we learned that the offficer was in no way alarmed at his predicament and, indeed, had assured Howe that Hitler would be in London within two weeks. He didn't expect to remain a prisoner for long and for this reason thought it necessary to carry only toilet requisites in the event of being shot down!

"Cocky little blighter," muttered George when this information was relayed to him. "It's just what we need to hear to put a bit of urge back into our tired minds and bodies. Two weeks, he'll see!"

The cockiness of this German pilot certainly had the opposite effect from that which he had hoped to convey. To those of us who were feeling low and near breaking point it was like a shot of adrenalin, and with a rejuvenated spirit we faced the next day. I was to need a stimulant to face what was in store for me.

CHAPTER ELEVEN

Bombs Away

THE morning of August 31st was strangely and ominously quiet in the Hornchurch Sector, particularly in view of the good weather, and it was not until about midday that the squadron received the order to scramble. We had just taxied into position for take-off, and were all lined up ready to go, when a counter order was passed over the R/T. No sooner were we again parked in dispersal with engines stopped than a wildly gesticulating telephone orderly indicated that we were to start up again. In a matter of seconds all twelve aircraft were again taxi-ing to the take-off end urged on by the Controller's now near-hysterical voice shouting over the R/T "Hornet aircraft get airborne as quickly as you can, enemy in the immediate vicinity."

Hurriedly, desperately, for I had no wish to be caught taking off, I swung my aircraft into wind only to find my take-off run blocked by a Spitfire, the pilot of which was looking vaguely around for his position in the formation. "Get to hell out of the way, Red Two," I bellowed, recognizing my number two from the letters on his aircraft. It was a second or two before he made up his mind to move; immediately he did so I opened the throttle and careered across the airfield in pursuit of the squadron which had by now cleared the far hedge, and with wheels retracting was turning and climbing away from the airfield.

I was not quite airborne when a bomb burst on the airfield, ahead of me and to my left. "Good, I've made it," I thought. To this day I am not clear exactly what happened next; all I can remember is that a tremendous blast of air, carrying showers of earth, struck me in the face and the next moment thinking vaguely that I was upside down. What I do remember is the impact with the ground and a terrifying period of ploughing along the airfield upside down, still firmly strapped in the cockpit. Stones and dirt were thrown into my face and my helmet was torn by the stony ground against which my head was firmly pressed.

Finally the aircraft stopped its mad upside-down dash leaving me trapped in the cockpit, in almost total darkness, and breathing petrol fumes, the smell of which was overpowering. Bombs were still exploding outside, but this was not as frightening as the thought of fire from the petrol now seeping into the ground around my head. One spark and I would be engulfed in flames.

"Al, Al, are you alive?" urgently, and to me miraculously, the voice of Pilot Officer Eric Edsall, who had been my number three in the section, penetrated to my dazed senses.

"Yes, but barely. For God's sake get me out of here quickly," I answered breathlessly, desperately afraid of fire.

"Can you reach the release wire on the door, Al? If you can free the catches I might be able to lever it open; I can just get my hand underneath it."

It was no mean feat to move my right hand across, locate the spring loaded release wire, and exert sufficient pressure to free the locks. But somehow I managed it, and after a tremendous struggle Eric managed to force the door outwards. The next problem was to free myself from the parachute harness, as the small aperture created by the now opened cockpit door was barely large enough to wriggle through, without the extra impediment of a parachute pack. This too I eventually managed, and after a frantic struggle squeezed my way out into the blessed fresh air.

"Come on, let's get off the airfield quickly, our 'Mae Wests' will attract the Hun fighter pilots," said Eric breathlessly. "You'll have to help me though, I've done something to my leg and can't walk. I crawled across here to get you out."

I was in no fit state to look after myself, let alone support Eric. Indeed, I was so dazed I wasn't sure which way to go but, with Eric supporting himself around my neck and giving the necessary directions, we struggled through the bomb craters to the safety of the nearby squadron hangar, and thence on to station sick quarters. Sick quarters bore all the signs of a casualty clearing station, a queue of injured airmen and stretcher cases filling the passageway. There seemed little point in staying there in the face of more serious casualties so, having left Eric in capable hands, I returned to the mess, bathed my raw forehead, and retired to bed to await the arrival of the Medical Officer at lunch time. A patch of skin and hair, about the diameter of a tennis ball, had been removed from the right side of my head just above the temple, and my neck and face bore numerous small cuts caused, no doubt, by the small pebbles thrown into the cockpit by the initial explosion. My neck had stiffened up considerably and I could barely turn my head.

Colin was the first to burst into my room on the squadron's return. "You know, Al, when I saw the remains of your aircraft on the airfield, I took it for granted that you had been killed and then I really saw red. To think that some b____ fool had made a mess of our scramble orders and that aided by Sergeant Davies (my number two), you should get killed as a result, was just too much to stomach."

"Thanks for the kind thought, Colin, but as you see there's life in the old dog yet. Now that you mention him, what's happened to Davies?"

"There's no sign of him. Whether he got off safely and was shot down later or was blown to smithereens, we don't know."

"Did you get a close look at my aircraft, and Eric's? I didn't get time to observe the extent of the damage."

"I certainly did. The port wing on your aircraft was blown off – that's what caused you to flick on to your back – and the engine was either blown off, or torn off when the aircraft hit the ground again, because it is quite a few yards away from the wreck. You can thank your lucky stars that it was because there was so much petrol around the aircraft that it only needed a spark and you would have been incinerated. The tank hadn't burst but a generous amount had come out of the broken petrol pipelines. Eric's aircraft also had a wing blown off, but he remained the right way up and slithered about the same distance as you did on his side. There's quite a furrow where you ploughed along upside down – about 100 yards I reckon. As for Davies, it's a mystery what happened to him."

"It was fortunate for me that I had the seat right at the bottom as I normally do for take-off, otherwise I'm sure my neck would have been broken. From what you say it seems as if a bomb must have dropped immediately in front of the section, perhaps it hit Davies."

"Probably, but it's hard to tell. Your Spitfires are lying in the middle of a line of bomb craters which run diagonally across the line of take-off. It must have been a great relief to you, Al, when Eric got the cockpit door open."

"It was. I must remember to tell Jeffrey Quill when I see him how pleased I am that his firm chose to incorporate a side door in the Spitfire cockpit. If there hadn't been one it would have required a crane to lift the aircraft to get me out. Just as well for me it wasn't a Hurricane which has no side door."

The mystery of Davies was solved about an hour after the incident, and about the time Colin was talking to me. He walked into the dispersal hut unharmed, much to the amazement of the squadron pilots. Apparently, he had been blown outside the airfield boundary into the River Ingerbourne, which skirted the east side of the airfield, and still firmly strapped in his cockpit. In order to get back into the airfield he had to walk about two miles around the perimeter outside the Dannert wire which surrounded the airfield, hence the delay in reporting his whereabouts.

George was my next visitor. "I can only stay a minute, Al, I'm up for a quick lunch and must dash off again on readiness. Glad to see you in one piece, or nearly so – that's a large slice off your head. Must tell you about my cow before I go, it will amuse you."

"Your cow, that sounds a bit odd to me, George. I can't see how a cow can have any connection with what's going

Wing Commander Alan C.Deere,
DSO, OBE, DFC and Bar

Kiwi I – the author's Spitfire

The author and *Kiwi I*, Hornchurch, 1940

Spitfires on patrol during the Battle of Britain

Individual pilots scores P. 90.

54 SQUADRON

DATE	PILOT	DESTROYED	PROBABLE
1940 March 31st	F/L Pearson ✓		1 Do 17
May 21st	S/L Leathart		1. Ju 88.
	P/O Allen.		1 Ju 88
23rd	F/L Deere	1½ Me 109.	1½ Me 109
	P/O Allen.	1½ Me 109.	1½ Me 109.
24th	S/L Leathart.	1 Me 109.	
	F/L Pearson	2 Me 109.	
	F/L Deere	1. Me 109.	
	P/O Allen	1 Me 109.	
	P/O Gribble	2 Me 109	
	Sgt Buckland ✓	1 Me 109.	
	F/Sgt Tew	1 Me 109.	
	Sgt Norwell	1 Me 109.	
	Sgt Phillips ✓	4 Me 109.	1 Me 109.
	Unclaimed by any one pilot.	1 Me 109. 15	
	P/O Gray		2 Me 109.
	P/O McMullan		1 Me 109.
25th	F/L Pearson	1 Me 110	
	P/O Allen	2 Me 110.	
	P/O Gray	½ Me 109	
	Sgt Norwell	½ Me 109.	
	F/L Deere	1 Me 109.	
	Unclaimed by any one pilot	1 Me 109.	
	S/L Leathart		1 Me 110.
	F/L Way		1 Me 110.
	P/O Mc McMullan		2 Me 110.

Facsimile of the first page of 54 Squadron official records
showing early successes in the Battle of Britain

Group Captain A.G. "Sailor" Malan, Squadron Leader (later Wing Commander) Jack Charles and the author, Biggin Hill, 1943

Canadian and French RAF pilots tie for the honour of 1000th enemy victim for Biggin Hill Sector, 1943.
Photo includes Squadron Leader Jack Charles, DFC (third left), Commandant René Mouchotte, Croix de Guerre, DFC and Bar (fourth left),
Group Captain A.G. "Sailor" Malan, DSO and Bar, (fifth left) and the author (sixth left)

Pilots of 611 Squadron celebrate the 1000th enemy aircraft destroyed, Biggin Hill, 1943

Squadron Leader Jack Charles chalks up the 1000th enemy aircraft, Biggin Hill, 1943

on, unless you have bought one to supply early morning milk to the pilots."

"Not a bit of it, old boy, this is an entirely different story. Just let me tell you. Well, we managed to catch up with those Huns who bombed the airfield, somewhere between here and Southend. Norwell and I fastened on to a Me 109 which we chased at tree-top height across Essex, taking a pot shot at him whenever the trees would allow." (Jock Norwell was a Sergeant Pilot in the squadron and an amusing and valuable addition to our ranks, having been transferred from 74 Squadron earlier in the year.) "In the course of our chase we crossed a meadow full of grazing cows and unfortunately for one of them I chose that moment to fire another burst. A cow was right in my line of sight and took the full blast. It went up vertically for about 20ft, just as if someone had ignited a rocket tied to its tail, before plomping back to earth. I'll bet there's still a look of amazement on that cow's face when the farmer finds it."

"I take it you're claiming one cow destroyed in your combat report. Seriously though, how many Huns did the squadron get on that sortie? Sufficient I trust to make amends for what they did to my section, to say nothing of my poor head."

"I'm not quite sure, but at least three. Colin, I believe, got two, but I didn't wait to hear the full story. I'll find out and let you know this evening. Must away now, Al, see you later."

In all, about sixty bombs were dropped in a line from just outside the perimeter, across the airfield, through the 54 Squadron dispersal area and beyond into the Elm Park housing estate. Cratering on the airfield was considerable, but a few buildings only were damaged. There were fatal casualties among airmen on the domestic site, while on the airfield four Spitfires, all 54 Squadron, were destroyed in the dispersal area. As 'Prof' put it when I spoke to him later about the bombing, "On return, the dispersal was a shambles where we had been. We would certainly all have been killed by bombs. As it happened the only fatal casualty was the squadron canary!"

Hornchurch was bombed again later that day. Half asleep in my bed, having been doctored and doped, I was dimly aware of the air raid sirens blaring on the camp and decided that the air raid shelter was the safest place to be as the chances were that Hornchurch would again be the target, and it was. I hastened to the shelter behind the mess which was for the use of the mess staff and the airwomen who slept in billets nearby. The civilian mess staff, headed by Sam our popular and bluff chef, were already safely installed and seated in two rows along either side of the shelter and engaged in the usual speculative conversation.

I had no sooner seated myself when a pair of female legs appeared unexpectedly on the top rung of the iron ladder which lead into the air raid shelter from the emergency escape exit at the far end. Shapely ankles were followed by a figure draped in a dressing-gown and obviously in some haste. Having successfully negotiated the descent, she jumped thankfully on the floor of the shelter and turned to face the audience to display all of mother nature's charms, so embarrassingly revealed through her dressing-gown which had, unfortunately, become unfastened. The poor girl was covered in confusion and the situation was made no less embarrassing by the ribald remarks which Sam tossed to the assembled company. The unfortunate airwoman, who was an operations-room plotter, had been caught in her bath when the sirens sounded and deemed it wise to make all haste to the shelter. A wise but, as it turned out, an embarrassing decision, and not one made any easier to laugh down by her admission that she didn't know there was another entrance to the shelter. In the circumstances, the bombing attack which then developed was suffered rather light-heartedly.

That night I was plagued by ghastly nightmares of falling bombs and burning aircraft and awoke on at least two occasions bathed in perspiration and with the bandage around my head wringing wet. Dawn was a welcome sight even if its arrival was accompanied by the roar of Merlins from a squadron of Spitfires being warmed up for the day's work. I dropped off to sleep again as quiet once again prevailed, and eventually slept through till lunch which I took in the dining-room, having decided to visit the sick quarters to ask the Medical Officer to clear me for flying. He was not at all pleased with the suggestion and even less so when I intimated that I thought I was fit to fly right away. After much persuasion on my part, he reluctantly agreed that I could return to operations tomorrow.

"You look a fine sight with your bandaged head and plastered wrist and I'm a damn fool to let you fly, let alone fight," was his joking sally as I departed his office, having first been freshly bandaged.

I was climbing into my aircraft the following morning when the Flight Sergeant handed me a sealed envelope saying as he did so, "A message from Mr Gribble, sir." We were late getting off and there wasn't time to read the note before arriving at Rochford, to which we had moved for the day's operations. I supposed George, who was standing down for the morning, wanted to pass on some instructions about details of his pilots for the morning's sorties. I should have known that it was some form of joke. Inside the envelope was a railway warrant made out in my name with Hornchurch as the station of arrival, and the station of departure left blank. There was a note attached which said: "Thought you might need this, Al!"

Although the squadron was jumped on its first sortie of the day, and I had the utmost difficulty in extricating myself from the 109s, I did not require the warrant for my return. Soon after take-off we were bounced by a large formation of 109s as we climbed up to engage a formation of about thirty bombers which eventually attacked Hornchurch. However, supported by other squadrons, we harassed the bombers and escort so much *en route* to their target that only six bombs fell anywhere near the airfield, and these caused no damage.

September 3rd marked the final day of operations for

54 Squadron in the Battle of Britain; a day on which the squadron did four further sorties before being relieved later that evening by 41 Squadron.

On one of the four occasions on our last day of operations, we were ordered off as soon as the aircraft were refuelled from a previous engagement and instructed to engage a raid returning from North Weald, which had been heavily hit. A few miles east of Hornchurch, and at about 13,000ft, we met up with the tail end of the escort; about a dozen 110s, all weaving desperately to avoid the bursting AA shells being poured among them from a battery near the Thames. The squadron had taken off singly, in pairs and in whatever order the aircraft became refuelled, so there was no question of a co-ordinated attack. In fact, I was alone at the time of sighting and fondly imagined that I was the first squadron aircraft on the scene. I had singled out a Me 110 and was taking great care to get my opening range accurate – an unusual pleasure afforded by the absence of 109s – when to my amazement a Spitfire, diving vertically from above, opened fire on my intended target which burst into flame and spun away to destruction. The damage done, both to the Me 110 and my pride, the Spitfire broke up and away in front of me and I saw from its marking that it was Colin Gray who had beaten me to it. "He would," I thought angrily, but reluctantly admitting to myself that it was a remarkable piece of shooting.

I managed to catch up with the remainder of the 110s who had, by now, been joined by some 109s which sat threateningly above. This made it a decidedly more difficult operation but I managed to get a 110 probably destroyed and another damaged, before returning to base with my ammunition exhausted. The first Me 110 could only be allowed as "probably destroyed" for although I was convinced it had dived out of control, probably into the Thames, there was no confirmation from the ground of one having crashed in the area at the time of combat. Colin added a Me 109 destroyed to the Me 110, which I had seen him destroy and which became the subject of much controversy. He put in his claim in the normal way, and I certified that I had witnessed the combat and confirmed the destruction of the Me 110. Later that day, we were informed that an AA Battery near the Thames had claimed the aircraft. Although the AA guns were firing at the time, there was absolutely no doubt in my mind that Colin had been the destroyer. In the end, the victory was credited to the guns – much to our annoyance – on the basis that they had done sterling work and needed encouragement. So did we.

For the third time in four months 41 Squadron arrived to take our place in the front line of operations. It was late that evening when they eventually landed, having been diverted to Duxford *en route* because of a raid in progress at the time of their expected arrival in the Sector. We were delighted to see them and must have looked it. Some years later when discussing the moment with Wing Commander Tony Lovell, who was later killed, he recalled his impressions of the occasion in these words: "We were amazed at the eagerness of you chaps to get away from Hornchurch, but we soon learned why. None of you looked as if you had slept for a week" (which I hadn't properly) "and you, Al, with your bandaged head and plastered wrist were an unnerving sight to our new pilots who hadn't tasted combat. They wondered what had hit them, or was about to hit them. It wasn't long though before most of us felt like you looked."

The Hornchurch diary of the period records the departure of 54 Squadron in these words:

"In the late afternoon, 54 Squadron left us for a period of rest and recuperation at Catterick. During the previous fortnight, they had been bearing the brunt of the work in the Sector for they had to hold the fort while the various new squadrons arrived and settled down into the Sector routine. With the exception of two very short breaks, they had been with us continuously during the first year of the war, and in this period had destroyed 92 enemy aircraft."*

Despite the numerous replacements during August, eighteen pilots all told, only sixteen pilots remained for the move to Catterick, a grim reminder of the intensity of the month's fighting. For some the Battle of Britain was over, myself among them. Others, however, returned within a month of our arrival at Catterick to reinforce depleted 11 Group squadrons, although 54 Squadron did not return to Hornchurch again until later in the year, when the Germans had switched to night bombing.

Safely installed at Catterick the pilots of 54 Squadron rested tired minds and bodies, while in the south the last intake of fresh squadrons into 11 Group faced up to the continuing onslaught. But the time in which an invasion was possible was passing. Quick results were required. And thus it was that on the 7th September the Luftwaffe abandoned its offensive against the sector airfields and began the assault on London; a most satisfactory decision from Lord Dowding's point of view and a tacit admission that the plan to defeat Fighter Command had failed. It was a battle now not only against the British Air Force, but against the British people. But they too could 'take it' and Hitler's hope that the destruction of the capital by itself might bring victory without the hazards of an invasion was never realized. On the 17th September 'Operation Sea Lion' was postponed indefinitely; on October 12th the invasion was definitely called off. The Battle of Britain had been won and the victorious German land forces massed along the French and Belgian coasts were denied the dramatic consummation of their triumphs – the chanting of their war song *wir fahren gegen England* as they spilled from invasion barges on to the English beaches.

*The top scoring squadron at the time

CHAPTER TWELVE

A Personal Opinion

THE Battle of Britain has been the subject of much misconception and not a little controversy, and it may therefore be of interest to record the personal views and opinions of one who was an active participant.

The misconception arose over the extent to which Fighter Command's forces became depleted and the controversy centres mainly around the strategy of the Commander-in-Chief and the tactics employed by the Air Officer Commanding 11 Group, the principal commanders in the Battle.

That the main shortage was of pilots, and not aircraft, will be clear from earlier chapters. After the Battle, there was much wild talk about shortage of aircraft. Though losses in the air and on the ground were indeed heavy, the replacement position in the critical period when our sector airfields were under attack, was such that squadrons were never kept waiting for new aircraft.

On the other hand, the pilot position was critical. The position in which 54 Squadron found itself towards the end of August, particularly in relation to shortage of leaders, illustrates the point, which is confirmed by the History of the Royal Air Force in these words: "By the opening week of September Dowding's squadrons had, on the average, only sixteen operational pilots out of their full complement of twenty-six." When we consider quality as well as numbers, the gravity of the pilot position becomes even more apparent. The newcomers, though magnificent material, did not match their predecessors in flying experience nor in their knowledge of the technicalities of air fighting.

Dowding's main problem then was not aircraft, but pilots. And it is against this background that his handling of squadrons must be judged. I can only offer the experience of

54 Squadron as an illustration that the Commander-in-Chief was well aware of the strategic implications of having to fight a prolonged battle with hopelessly inadequate forces. 54 Squadron was rested at just the right moment on the two occasions before its final departure from the Battle. On the last occasion, however, I indicated that the squadron should have been moved out of the line sooner than it was. But this was merely to emphasize the critical position reached by the end of August, when Dowding was faced with the problem of a fresh squadron becoming depleted and exhausted before any of the resting and reforming squadrons were ready to take its place.

The second major problem he faced was how and where to concentrate his squadrons. His decision to concentrate only a portion of his available forces in the most threatened area – No. 11 Group – and to relieve tired squadrons as considered necessary from the less hard-pressed Groups has also been sniped at by many armchair critics, particularly those who supported the Leigh-Mallory* concept of concentrating all the power in the threatened area. What would have been the outcome of the strong German raids against the north-east coast on the 15th August had there been no forces in position to meet them? It is easy to be wise after the event, but I suggest that had these raids been unopposed, or met by only token forces, there would have been an outcry against Dowding from the Air Staff and the Government. The vital question affecting Dowding's whole outlook was: How long is the battle going to last? No one could give him the answer: only time would tell and time was working on the side of the enemy with his numerically superior forces.

The tremendous odds faced by the pilots of the 11 Group squadrons gave rise to criticism of Air Vice-Marshal Park's tactics. I am in a position to comment at first hand on one aspect of these, and that was the policy of using selected Spitfire squadrons to draw off the enemy escort fighters thus enabling the remaining squadrons, and this included

---

*Air Vice-Marshal Leigh-Mallory, AOC, No. 12 Group during the battle

the 12 Group Hurricanes, to concentrate more effectively on the bombers. Though this decision meant a much tougher and unrewarding job for the Hornchurch Spitfire squadrons, I do not recall a single pilot saying other than he thought it an excellent idea. I strongly support this view, and on numerous occasions witnessed the rewards reaped when enemy bombers, shorn of the majority of their escort, were set upon by the defending Hurricanes which, excellent as they were, could not have coped so effectively without the intervention of the Spitfires.

It was over the question of mass formations – or wings of squadrons, as they later became known – that a really vital issue arose. Douglas Bader was the chief instigator of the use of wings in the Battle of Britain, and had sold the idea to Air Vice-Marshal Leigh-Mallory. Although concentration of force, which the mass formations implied, is a foremost principle of war, it did not apply under the conditions which affected the defence of these shores in the Battle of Britain, at least through the medium of wing formations. The wing was not new to Park – he had used it in the closing days of the Dunkirk fighting – and it must be assumed therefore that he had considered, but discarded, the use of mass formations, undoubtedly for reasons of speed and flexibility. The sober truth is that, at this stage of the war, the information from the radar chain was neither sufficiently complete nor sufficiently reliable to permit the added option of the policy with success. Although the initial build-up of a raid was quite often reported over the Pas de Calais, the strength and composition could not be accurately determined.

Was it 200 bombers? Was it 30 bombers and 170 fighters? Or, was it just 200 fighters? There was no way of telling. It would have been blind folly therefore to have hurled masses of defending fighters into the air on each and every occasion that a build-up occurred. Had this been done, larger and more serious threats could have developed in say, the Portsmouth and Harwich areas and few, if any, forces would be left with which to meet them. Or alternatively, had the raid not developed as expected, large numbers of fighters would have been on the ground refuelling when they might have been most urgently needed.

From personal experience, there were very few occasions in the 11 Group area when it would have been possible to scramble and assemble two squadrons as a wing – let alone five as finally used from Duxford – in time to make an effective interception before the enemy bombers reached their target. Almost one hundred per cent of the interceptions by the Duxford wing were over or just short of the target, and sometimes after the bombs had fallen, which supports the contention that much vital time was lost in forming up, and proceeding to the target, in mass formation. On this basis, I wonder how many of the 11 Group Sector airfields would have been in commission on the 7th September, when the Germans finally ceased bombing airfields, and how many aircraft would have been destroyed on the ground or caught in the act of getting airborne, had Park relied on wing formations to fight his battle? Finally, with the forces allotted to him by the Commander-in-Chief, Park's password was 'economy of effort' and in this context it is of interest to note that in a series of ten large formation sorties from Duxford into the 11 Group area, nine were unsuccessful and the tenth destroyed one Me 109!

From a fighter pilot's point of view, I hold that Bader's wing concept was wrong, and I consider that the German fighter tactics against the American daylight bombers prove my point. The Germans faced the same problem in 1943 as did Fighter Command in 1940, but with vastly more experience behind them, a more sophisticated radar control system, and a longer period of defensive operations in which to experiment and learn. Most important of all, they had adequate early warning of attacks on their Homeland and time in which to concentrate their mass formations where and when they wanted them. In the end, having tried the mass formation technique, they resorted to small mobile formations of fighters concentrated in time and space, but operating independently. They found that too many fighters tied to a single leader sterilized flexibility of action and thought on the part of individual pilots, and usually resulted in only the leader getting a decent shot at the raiding bombers before the rest of the formation was set upon by the escorting fighters. Certainly, when on the offensive in the later stages of the war, and using the wing concept, I found that the maximum number of squadrons that could be efficiently handled in combat was two, not five as used in 1940-1941. I know that most wing leaders agree with me, and certainly those who had the benefit of later experience. Johnnie Johnson was one and in his book *Wing Leader* he supports this view. Douglas Bader, I know, won't agree.

In any discussion of the Battle of Britain, it is important to remember that the aim of the Luftwaffe was to destroy Fighter Command in the air and on the ground and by so doing open the way for a sea-borne invasion of England. Dowding's task was, therefore, twofold:

(1) To prevent the destruction of his forces, and
(2) In the process, inflict the maximum of destruction on the enemy air forces.

To achieve the second only was not in itself sufficient; he must also ensure that Fighter Command remained strong enough to influence events should an invasion be launched. Park's tactics were, of necessity, based on the overall aim of his Commander-in-Chief and not, as some people fondly imagine, to destroy the German Air Force, a task beyond the slender resources of his Group and, for that matter, of the Command. That the strategy of Dowding and the tactics of Park were successful, is proven by the fact that by the end of August, when according to German estimates Fighter Command would be defeated, the 11 Group squadrons were still inflicting heavy losses on the enemy, and all the Sector airfields were intact. From the outset, both commanders were quite clear what each had to do; they saw no point in boasting to the world that large numbers of German aircraft had been shot down if, in the process, it entailed the destruction of Fighter Command and its base organization, thus making it possible for the Germans to launch an invasion. And there can be little doubt that they would have done so, as captured documents now reveal, had the Luftwaffe won this most decisive of all air battles.

Victory in the Battle of Britain was achieved by a narrow margin; how narrow, very few people realize. Its achievement should have brought just reward to the two commanders who had been the architects, but for Dowding there was the dubious appointment to serve on a mission to the United States, and for Park, command of a training Group. Dowding and Park won the Battle of Britain, but they lost the battle of words that followed with the result that they, like Winston Churchill at the post-war polls, were cast aside in their finest hour.

CHAPTER THIRTEEN

Mid-air Collision

IT was fitting that 'Prof' should be at the head of the squadron when it arrived at Catterick in the late evening of September 3rd, despite the fact that he had officially handed over command ten days previously. For the third and last time in the space of four months 54 Squadron was installed at Catterick to afford its pilots a rest from the arduous operations in the south.

A very, very tired group of pilots climbed wearily down from their Spitfires and, with a feeling of relief, flung themselves into the chairs in dispersal, relaxed for the first time in four weeks. An unnaturally subdued George, dropping parachute and Mae West on the floor, sank into the chair next to mine and said:

"You know, Al, I don't really know how I survived that last week. My eyes got so tired that I was seeing double on the last few trips. God, how frightened I got towards the end, I had an overwhelming urge to run every time I saw those massive Hun formations; how I didn't give way to the urge, I just don't know."

"I know exactly what you mean, George. From the bombing incident onwards I was in a complete daze. I think I was past being frightened, I was just too tired to care what happened. Somehow I felt that what was to come couldn't be worse than what had gone before. In the end, I just kept going from force of habit."

"Ah well, as the old proverb says, 'He that endureth is not overcome.' What was it that Ovid said? Let me see, I should know, I sweated enough blood over Latin at school. Ah yes, I remember: 'Much and long I have endured'," quoted George very dramatically. "A very apt observation on the last month's operations, I think you'll agree."

"Very apt, George, but what do you think our chances are

of surviving another round?"

"Damn all, I should think. So much so that I am not going to worry what Mr Lloyd (as RAF officers usually referred to Lloyds Bank) thinks of my bank balance at the end of this month. I'll be back at Hornchurch again by then and bank balances will be the least of my worries."

On this light-hearted note we adjourned to the Officers' Mess where we were greeted by the now familiar faces of the mess staff who, displaying more than the usual pride in the job, conducted us to our various rooms. We partook of many a thirsty beer that evening; beers consumed and enjoyed for the first time in weeks, without the nagging fear of how to face the events of tomorrow.

We were soon into the relaxed routine of this quiet Sector but, as a result of the German attack against the north-east on 15th August, the squadron was required to keep one flight at readiness at the satellite airfield of Greatham, on the coast near West Hartlepool. It was a boring business having to spend the whole day at Greatham with, as it were, only a telephone for company and one which, unlike its counter-part at Rochford, very rarely ever rang. Agreeably, towards the end of September, when the Germans had turned to night bombing, this state was relaxed to the extent of allowing one section on training flying while the other remained at readiness.

I had an odd experience during one of the very few scrambles from Greatham. I intercepted a Junkers 88 near Whitby but before I could fire a shot, and after he had dropped his bomb, the pilot sought the safety of the clouds and headed off eastwards out to sea. There was absolutely no point in trying to ferret him out of the cloud, so I orbited in the vicinity awaiting orders from Control. My number two, a Polish pilot who had but recently joined the squadron and was seeing his first German aircraft since his arrival in England, had tasted blood and could not be restrained. He shot into cloud after the Hun, despite my orders to the contrary, and was never seen nor heard of again. A plot was followed from the position where they both entered cloud until the track was lost about forty miles off the coast. I suspect the Pole just flew on, further and further out to sea and discovered too late that he was short of petrol and out of R/T range. Perhaps he got the Junkers in the end, but I doubt it. Like many similar incidents during the war, his disappearance remains a mystery.

Squadron Leader Pat Dunworth assumed command of 54 Squadron a few days after our arrival at Catterick, and 'Prof' departed to Air Ministry where he was destined to polish a chair for the next year. In dribs and drabs the injured pilots returned. First Jack Coleman, fully recovered from his bout of malaria; next Allan Campbell, his bruised and battered ear bearing permanent signs of his lucky escape; then Charlie Stewart none the worse for a long immersion in the English Channel; Sergeant Lawrence recovered from a similar experience; Pete Matthews, another enforced sea-bather; and so the procession went on as others, bearing varying scars of combat but all fully fit again, reported back to try their luck a second time. It seemed as if the squadron would be its old self again in next to no time, but then the blow fell. A signal was received from No. 13 Group, our parent Group while at Catterick, stating that 54 had been designated a 'C' Class Squadron, and posting a number of our more experienced pilots to squadrons in the south.

To those who had been in the squadron long enough to be proud of its record and achievements, and this applied more particularly to the four survivors of the squadron that first went into battle, it was a bitter blow.

"How could they do this to us after what the squadron has done," wailed Colin. "To think, we are now 54 Training Squadron. What a come-down, and what an existence."

"Yes, dammit, that's shattered all my plans for a large overdraft," muttered a despondent George.

That 54 Squadron should be singled out to suffer such an ignoble fate, seemed to us a peculiar form of gratitude. In fact, had we but known at the time, it was a decision reluctantly taken by the Commander-in-Chief and forced on him by the really serious pilot position now facing Fighter Command. The stage had been reached – as discussed in the concluding paragraphs of the previous chapter – whereby none of the resting squadrons was ready to take the place of those which had been most heavily hit, and I must admit 54 Squadron was not then ready to return. It was only after careful consideration that Air Marshal Dowding made this decision which he knew would be unpopular with the squadrons. As he says in his Despatch on the Battle:

> "I considered, but discarded, the advisability of combining pairs of weak units into single squadrons at full strength, for several reasons, one of which was the difficulty of recovery when a lull should come. Another was that ground personnel would be wasted, and a third was that the rate at which the strength of the Command was decreasing would be obvious.
>
> I decided to form 3 Categories of Squadron: –
>
> (a) The units of 11 Group and on its immediate flanks which were bearing the brunt of the fighting.
>
> (b) A few outside units to be maintained at operational strength and to be available as Unit Reliefs in cases where this was unavoidable.
>
> (c) The remaining squadrons of the Command, which could be stripped of their operational pilots, for the benefit of the A Squadrons, down to a level of 5 or 6. These C Squadrons could devote their main energies to the training of new pilots, and, although they would not be fit to meet German fighters, they would be quite capable of defending their Sectors against unescorted bombers, which would be all that they would be likely to encounter."

Thus it was that 54 Squadron became a 'C' Class Squadron. In next to no time we were down to five of the original pilots, and in place of those who had been drafted south there were many new faces, fresh from Operational Training Units. Our training task was under way.

George and I worked out a syllabus of training which concentrated on cine-gun exercises, and only included formation flying as a means of judging a pilot's confidence and ability to fly in cloud in formation and to carry out fast climbs to height. From the moment the pilot got into his aircraft he was briefed to switch on his reflector sight and from then onwards he was made conscious of the fact that his primary aim was to bring his sights to bear on the enemy. No matter what the exercise, we invariably finished up with the pilots in line astern formation, at about 200 yard intervals, and briefed that not only must they follow the leader but that they must endeavour to keep taking cine-gun shots while so doing. In this way we hoped they would soon get out of the inbred training habit of flying their aircraft always in relation to the horizon and with constant reference to instruments, rather than by feel and instinct. We wanted them to be able to get their sights on a target and to keep them there without worrying about the attitude of their own aircraft in relation to the horizon or the ground. The principle must be that the aircraft is but the agent to carry guns, and the latter must be brought to bear whatever the antics of the target.

It was amazing how quickly the cine-camera results, and the flying, improved. Furthermore it was soon apparent which of the new arrivals were going to make really good fighter pilots. It was up to the squadron to say when a particular pilot was ready to go south, and the doubtful ones were kept back as long as possible. A pilot was certified as fully operational only after he had passed the most stringent tests, the final one of which was a dog fight with his flight commander or his deputy. In the course of one of these final tests, I had another remarkable escape.

A particularly promising pilot by the name of Sergeant Squires was keen for me to take him on his final test, and I agreed. We climbed to 10,000ft and I told him to position himself astern and below at about 250 yards, using the range-bar on his reflector to get his distance. A dog fight now ensued with me doing everything I knew to get him off my tail until, as usually happens in aerial combat, I found myself down to about 3,000ft which was well below the safety height we had set for this exercise.

"OK, Red Two, I'll climb up again to 10,000ft and we'll have another go. You are doing fine, but please keep your distance at about 250 yards, you are getting far too close."

Squires acknowledged this message and dropped back to the required distance. When at the desired height, I again started throwing the aircraft about, determined this time to get him off my tail. It is most difficult, and indeed almost impossible, with the rear vision afforded from the cockpit of a Spitfire, to keep an aircraft behind and below in sight for every second of a dog fight. After a series of hectic manoeuvres culminating in a steep turn, I could not see Squires and in order to check if I had been successful in shaking him off I reversed my turn quickly. For a split second I caught a glimpse of the nose of his aircraft right on top of me and the next second he had flown into me. His airscrew chewed clean through my tail plane and immediately my Spitfire whipped into a vicious spin, completely out of control.

In a matter of seconds I had jettisoned the hood and proceeded with the business of baling out having, of course, first carried out the necessary preliminaries of releasing my cockpit straps and freeing my R/T lead. To get out of the aircraft was not going to be easy, as I soon discovered. I was spinning at an unnaturally fast rate, and descending at a very high speed. Try as I might I couldn't overcome the centrifugal force which kept me anchored to my seat, and no amount of pulling with my hands on the side of the cockpit would overcome it. Again and again I tried until quite unexpectedly I floated out of the cockpit. I can only think that at some stage of the spin the centrifugal force was less, and I had chosen the right moment to exert a little more strength. Anyhow, I was free, but only for a second or two. I was blown on to the remnants of the shattered tail unit where I stuck fast. I twisted and turned, kicked and fought with every ounce of my strength until finally I broke free.

Instinctively I reached for the parachute rip-cord handle and it was then that I realized that my parachute had been partially torn from my back. The handle was not in its usual place and the whole parachute pack was whirling around my head as I tumbled over and over, the ground uncomfortably close. I can distinctly remember saying to myself at this juncture, "Fancy being killed this way." Meaning, of course, not in combat.

When all seemed lost, my parachute miraculously opened of its own accord – partially as it turned out – and only just in time, for I seemed to hit the ground at the same moment. I was horizontal when I struck and this position, coupled with the fact that I ended up in a farmer's cess-pool which cushioned the impact, probably saved my life. I very nearly drowned in the foul stuff (but in the circumstances, perhaps sweet!) as with a badly injured back making it agony to move, I had the greatest difficulty in crawling free. A passing motorist came to my assistance, and together with his wife, helped me into his car and was good enough to drive me back to Catterick some seven miles away.

I was rushed off to hospital in the station ambulance and an immediate X-ray revealed no breaks, but disclosed a chipped coccyx. The damn thing has been a nuisance ever since and was to be the source of acute discomfort, and pain, on later operations when fighter aircraft were equipped with dinghies and the pilot had perforce to sit on a hard-packed dinghy which replaced the hitherto comfortable sorbo-pad that was fastened to his parachute pack. My back was also badly strained and that injury, too, persists and is the cause of many sleepless nights.

On inspection the parachute was found to have been torn

across one end of the pack and somehow the auxiliary chute – a small spring-loaded chute packed on top of the main parachute to assist in pulling out the canopy – had worked free and pulled the canopy out one side of the pack. Not only was the steel wire rip-cord still encased in its protecting outer cable but its double ends, which pass through the eyelets that hold the pack together, were bent double, and it is most unlikely that I would have been able to pull them clear of the eyelets, thus freeing the auxiliary chute, even had I been able to reach the rip-cord handle.

Sergeant Squires' aircraft had caught fire on impact but he had full control and was able to bale out successfully, landing uninjured. On his first operational trip he was shot down by flak and taken prisoner-of-war.

A seven-day stint in bed followed, but in the mess. There I had the companionship of the cheerful George and Jack Coleman, Colin having by this time gone off to command a flight in 43 Squadron at Acklington.

"If I were you, Al, I'd pack it in," said George who sat comfortably on the end of my bed blowing smoke rings and spearing them with his fore-finger. "There's one thing you must do, and that is to do away with that Kiwi emblem on the side of your aircraft. It certainly doesn't seem to have brought you any luck. Anyhow, the wretched bird can't fly, and it seems all wrong to have it on an aircraft. Don't you agree?"

"As a matter of fact, George, I think I do. I'm not superstitious, but there is something in what you say. It may be that the letter 'B' (the flight letter of the aircraft I always flew) has something unlucky about it too, but to start with I'll just dispense with the Kiwi." And I did.

My first trip in a Spitfire after my return to duty was an unhappy one. I felt most unsafe and whenever another aircraft was anywhere near me in the sky, I broke out in a cold sweat. This feeling went on for a week and I was so acutely affected by it in the course of a squadron formation practice that I broke away and returned to land. It was no

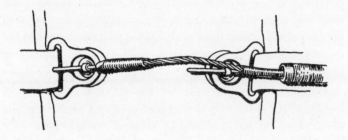

Diagram showing rip-chord pins in position on parachute pack

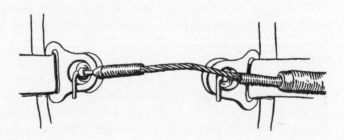

Diagram showing how the rip-chord pins were bent around the eyelets

good going on, my nerves were all to hell and the sensible course was to go to the squadron commander and ask to be taken off flying for a bit. After about three days of sheer misery, an unusual sensation for me when flying, and trying to make up my mind what to do, I took the plunge. The squadron commander referred me to the Station Commander who was most considerate and said that the question of giving me a rest had been discussed before the last incident, and 'Prof' had recommended it before he left. He went on, "I now understand that you are to be made a Squadron Leader and employed as a Controller in Station Operations while off flying. It would be a good idea for you to get away from the station for a bit first, and take up your new duties in a week's time. Have you anywhere to go on leave?"

"Yes, sir, I have friends in Bucks. I think I'll go there for a week," I answered gratefully.

I caught the train the very next day and arrived at Little Missenden that evening for my second leave of the war. Little Missenden House had by this time been handed over to the Red Cross as an emergency war hospital and the Dumas' were living in the gardener's cottage. I was most welcome nevertheless, and made a great fuss of, which was just what I needed in my very low state. It was grand to be able to sleep late in the mornings after such a long spell of early risings and to have a whole day with nothing to do except, of course, my frequent visits to the nearby local where I was a regular customer for beer. With the responsibility of running a flight no longer hanging over me, a weight seemed to have been lifted from my shoulders, and in a matter of days I was feeling more like my normal self. I knew, however, that it was wise to remain off flying for a while longer and was not too depressed at the thought of spending my days, and as it turned out many nights too, in a stuffy operations room.

I returned to Catterick on 11th January, 1941 and on the following day made my appearance in the Operations Room for the first time. It was a pleasant surprise to find that in my absence, and through the efforts of George and the new squadron commander, Colin had been posted back to 54 Squadron to take over my flight. I wouldn't have wanted to hand over to anyone else. Controlling I found most interesting, and exciting when there were enemy raids to be dealt with. This happened only infrequently in the Catterick Sector, and usually at night. To me, one of the more pleasant aspects of the Operations Room was the bevy of beautiful WAAF plotters with whom one worked. They certainly proved an attraction to the squadron pilots who, from the time I took up duty there, became regular visitors. George, in particular, frequently occupied the guest chair next to the Controller to, as he put it, "Keep an eye on Al's glamour crew."

The monotony of my first month as a Controller was relieved by a very pleasant interlude. I was summoned to the Palace to receive the Bar to my Distinguished Flying Cross which had been awarded in the middle of August. Colin Gray, who was to receive the same award, had also been summoned to attend and we made the trip together. It was a wonderful opportunity to show my gratitude to the Dumas family for their many kindnesses and I invited Mrs Dumas as my guest to the Investiture. Though a much more formal affair than my first appearance before the King, it was nevertheless a thrilling occasion and one which I was proud to have the honour of attending.

On this visit to London I had the unique experience of making a recorded talk for the BBC on my impressions of the Battle of Britain. There was a little bother with the producer about sticking to the script, which had more or less been written for me by the Air Ministry, but as the remuneration was worthwhile I was persuaded to play ball. The talk was broadcast one evening shortly after my return to Catterick and needless to say I was not to be found at the appointed time; I couldn't face up to the smirks and gibes of George and Colin who were assembled in the mess ante-room expectantly awaiting the event.

The winter of 1940-41 was a very severe one in the north of England and the station personnel, pilots included, spent most of their time on the airfield shovelling snow from the runway to keep it clear for flying. It was certainly a primitive method of keeping a runway clear for flying and not one which appealed to either officer or airman as, hands frozen and backs aching, one and all laboured incessantly against the falling snow, and almost always fighting a losing battle. Why weren't there mechanical means to do the job? Simply because grass airfields were the rule in Fighter Command up to and including the outbreak of the war and the method of snow clearances on these was to tramp the snow hard; and if the fall was such that this was impossible, flying was suspended. Snow-ploughs of a sort were available but they were most inefficient, consisting only of an attachment to the front of an ordinary three-ton truck or petrol bowser, and more often than not the vehicle was unserviceable. Operational commitments quite often meant flying when the airfield surface was unsafe and a number of fighters were written-off or damaged, particularly in the early months of the war, because of accidents on the ground caused through snow and ice. To this day, the problem has not been fully solved.

The snow continued falling in Yorkshire until about the end of February and very little flying was possible over the two months of the new year. This made my enforced rest from flying a little easier to bear as a great deal of my off-watch time was spent down at dispersal, when not on the snow clearance party, playing cards and swopping stories with the squadron pilots. Under more normal flying conditions, the squadron's new training commitment – it had now ceased to send pilots south and was working up to squadron strength again before returning to Hornchurch – would have left them little time in which to play cards. Although I was now a spectator, it was heartening to see pilots posted in as permanent squadron members again thus enabling them to absorb the atmosphere and comradeship of a unit in which they would remain for their first tour of operations. Just before its departure south 54 Squadron's pilot strength reached its highest to date. As the squadron commander said, "There are now twenty-eight pilots in the squadron and no less than seven are fully operational day and night!" The acute shortage that existed at the end of the Battle of Britain was over, and the training pipe-line was beginning to spew forth a steady flow of new recruits.

As the big day of 54 Squadron's return to Hornchurch grew closer, I began to feel depressed at the thought of not going with them, and the prospect of life at Catterick when they had departed did not appeal to me. Since the last baling out incident, I had flown only infrequently and still did not feel happy in the air. Had it been otherwise, I would have pressed my claims to go with the squadron, although this would mean reverting to Flight Lieutenant. Common sense prevailed, and I sat back, dreading the day when they took off from Catterick for the last time. To date, my whole war had revolved around the activities of 54 Squadron and despite the fact that in its present form it bore no relation to the squadron I had known, only George and Colin being now left, I still felt a part of it.

On the 23rd February, 1941, after a delay of three days caused through bad weather, 54 Squadron passed out of my life for the rest of the war. Amidst thick snow, and in a biting wind, I stood at the end of the runway as pair after pair of aircraft lifted into the air above my head and turning on to a southerly course disappeared into the murk of the snow-laden sky. With two fingers raised in Churchill's 'V' sign, and his smiling eyes bidding me a fond farewell, George's aircraft passed by in a last salute. I was never to set eyes on him again.

Slowly I plodded through the snow and across to the dispersal hut now occupied by the pilots of 41 Squadron who had landed a few hours previously to enable their aircraft, a newer version of the Spitfire, to be handed over to 54 to take south with them. 41 Squadron was certainly a mixture of new faces and there were very few whom I knew. Don Finlay was the squadron commander, now fully recovered from the injury received when he was shot down leading 54 Squadron, and he greeted me with the words, "I hear you are now a Controller, Al. I trust you have the business weighed up because we'll be depending on you to find us some Huns." The only other members of the squadron I knew well were the two flight commanders, Tony Lovell and 'Mac' McKenzie both of whom were survivors of the original squadron that had landed at Hornchurch at the end of May to relieve 54 for the first time. Norman Ryder, who for so long had been the operational prop in the squadron, had been promoted and now commanded 56 Squadron at North Weald.

Better weather gradually returned and with it increased enemy activity, but mostly at night and only very scattered in our part of the country. The night squadron at Catterick, 219 equipped with Beaufighters, were constantly in the air and we were kept fairly busy in the Operations Room vectoring them after scattered enemy raids directed against the industrial areas to the north and south. The Spitfires also were used, but only under moonlight or very favourable weather conditions, when they were ordered off against mass raids. It was a lonely business in a single-seater aircraft at night, flying up and down a patrol line with nothing but your thoughts to keep you company, and no one to whom you could talk. The monotony was only broken if the Controller chose to pass information on raids or any other matters of interest to the patrolling pilot. This we normally did, knowing full well the uneasiness of a pilot when he was left without any information, or contact with control. One of the 41 pilots with whom I became particularly friendly while at Catterick was Flying Officer 'Mitzi' Darling and whenever he was on patrol, and there was nothing doing, I would maintain a strict R/T silence until 'Mitzi' could stand it no longer. Eventually, his troubled voice would come through on the R/T, "Control from Acorn 17, are you still receiving me?" to which I would make no reply. Again, after an interval, the same message would be received but in a more insistent tone of voice; but still no reply. Back in the Operations Room, I always imagined poor old 'Mitzi' squirming in the cockpit in anxiety, and after a further period of silence would call to ask if he was still receiving me. On one such occasion, 'Mitzi's' exasperated voice disturbed the tranquility of the Operations Room with, "Al, you b____, I know you can hear me and if you don't answer I'm coming home." I had to take some action then or else answer to the Station Commander, who was quite likely to pop into the Operations Room without warning, and ask for details of the Spitfire on patrol.

I was now beginning to fly more and more, and had taken on the task of teaching Captain Peter De Mey, an attached Army officer, how to fly the station's Magister, a training type aircraft. This interesting interlude really brought home to me the reasons for the extremes of temper demonstrated by flying instructors and which, hitherto, I had fondly imagined were uncalled for. There is nothing more exasperating than teaching a person to fly – unless it is teaching a dyed-in-the-wool soccer player the off-side rules of rugby football – and even though Peter was a most apt pupil, I quite often lost my temper. However, it was another means of restoring my lost confidence and for this reason was a valuable way of spending my spare time. I might add that as a result of the teaching I gave him, Peter managed to get himself into the Glider Pilot Regiment which had long been his ambition. I often wondered if they knew he was colour blind!

Quite frequently I flew with 41 Squadron and paired up on more than one occasion with Pilot Officer Bennions who had been injured while flying with 41 and was doing a stint on the ground. Benny had lost the sight of one eye, but this did not deter him from flying on every possible occasion. He was an exceptional pilot and a wonderful shot and I firmly believe if it hadn't been for his unfortunate eye injury he would have been among the top scoring fighter pilots in the war. I managed also to get on a night detail with 41 and was lucky enough to choose the night on which Hull was bombed. My orders were to patrol over Hull, at a safe height above the anti-aircraft fire, and to go after any bomber I could pick out against the fires below. From 20,000ft, where I reckoned to be safe from the guns, I gazed down on an inferno that was Hull. The centre of the town seemed to be the aiming point for, as I watched, bomb after bomb burst in or near the conflagration which lit up the surrounding areas. It was impossible to pick up the enemy bombers, at least I found it so, and one felt helpless darting this way and that way after imaginary silhouettes which appeared to flit across the flaming background of fire. Although there were countless enemy aircraft reported over Hull that night, I failed to see a single one.

Towards the end of March, I decided that it was time for me to return to operations, and accordingly I lodged a formal application with the Station Commander, Group Captain Eccles, who promised to send it on to Group. I was quite enjoying my term as a Controller, and the social freedom it afforded, but the urge to get back to flying was now in the ascendancy. I was fully aware that a return to flying would mean reverting to Flight Lieutenant rank but I hoped to get my own squadron before the end of the year. And so it turned out.

CHAPTER FOURTEEN

Rest and Return

W HEN two weeks had passed without news of my
return to flying, I again asked for an interview with
the Station Commander who promised to make enquiries.
With the day fighter war at a temporary standstill in the south
– although the offensive sweeps over France were now under
way – and the pilot position much more favourable, there was
a chance that I might be left on the ground indefinitely, and
this I was determined to avoid at all costs.

It was during this waiting period that I first met the girl I
was to marry. An Army Captain, who had been a regular
visitor to the Operations Room to watch the night
operations, and with whom I had become friendly, was
insistent that I meet his girl friend at the first available
opportunity. The introduction finally took place one night
when, in company with Flight Lieutenant 'Mac' McKenzie,
I was dining at the Morritt Arms Hotel near Barnard Castle.
My army chum, who was also there with his girl friend,
called me across and said, "Al, I would like you to meet a
friend of mine: Miss Joan Fenton – Squadron Leader Alan
Deere." The usual formalities were exchanged, and that was
that. "Certainly," I thought to myself, "he wasn't
exaggerating when he said she was pretty." Joan and I met
again by chance a week or so later and then again at a party
in the Officers' Mess at Catterick. A close friendship soon
developed and we began to see each other on every possible
occasion until my departure from Catterick to return to
operations. I knew by then this was no light-hearted affair; I
was firmly and deeply committed.

Life at Catterick now held a new interest, and for the time
being my thoughts were diverted from a return to operational
flying. Whereas previously my social activities were
confined more or less to the orbit of the station, I now spent

most of my spare time with Joan going to race meetings, at which I was always unlucky, and to dances and parties in the Darlington area where Joan lived with her parents. They were happy days, and it was with a certain amount of misgiving that I heard the news of my return to a squadron.

"Deere, you have been posted as a flight commander to 602 Squadron with effect from 7th May," were the words with which the Station Commander greeted me when I was ushered into his office by the Station Adjutant. "You are to report to 13 Group *en route* to Ayr, where the squadron is based, for an interview with the AOC. You can start clearing tomorrow, and report to Group the following day in the rank of Flight Lieutenant. The Adjutant will make the necessary arrangements with the AOC's Personal Assistant for an interview." Then on a less formal note, "The best of luck, and good hunting."

I rang Joan straight away – I had previously warned her that I was likely to go any day – and arranged to meet that evening to discuss plans for her travel up as far as Newcastle, where we could have a final lunch together. Joan was herself waiting news of an application to join the American Ambulance, Great Britain, a voluntary organization whose ambulances were bought with funds raised in America, and driven by British girls.

In many ways, I was quite sad at the thought of leaving Catterick where I now had many friends. However, the thought of the comradeship of squadron life again more than offset any misgivings at leaving. As planned, Joan travelled up to Newcastle with me and waited there while I went by car out to the Group Headquarters, just outside the town, for my interview. The AOC, Air Vice-Marshal Jock Andrews, was extremely pleasant and said that he had hoped to offer me a squadron but that there wasn't a vacancy just yet. In the meantime, he was sure that I would be happy with John Kilmartin who was the squadron commander. He, too, had not long returned to operations and between us we should make something of the 602 Squadron before it returned to 11 Group. The interview over, I joined Joan for lunch. Two hours later I was bound for Ayr and a second tour of operations.

John Kilmartin, or Killy as he was known, was at the railway station to greet me on arrival at Ayr. Killy and I had been fellow trainees before the war, and more recently he had served with 43 Squadron in France where his exploits had earned him the Distinguished Flying Cross. It was nice to see him again and I felt sure that it would be a happy squadron with him in command. On the way back to the airfield he told me that 602 Squadron was now an auxiliary squadron in name only; there were only a couple of the original pilots still in the squadron and a very few of the ground crew. The Battle of Britain had taken a fairly heavy toll of the pilots, and some of the more senior survivors had been promoted and gone to take squadrons and flights elsewhere. There seemed to be a good spirit in the squadron, and he was happy that before long it would be considered fit to return south for operations. I hoped so too.

After booking in with the Station Adjutant, I was seen by the Station Commander, Group Captain Loel Guinness with whom I had served for a short time at Catterick. In the course of conversation the incident connected with the shooting down of the He 59 by my flight in July was mentioned.

"If it was your flight that shot it down, Al, I've got some photographs that will interest you," he said. "My yacht was taken over by the Admiralty at the outbreak of war and is doing odd jobs around the Channel approaches. On the day that the He 59 landed on the sea near Deal, she was in the vicinity and it was her skipper who rescued the aircraft's crew. He took some photographs which he sent on to me – you can have them."

Ayr was a fairly newly opened station and the accommodation consisted entirely of Nissen huts. To one who had, so far, been accustomed to the comfort of pre-war stations, it was a most spartan existence. In May, however, and with the good weather that prevailed over that part of the Scottish coast, the early morning walks to the ablutions, centrally situated at the domestic site, were bearable. The thought of having to do the trip in the winter was no encouragement to remain at Ayr too long, and I sincerely hoped that the squadron would move south before the summer was out, as was expected.

I had promised 'Mitzi' Darling that as soon as I was settled at Ayr I would try and arrange for him to be transferred from 41 to 602 Squadron. He was keen to get back on operations and foresaw a long sojourn at Catterick with 41 Squadron which had only recently returned from Hornchurch and was not likely to be in 11 Group again for some time, certainly long after 602 were expected to return. There was a good deal of inexperience in my new flight and a seasoned deputy would be invaluable during the work-up period and, of course, essential in the south. Killy took the matter up for me and through his efforts, and a certain amount of discreet telephoning on my part to the responsible 'P' Staff Officer at Group, we got results. Within a month of my arrival at Ayr, 'Mitzi' was installed in my flight.

It was grand to be back in harness again and I soon settled into the familiar routine of squadron life. Three days after my arrival I was airborne on my first scramble since my return, to investigate an aircraft reported as flying west towards Glasgow. It became obvious from the variety of vectors given to me by the Controller that plots on the aircraft were intermittent and not very reliable. I was not surprised therefore when after some fifty minutes flying I was instructed to return to base and land.

When I spoke to the Controller on landing he informed me that an aircraft had been spotted by the Observer Corps and reported as a Me 110 and that the reason for the scanty information passed to me was because of the paucity of Observer Corps plotting over the less populated areas in the

Scottish hills. He further said that an enemy aircraft had in fact crashed near Glasgow and that the pilot, who had baled out, was being held by the local police. I cursed my bad luck at having missed such a lovely target, and thought no more about it. Imagine my surprise when I read in the paper a few days later that a Me 110 had crashed near Glasgow, and the pilot was none other than Rudolf Hess. An Me 110 unescorted was a wonderful target; with Hess aboard it was probably the prize fighter pilot target of the war, and I hadn't even got within sighting range.

In consultation with Killy and the other flight commander, Flight Lieutenant Glyn Ritchie who was one of the original squadron members in its auxiliary days, a programme of training was based on the new formation tactics now being introduced into Fighter Command. In the short time that I had been grounded, Fighter Command had gone over to the offensive, and wing formations were now firmly established. Within the wing, the squadron had changed and sections of three aircraft were no longer the basis of the formation. 'Sailor' Malan was the first fighter leader to appreciate the advantage of basing squadron tactics on sections of four aircraft, spaced in such a way that each of the three sections, although an integral part of the squadron, had freedom of action in combat. The element of two, on which this formation was based, was a direct copy of the tactics so effectively employed by German fighter formations whose leaders must be given full credit for their foresight in introducing the pair as the best fighting unit. If 602 Squadron was to form part of a wing immediately on its arrival in the south it was essential that all the pilots were fully conversant with the new procedures, and training flying was therefore directed to this end.

On the morning of 5th June, I was airborne with the squadron on a climb to 30,000ft to practice some of the new tactics when I met with yet another accident, and so soon after my return. A forced landing under normal circumstances is a quite straightforward event and one which most pilots experience in the course of their flying career. It will be remembered I had to carry out one shortly after my arrival in 54 Squadron. However, the circumstances under which I was called upon to execute one on this particular occasion were usual only in so far as I had plenty of height and full control, the rest wasn't so straightforward.

On the climb to height, and at about 10,000ft, my engine began to vibrate so violently that I was forced to throttle back immediately. A quick glance at the oil pressure gauge revealed that my oil pressure was dangerously low but before I could check further there was a tremendous bang followed by a gush of oil over the engine cowlings and windscreen. I switched off immediately. My position was about ten miles off the coast and my height roughly 10,000ft. The question was could I reach land, and if so, would I have sufficient height to execute a successful forced landing? The alternatives were to bale out or ditch the aircraft. The former I discarded because the sea was very choppy, I carried no dinghy (they weren't issued at this time) and there was no shipping in sight. The second alternative didn't appeal to me at all for I distinctly remembered chatting to Norman Ryder about his miraculous escape when he ditched a Spitfire off the east coast earlier in the war. He says he remembers seeing about four different shades of sea water as he went down and down in his Spitfire struggling to get free of his harness and parachute, and wouldn't recommend ditching to anyone. Besides, I had a strong desire to try and save my aircraft and if at the last moment I saw I wasn't going to make the coast, I could turn away and ditch near the shore. My mind made up in a matter of seconds, I turned towards land.

It was unfortunate that the nearest stretch of coastline was the Heads of Ayr whose craggy tops, even from ten miles, looked uninviting. But I had insufficient height to reach any other part of the coast and must therefore take the most direct route. I could only hope that beyond the clifftop there was a reasonable stretch of flat ground in which to crash-land. I reckoned on covering a mile for every 1,000ft of height lost, but with a dead airscrew this would be reduced somewhat. It would be touch and go. Right up to the last moment I was undecided whether to turn away and ditch or to carry on, and I don't know now why I determined on the latter course.

In the event, I cleared the top of the cliffs by the nearest fraction only to be faced with the ground falling steeply away behind into a series of small fields separated by formidable stone fences. There was no height in which to manoeuvre and I had perforce to keep on going straight ahead. When only a few feet above the ground, I could see that unless I took some action I would fly into the stone fence now directly ahead of me. There was no question of turning at that height, and my speed was insufficient to allow me to ease the aircraft over the obstacle. There was only one thing to be done; sit her down prematurely. Thereupon, I pushed the stick firmly forward – an unpleasant sensation when only a few feet above the ground and still doing about 90mph – and immediately the airscrew bit into the potato crop below, throwing a shower of freshly dug potatoes in all directions. For a brief second, it seemed, the aircraft stood on its nose and in the same movement pitched over on to its back. Once again, my Sutton harness held firm, and it saved me from breaking my neck. My head was only lightly pressed against the ground and I could move my arms sufficiently to reach the door release and so free the spring-loaded catches. Unlike the Hornchurch bombing incident, there was no one to assist me from the wreckage and it was lucky that I was able to move sufficiently to free the door; it would have been unpleasant hanging upside down indefinitely. On this occasion, however, I had no fear of fire as the engine had been stopped for quite a time and there was no smell of petrol indicating a burst tank or broken petrol pipe lines.

Having released my parachute harness, I rather gingerly pulled the Sutton harness release pin in order to ensure that when the weight of my body was transferred from the harness shoulder straps I didn't take it all on my neck. Pilots had been known to break their necks through thoughtlessly doing this when in a hurry to get out from an aircraft which had turned over on landing. Even with the hardly perceptible drop I felt the slight shock on my neck as my head dug into the soft earth, and was pleased that I had taken all precautions to minimize it. In a matter of seconds I was through the small aperture afforded by the now open cockpit door, and gratefully breathing the pure air outside.

There was no one in sight – I might have hung upside down for some time – so I commenced to walk towards a building which turned out to be the club house of a nearby golf course. A woman, the sole occupant, greeted me as I entered with the words: "Good gracious, where did you spring from?"

"I've left my aircraft in that potato crop just across the way there," I answered rather smugly. "I'd love a drink, I feel a little shaken."

"I'm sorry, all I can offer you is tea. The club is teetotal."

"Just my luck," I muttered to myself, and aloud, "thanks that will do fine."

There was barely time to consume my cup of tea before Group Captain Guinness arrived on the scene in his car to drive me back to the station. We walked out to the aircraft to collect my parachute and to have a look at the damage. Without removing the engine cowlings, it was not possible to see what had caused the engine failure so we satisfied ourselves with an outside examination of the damage caused by the crash landing. The airscrew blades were, of course, bent double but otherwise the aircraft seemed in reasonable shape, except for a slight buckling of the tail fin which had taken the impact when the aircraft turned over.

"You were damn lucky you didn't hit that wall, Al," said the Station Commander, eyeing the few yards which separated stone wall and aircraft. "If you had, you wouldn't be standing here now."

"You're right there, sir, I'm trying to make up my mind whether I was lucky or unlucky this time. It was luck that I had sufficient height to make land and that I didn't break my neck when the aircraft turned over so violently. On the other hand, trust me to have chosen the one aircraft in the flight which was destined to have an engine failure. I will be interested to know what caused it."

Examination of the engine revealed that a connecting rod had come through the block. This was an unusual failure in a Merlin and gave cause for alarm. It was thought that faulty material must have been the cause of such an unusual occurrence and as the engine had been shadow-factory-produced it was therefore packed up and sent away for a thorough investigation. I never did hear the result.

I must confess that I was a little shaken by such a narrow squeak so soon after my return and hoped that it would not be the fore-runner of another spate of escapes. It proved one thing: it made no difference not having a Kiwi emblem on my aircraft – I had discontinued this practice on joining 602 Squadron.

Flying Officer Hopkin, John Willie of 54 Squadron days, greeted me on my return to dispersal with the words, "It's just like old times, Al: first I greet you on arrival here as my flight commander and then in the next breath congratulate you on yet another escape."

"You can't say we didn't give you a good escort on the way down," interjected 'Nuts' Niven, another auxiliary survivor in the squadron. "No doubt you saw the whole squadron circling overhead. A few prayers were being said on your behalf and it looks as if they were of some use."

"I knew you were above but I wasn't paying much attention, 'Nuts'. I was in such a flap to know whether to try and reach land or to bale out while I still had plenty of height. I'm pleased now I kept to my original decision to make for the coast. Anyhow, the sea looked awfully rough, and cold."

Shortly after this incident there was a break in our training routine when the squadron was ordered to proceed to Limavady, Northern Ireland, for a special operation. We were to provide a continuous escort of four aircraft over the battleship *Prince of Wales* which was returning to Scotland for minor repairs after her engagement with the German battle cruiser Bismarck. My flight was the first out on patrol and we found her about fifty miles out to sea from the north-western tip of Ireland. The battleship, and her destroyer escort, presented a wonderful sight as with smoke pouring from their funnels they steamed at full speed in the choppy sea, the destroyers practically disappearing from view as they charged into the great troughs of water. We stayed on patrol for about forty minutes at the end of which time we were relieved by the other flight. This procedure went on most of the day and until the ships were well within sight of the Scottish coast. It was a pleasant interlude in our training programme and the first occasion on which I had set foot on Irish soil, the land of my fore-fathers.

The squadron was really taking shape now and it was therefore most unfortunate that we should have to change squadron commanders at this juncture. Air Ministry had seen fit to post Killy to West Africa, much to his annoyance, and Pat Meagher, a supernumerary Squadron Leader in 41 Squadron, was to relieve him. I had hoped that I might get the squadron, but Pat as a substantive Squadron Leader had a prior claim. I had got to know Pat at Catterick and though I was pleased he was getting a squadron, I was very sorry to see Killy go just as it seemed we were ready to go south. AOC Pat was soon in harness and the training programme proceeded as before.

At about this time I received one of my periodic letters from New Zealand and was distressed to learn that my brother Brian, who was serving in the New Zealand Army, was missing in Greece. He was later reported as a prisoner-of-war. It must have been a worrying time for my parents with five sons in uniform, and all overseas. Fortunately, we all came through the war safely, despite my many narrow escapes and the fact that two of my brothers finished up as prisoners-of-war in Germany. The sixth brother was too young to join but was awaiting call-up when the war ended. On top of this sad news about my brother, I had been informed by telephone from Hornchurch that George Gribble was missing, believed drowned. Apparently, he had engine failure when about to engage some Messerschmitts over the Channel and was heard by his number two, who because of the presence of the Huns was unable to go to his assistance, to say over the R/T that he was going to bale out. He did not carry a pilot dinghy – they were still not in general issue – and was never found. The epitaph of this gallant officer, who to me typified more than any other the spirit of the Battle of Britain pilot, is imprinted in 54 Squadron's Record Book in the following words: "Flight Lieutenant D G Gribble, DFC, was the last member of the old 54. His exploits are recorded on nearly every page of this History. It only remains to be said that his personality was everywhere identified with the name of the squadron and no one who knew or heard his happy laughter would ever forget the affection they felt from the first." George died young, at the early age of twenty-two, but already a veteran in combat.

There was great jubilation in the squadron when in early July it was announced that we were to move south to Kenley. There was just ten days allowed before the move to enable the squadron to reduce its flying programme to a minimum and to concentrate on getting one hundred per cent serviceable aircraft on departure day. The announcement was made on the Friday evening in the mess and called for no small celebration in the course of which I learned from a pilot in the Defiant night fighter squadron, also based at Ayr, that one of their aircraft was flying to Catterick first thing the following morning and would be returning on the Monday. He was sure I could go as a passenger in the rear turret. The thought of flying over the Scottish Hills in the rear turret of a Defiant, and with a pilot whom I didn't know, was a little unnerving to say the least. As, however, it would be my last chance of seeing Joan before we moved south I accepted on the spot, knowing full well that I couldn't take a Spitfire away for the weekend because of the likelihood of being stuck at Catterick through bad weather. In the sober light of day, or more accurately on the following day of indifferent weather, I wasn't sure that I hadn't been a bit hasty. It was too late to back out now, and in any event there was no denying that I was keen to see Joan again before returning south. The trip there and back was accomplished safely.

Joan, I discovered, had got her orders also and was off the very next week to Birmingham to start work as a driver with the American Ambulance, Great Britain, a service she was to remain with until the end of the war. We had hoped that when her orders arrived she would be assigned to the London area but consoled ourselves with the thought that there was a good train service between Birmingham and London.

The day of our departure was gloriously fine and this added to the high spirits of the pilots who were laughing and joking like schoolboys about to go on a picnic, as they busied themselves over last-minute preparations about the crew room. What a mixture we were: New Zealanders, Australians and Canadians of the old and trusted Dominions rubbing shoulders with Englishmen, Scotsmen, Welshmen and Irishmen, all moulded into a happy fighting team. Later the squadron was to have French and Norwegian pilots added to its numbers and they, too, fitted in happily and smoothly as most welcome members of the team. It was my experience during the war that fighter squadrons with a mixture of nationalities were invariably happy and successful units. In a cosmopolitan squadron there was a friendly and healthy rivalry between the representatives of the various countries concerned, and an individual urge to do better than the other chap. The success enjoyed by the Royal Air Force in the war was due, in part, to the sensible attitude adopted towards pilots of foreign nationalities who formed a not inconsiderable part of our new aircrew strength. Appointments to command wings and squadrons was made purely on merit and irrespective of nationality with the result that some of the RAF's most successful leaders were foreigners. Mike Donnet, a Belgian; Bernard Duperier, a Frenchman; Colonel Berksted, a Dane; these are a few of the names that come to mind – all skilled wing leaders with Royal Air Force units under their command.

At long last the great moment had arrived, and we were all set to go. At the appointed time I pressed the starter button, a few jerky revolutions of the airscrew, and the engines burst into life to the accompaniment of the many spitting Merlins of other Spitfires in the dispersal area. A few moments to warm up the engine, chocks away, and off down the taxi-track to the take-off end of the airfield where I pulled to one side to await the arrival of the squadron commander. On my immediate right 'Mitzi's' aircraft ticked-over contentedly while on his expressive face there was a quiet smile of satisfaction. I had no doubt that the happy thoughts which were the root of the smile were attuned to mine which at that moment dwelt on the prospect of the busy life on an 11 Group airfield. Unexpectedly, the Controller voice awoke me from my reverie:

"Control to Blue One, are you receiving me?"

"Blue One to Control, receiving you loud and clear. Pass your message."

"Hello, Blue One, Red Leader is unable to start his aircraft and you are to take over and go ahead as planned. Is this understood?"

"Blue One to Control, your message received and understood."

"I'll bet Pat is cursing," I thought to myself as I swung my aircraft into wind and waited for the rest of the squadron to form up behind me before giving the order to go. A thick haze obscured the ground between Ayr and Catterick and I was so busy trying to check pin-points *en route* that I was unable to sit back and enjoy this first leg on the trip. The haze thinned out sufficiently once over the hills and before long I picked out the familiar outlines of Catterick airfield ahead. The minimum amount of time was spent at Catterick for refuelling and we were away again within the hour, finally arriving at Kenley in the late afternoon.

Kenley was one of the vital Sector airfields in the Battle of Britain and I could plainly see the scars of bombing as we circled prior to landing. The runway in use was short compared with the extra long one at Ayr, and it was with a certain amount of difficulty that we all finally landed intact.

Wing Commander John Peel, the Wing Commander Flying and a fellow Battle of Britain pilot, met the squadron on arrival and made us feel at home from the outset.

"Welcome to the Kenley Wing," were his first words to the pilots now assembled in their allotted dispersal hut. "The squadron won't be required to operate tomorrow so take your time getting settled in tonight. Tomorrow afternoon there will be a familiarization briefing on the shape of things down here and on the type of operations you can expect. You can expect plenty of operational flying, perhaps not all to your liking." On that last rather ominous note the wing leader departed.

The aircraft safely parked in the dispersal pens, 'Mitzi' and I strolled the few hundred yards to the Officers' Mess, a large comfortable pre-war building which promised much after the bareness of the temporary mess at Ayr. There was a sort of happy atmosphere about the mess which we both sensed on entering and I think 'Mitzi' expressed our first impressions when later that evening over a pint of beer he said: "Al, I'm going to like this place."

On the Offensive

THERE were three squadrons in the Kenley Wing: 485 (New Zealand), 452 (Australian) and 602 (City of Glasgow). We were a cosmopolitan squadron in a cosmopolitan wing. Only two of the three squadrons were based at Kenley airfield, the third operating from the satellite airfield of Redhill on a rotational basis of three months per squadron. When 602 Squadron joined the wing, 485 Squadron, led by Squadron Leader Marcus Knight, a New Zealander in the Royal Air Force, was at Redhill.

On the day after our arrival, the squadron was assembled in the wing briefing room for an introductory briefing by the Wing Commander Flying. Together with 'Sailor' Malan and Douglas Bader, John Peel was one of the three original wing leaders in No. 11 Group. On this first occasion, and on subsequent briefings by him, I was impressed with his quiet, efficient manner and the friendly atmosphere he created in the briefing room. A tall, good-looking officer, John Peel typified my idea of his historical namesake and whenever he stood on the briefing dais my thoughts invariably shifted to a happier form of hunting than that on which we were now engaged.

"Good morning, everyone," said John entering the room. "Welcome to your first briefing as members of the Kenley Wing. We will get straight down to business, which is to put you in the picture on the names and types of the various escorts you will undertake in the wing. We'll have questions afterwards to cover any points I may have missed."

The briefing that followed was far too comprehensive to repeat in detail in these pages. Only a few short paragraphs on the escorts used are necessary to enable the reader to follow the daylight offensive operations now being undertaken by Fighter Command and No. 2 Group Bomber Command.

There were four types of escort directly concerned with

bomber protection, the wings undertaking them being ordered to adhere strictly to bomber courses and timings to and from the target. Other escorts were of a more indirect nature and designed primarily to shoot down enemy fighters enticed into the air by the bombers. In order, the first four types of escort were: the close escort, which surrounded the bombers; the escort cover, providing cover for the close escort fighters; the high cover, to prevent enemy fighters positioning themselves above the two lower fighter formations; and lastly, the top cover which, although tied to the bombers' route, had a roving commission to sweep the skies clear of enemy fighters threatening the immediate area of the bomber attack. The three remaining types of escort were undertaken by independently routed wings which were responsible for the tasks designated by the names given to each. These were: target support, withdrawal cover, and fighter diversion. Supporting fighter sweeps, routed into an entirely different area, were also employed when the penetration of the raid was sufficiently deep to encourage the Germans to send reinforcement fighters from bases not in the threatened area of operations.

The tactics adopted within the framework of the overall task assigned to each particular wing were entirely a matter for the wing leader concerned. It was usual, however, when on close escort duties for a wing to be split, and for one squadron to be given the job of flying alongside the bombers. This squadron was in turn split; a section of four aircraft being positioned on either side of the bomber formation and a third slightly above and behind. The other two squadrons in the wing normally operated above and behind the gaggle then formed by the bombers and their close escort squadron.

This overall pattern of escort was a direct copy of that used by the Luftwaffe in the Battle of Britain. First we copied their system of pairs of aircraft, and now we adopted their escort tactics. But in the latter case I think we were at fault. The German aim in the Battle of Britain was to destroy

Fighter Command primarily by bombing, with aerial combat a necessary adjunct. Whereas the aim of the Royal Air Force in the 1941 daylight offensive was to entice the Luftwaffe fighters into the air with the object of destroying as many of them as possible. The bombing aspect of the operations was incidental, although directed at specific military targets. In effect, the bombers were bait; they were inadequate, both in numbers and in weight of bombs carried, to threaten seriously worthwhile enemy targets.

For the Germans to achieve their aim it was necessary to provide overwhelming fighter escort. Not so the Royal Air Force; our escort forces directly connected with bomber protection should have been the minimum necessary to guarantee their safety thus leaving the bulk of our fighters to freelance in the area of operations. On occasions, there were as many as 200 fighters concerned with the escort of a single Stirling bomber. This more than guaranteed the safety of the lone bomber but, in so doing, realized a poor return in terms of enemy fighters destroyed. However, these somewhat disappointing results cannot detract from the value of the RAF daylight offensive in 1941 to the overall air war. The Germans, always sensitive to the Royal Air Force flaunting its authority over France and the Low Countries, were forced to keep a disproportionate number of fighters in North-West Europe to the detriment of operations in other theatres, particularly on the Russian front.

To conclude his briefing the Wing Commander Flying stressed the importance of pilots adhering to the correct emergency procedures for pilots in distress.

"Don't forget," he said, "to go over to Channel 'C' and give the emergency call 'Mayday', followed by your squadron and individual call sign, if you decide to ditch your aircraft or bale out over the sea. There is a very good air-sea rescue organization in operation and aircraft and boats are alerted for all these shows. As soon as the emergency call of 'Mayday' is heard, the aircraft are sent off to search and the RAF Rescue

Launches, already at sea, are sent to the area. If for any reason you change your mind about baling out or ditching, remember to cancel the 'Mayday' call, otherwise aircraft and boats will spend hours in unnecessary searching."

John Peel had good cause to be thankful for the air-sea rescue organization. Shortly before our arrival, he had been forced to abandon his aircraft near the French coast and was picked up under the very noses of the Germans. The use of the pilot-type dinghy which was now in service had made this possible. At the outset of the air war over the Channel, German fighter pilots were equipped with pilot type dinghies and were also provided with a fluorescent pack containing chemical substances which stained the water around their dinghies bright green. Our pilots fighting over Dunkirk and in the Battle of Britain had none of these aids and relied entirely on their 'Mae Wests' when baling out or ditching at sea, and on the fortuitous presence of shipping to rescue them from drowning. A large number of fighter pilots were lost during these two phases simply for want of such rescue aids. The air-sea rescue service now in force stemmed from the efforts of Air Vice-Marshal Keith Park who, in co-operation with the Vice-Admiral Dover, had succeeded in borrowing some Lysander aircraft to work systematically with the launches and other craft. Few investments of aircraft were to yield more precious dividends.

The squadron's first offensive operation on the following day was a fighter sweep over the St. Omer area in conjunction with the Hornchurch and Biggin Hill Wings, the former led by its Station Commander Group Captain Harry Broadhurst, and the latter by 'Sailor' Malan. Our instructions were to "seek and destroy the enemy," a pet phrase of the then Air Officer Commanding No. 11 Group, Air Vice-Marshal Leigh-Mallory. On the climb out to the Channel, I was lost in contemplation of past events brought to mind by the many familiar land-marks slipping away below my climbing Spitfire. Each recalled a particular incident – Detling airfield, the farmer and his plum tree; the dark and broken-edged North Downs, a delayed parachute drop; Ashford town, an agonizing ambulance journey; and Manston, now below, the hectic days of August 1940 and the spirit and comradeship of the many friends killed operating from that most memorable of all airfields.

In wide battle formation the wing swept in an arc over the sunlit acres of Northern France and under a blue sky undisturbed by the presence of enemy fighters. Obviously the Luftwaffe was not to be enticed into the air by fighters alone and not even the anti-aircraft batteries acknowledged our presence, of which they were undoubtedly well aware. Slowly, or so it seemed from our great height, we crossed outward bound over the now peaceful beaches of Dunkirk, the white sands and foam-fringed sea recalling vividly to mind the chaos and destruction that existed there but one short year ago. As if in defiance, and to confirm that they were aware of our presence, the German anti-aircraft gunners in Dunkirk town fired a few desultory rounds at the retreating wings. The 602 Squadron pilots returned to base disappointed, yet in some ways relieved, that there had been no opposition on their first offensive sortie in this new phase of operations.

From now onwards, shows followed each other in rapid succession. Fighter sweep followed close escort; withdrawal cover followed target support; and diversionary sweep followed high cover, each task providing a new experience, some realizing dividends in enemy aircraft destroyed and others losses in Spitfires. The Kenley Wing had more than its share of the most hazardous, and certainly the most unpleasant, of the escort tasks, namely close escort. As a wing, close escort was an unwelcome commitment; as the squadron within the wing detailed as close escort squadron, the task was hated and feared. As 'Mitzi' so aptly put it, "We are just sitting ducks for flak and fighters." Unfortunately for Kenley, its squadrons were still flying Spitfire IIs while the majority of other squadrons were now equipped with the faster and better Spitfire VBs; these were rightly used in the more rewarding freelance roles.

The squadron's first commitment as close escort, I recall only too well. At the briefing for this particular operation I sat next to Flight Lieutenant Paddy Finucane, a flight commander in 452 Squadron who, when the target was announced, turned to me and said:

"I don't envy you your job, Al. A bombing raid on Lille always stirs up a hornets' nest of Hun fighters. They come up in their hundreds, fairly buzzing with evil intentions. It's bad enough being in the close escort wing, but in the close escort squadron it's murder. This is your first trip leading the squadron, isn't it?"

Paddy's pessimistic remarks increased my already nervous fears. Pat Meagher had been confined to his bed for the past few days with tummy trouble and I had been running the squadron. Prior to this show, John Peel had been leading it on operations but had now decided that it was time I had a go. It would be a tough first assignment, if things turned out as Paddy prophesied.

At 6am the wing was airborne for North Weald to refuel prior to rendezvous with the Stirling bombers over Clacton. The North Weald Wing led by Wing Commander John Gillan, who pre-war had made a record flight from Edinburgh to London in a Hurricane fighter, was to act as escort cover above our wing. As Paddy had forecast, the Huns reacted strongly; they first appeared about twenty miles inland from the French coast and from this point onwards the raid was under constant attack. In the very first attack Glyn Ritchie went down, streaming glycol and obviously out of control. Almost immediately afterwards, John Peel was hit and forced to return, while Sergeant Bell-Walker, who was flying as my number two, failed to hear the 'break' and received a cannon shell in his port wing but courageously carried on and completed the trip. The North Weald Wing above took the brunt of the attacks but despite their efforts occasional Messerschmitts broke through to bomber level only to be pounced on by 485 and 452 Squadrons coming in from the flanks. All the way to the targets the attack went on to the accompaniment of sighting reports, warnings of attacks, expletives and loud hurrahs announcing a kill.

"Two Messerschmitts 3 o'clock." (A reference to the clock used to report enemy aircraft.)

"See that bastard, Red Two?"

"Watch out, Blue Leader. They're behind us."

"Got you, got you. Look at him burn, Ken."

"Keep up, Yellow Four, or you'll get your bottom blown off."

"Here they come again, Beehive Squadron. Prepare to break."

"He's behind you, Green One."

"Which Green One? Give the call sign, you damn fool."

And so it went on, the shouting voices very often drowned by the background noise on the R/T, caused by repeated bursts of gunfire from the defending Spitfires. It seemed a slow and never-ending outward leg, but there wasn't a great deal of trouble on the return and the homeward leg was accomplished more quickly – or so it seemed.

Safely back on the ground at Kenley, I counted our casualties; Glyn Ritchie missing believed killed and three Spitfires damaged. In return, the squadron hadn't even a "damaged" to its credit. But that was the way of things when acting in the close escort role; our job was to protect the bombers not to destroy the Huns, and the bombers had all returned unscathed.

"I don't think much of close escort, not at all my idea of fun," said Flying Officer Niven entering the dispersal hut and unknotting his sweat-soaked scarf. A chorus of "Hear, Hear," greeted this remark.

"It's too much like cold-blooded murder to me," broke in Pilot Officer Max Charlesworth, "I've always thought that a Spitfire was a means of carrying guns to a target, not a gunnery target for the Hun fighter pilots. As for the flak, it was most unpleasant."

"I couldn't agree with you more," said 'Mitzi' wiping his brow. "That Hun who got Glyn came through the top escorts at a tremendous speed. One burst, and he was away. I'm afraid Glyn was killed in the first burst, certainly judging from the way his aircraft went down."

John Peel couldn't have chosen a more severe test for the blooding of a potential squadron commander. I was not at all sure that I had come through the test with flying colours but there seemed little else I could have done in the circumstances, and the bombers had not been attacked. The Wing Commander was obviously satisfied for on the very next day I was detailed to lead the wing, a great honour as a mere flight lieutenant. Our job was to act as withdrawal cover to a formation of Blenheims returning from Le Touquet, an easy task involving no penetration, and made more so by the absence of enemy fighters. Nevertheless, I was justifiably proud of being nominated to lead when not yet a squadron commander.

A spell of bad weather now intervened and the squadron was able to do a little training flying. New pilots were arriving in all the time to supplement our already generous quota – compared with the numbers in the early days of the war – and to replace others posted overseas. A replacement for Glyn Ritchie was among the new arrivals; Tommy Williams, a pre-war auxiliary, had a good operational background and proved himself to be a most able leader. With so many pilots at my disposal, it was an entirely new experience when making out the day's detail; the problem was to decide whose turn it was to go on an operation rather than, as in the 54 Squadron days, who could be spared for a rest. The tempo of operations too, was so different. Admittedly, the squadron was averaging two shows a day but with such a generous supply of pilots and, more important, experienced leaders, there was more time for relaxation and social activities. The long hours of readiness were over. Between shows, we adhered to a very leisurely routine of training and with an adequate supply of pilots were able to keep a regular leave roster in force.

When the weather was considered too bad for the normal type of operation, but suitable for flying, a type of operation known as a 'Rhubarb' was usually undertaken. This consisted of pairs of aircraft from the various squadrons in the Group operating at low level over the Occupied Territories on freelance missions in search of opportunity targets, using the cloud cover to escape should they encounter a serious enemy fighter threat. I saw no point in this type of operation which was usually unrewarding and, on a number of occasions, was the cause of an experienced leader falling to the enemy light flak guns. 'Rhubarbs' served only as a means of 'letting off steam' in that it enabled pilots to fire their guns in anger, more often than not against some unidentified target. I did two or three of these operations and cannot truthfully say that the vehicles and a train which I attacked were strictly military targets.

August 1st was a red letter day for me. I was appointed to command 602 Squadron, in place of Pat Meagher who had gone off to hospital, and on that very day I destroyed a Me 109, my first confirmed victory at Kenley. I must confess I was finding it most difficult to get decisive results in the present operations and though I had shot at Messerschmitts on a number of occasions, I had a couple of 'damaged' only to my credit. Aerial combat when tied to the bombers was mostly confined to short defensive bursts and a pilot needed to be an exceptional shot to produce conclusive results from such fleeting engagements. I was never more than an average shot and had always worked on the principle 'shoot when you see the whites of his eyes'. This principle stood me in good stead in the Battle of Britain when the Hun fighter pilot was more or less forced to stay and fight, but over Northern France, where the tactics were of his choosing, good deflection shooting was a must. The Messerschmitt which I had destroyed resulted from an engagement over Gravelines where my squadron had bounced some Huns climbing up out of a heavy mist. I was in range before the Hun pilot saw me, a long burst from my eight Brownings did the rest.

The Group Captain at No. 11 Group responsible for planning the offensive operations was Victor Beamish, the eldest of the four famous Irish brothers serving in the Royal Air Force. He was waiting at dispersal when I landed from a show on the following day.

"Hello, Al, just dropped in to congratulate you and to say hello to your pilots."

"Thanks, sir. We're always pleased to see you. Won't you come into the crew room and take a cup of our brew? It should be just about ready."

"Yes, I will," answered the Group Captain stripping off the faded blue overalls, which he always wore when flying, and placing them on an armourers' trolley standing nearby.

"Hello, Hopkin," he said, addressing John Willie on entering the crew room. "Congratulations on getting your flight." (John Willie had been promoted to take over my flight.)

Victor, as was his custom, chatted to each pilot individually before taking his leave. In the short time that we had been in the crew room, someone had removed the armourers' trolley, and Victor's overall with it. The Flight Sergeant who was despatched to find the overall soon returned with the missing garment, and handing it over to Victor said, "I'm sorry sir, the armourer thought they belonged to his mate."

A broad grin spread over Victor's rugged countenance as he answered, "Never mind, Flight, a perfectly natural mistake; I must get something more in keeping with my rank." An embarrassed Flight Sergeant was at a loss for a suitable reply.

Very little has been written about Victor Beamish who I consider was one of the great Royal Air Force personalities of the war. He lived for the Air Force and was dedicated to the defeat of Germany. It meant nothing to him to spend all night planning the day's operations and the next morning to appear on the very first show. Often I heard his voice over the R/T giving his special call sign and informing the wing leader that he was joining the formation but that he did not wish a number two detailed to fly with him, as he was quite happy by himself. Victor, a double DSO, and a DFC, was a great inspiration to all who served with and under him and his death in operations in 1942, while flying with 485 Squadron, was a sad blow to those of us who had the pleasure of knowing him.

Joan had taken my reversion to the rank of Flight Lieutenant as an insult to my ability; she could not understand why, once having attained the rank of Squadron Leader, I should have to lose the rank again, especially when the reduction was caused by a return to operations. My first thought therefore was to telephone her in Birmingham and tell her the good news. To my query, "Guess what, darling?" she answered, "You have baled out again." Somewhat amused I told her the true facts and suggested that we should meet in London to celebrate. Joan was an expert at wangling time off duty, and duly arrived in Town on the following Saturday. In company with 'Mitzi' and his girl friend of the moment, we spent a gay evening meeting friends in our various haunts in wartime London. It was a pleasant surprise to meet among them Dennis Gillam whom I thought was in hospital after being injured on operations. At the time, Dennis was commanding a four-cannon Hurricane squadron specializing in anti-shipping strikes. He was an expert in this form of attack and enemy shipping in the Channel had some unhappy encounters with Dennis and his boys. A very pleasant evening had to be cut short to enable 'Mitzi' and I to catch the last train back to Kenley. Just before leaving the Mess I had been warned that I was to lead the wing on a fighter sweep the following morning as John Peel would be away at Group. I needn't have hurried back because bad weather delayed the take-off and when the operation finally took place, there was no enemy opposition.

On his return from Group later that afternoon, John Peel called me to his office and said, "Al, I'm being taken off operations and Johnny Kent is taking over the wing. You know him, don't you?"

"Yes, I do, sir," I answered. "I'm sorry to see you go though, and I know the other pilots will be too."

Johnny Kent, the new wing leader, led the first Polish Squadron to be formed in this country in the Battle of Britain and, more recently, commanded 92 Squadron at Biggin Hill. His appointment to the wing certainly added to its cosmopolitan flavour; he was a Canadian who had joined the Royal Air Force before the war. Johnny soon launched himself into operations and on the second show with the wing, and leading my squadron, he shot down a Messerschmitt over France.

August 1941 was a month of gloriously fine weather and the intensity of operations was stepped up accordingly. The Kenley Wing was hard at it from dawn to dusk on most days but the tasks to which it was assigned were becoming a little more interesting. All three squadrons in the wing were now equipped with Spitfire VB's and thus there were fewer close escort tasks allotted to us. In fact, we had only one close escort job in the first two weeks of August. It would, of course, be to the hated Lille, and the opposition was intense. This show witnessed my first really narrow escape since returning to No. 11 Group. When at briefing the Wing Commander Flying announced the target as Lille and said that 602 Squadron would act as close escort squadron, I had a premonition that it would be tough going. I noticed 'Mitzi's' face turn white at the mention of Lille and the expressions on the faces of the other pilots in the room revealed the varying degrees of emotion caused by this announcement.

The towering banks of cumulus cloud, interspersed with layers of thin cirrus, which covered the route to the target, confirmed my worst fears. There was a sufficient amount of cloud to make escort difficult but not enough to interfere seriously with the operation. On the other hand, conditions were ideal for defensive fighters and the strong enemy reaction was proof that the Huns thought so too. The raid had barely reached mid-Channel before R/T silence was broken by the Controller to warn us of heavy enemy activity.

"Fairfax from Control; there are signs of heavy enemy activity in the St. Omer area. Your other friends have been ordered to proceed to the target area." The voice of Squadron Leader Cyril Raymond, (the well-known West End actor who was doing his war stint as a fighter controller) sounded ominously subdued as he passed this information. His reference to friends was a reassuring message to the wing leader that supporting wings had been instructed to cover our approach and withdrawal.

"Thank you, Control." I detected a note of anxiety in Johnny's voice as he acknowledged this message.

Shortly before we reached St. Omer, where the first attack developed, the escort cover fighters, and those above, were screened from view by intervening cloud banks. To make matters worse, 485 and 452 Squadrons were forced to reduce height in order to keep the bombers in view. The scene was set, action was soon to follow. The first warning of attack came in the form of a surprise yelp from Johnny Kent.

"Christ! There are Messerschmitts diving through the clouds ahead of us."

A stream of Hun fighters had broken cloud ahead of the bombers and, wheeling around to port, they lined up for an attack. I was on the port side of the bombers with my section of four and could see Johnny taking a squadron across to cut them off. Anxiously I watched two Messerschmitts, which had separated themselves from the main formation, turning in behind me for an attack and as soon as I was certain that my section was to be the target, I gave the order to break to port. With my vision greying out under the mounting 'G' loading, I pulled hard around to meet them. A menacing yellow spinner passed within inches of my wing followed closely by a second as the two attacking Messerschmitts broke up and away, their first attack thwarted by our quick turn. "They'll be back," I thought, and aloud, "Toddy Red Section stick with me, we must protect the bombers." So saying, I re-positioned my section in our escort position and waited for the next attack. It soon came.

"Break, Toddy Red – BREAK," an unknown voice screamed over the R/T.

Outwards and upwards I broke just in time to avoid a stream of tracer bullets which clawed through the air and disappeared beneath my port wing to be followed by the sleek grey outlines of a Messerschmitt 109 which dived away below me. Violently I reversed my turn and, more in anger than hope of a kill, gave the retreating Hun a quick burst.

"Toddy Red One, your number two has gone down in flames."

For a moment I was stunned; that stream of tracer must have been the overshoot from a burst of fire which was directed at my number two. "Poor old Bell-Walker," I muttered angrily into my mask, "he's been a damn good number two." There was no time for commiseration, for the Hun fighters, using the clouds to advantage, attacked again and again.

My neck and shoulders were aching through having to twist and turn in the cockpit to keep the enemy in view and my eyes were smarting from the perspiration which poured freely down my face. Yes, I was frightened, really frightened. "If only," I thought, "I didn't have to stay with the bombers." The urge to run was there, and only determination, fired by the presence of others, kept me in check. Now I knew what the German pilots must have suffered on their deep escort penetrations to the London airfields in 1940, subjected to constant attacks by the defending Spitfires and Hurricanes. How often I had gloated over their misfortune while, at the same time, admiring their tenacity in sticking with the bombers. Now it was their turn to gloat and our job to show them that we, too, could stick it out. All the way to the target the attacks continued and it was only through constant breaking and turning that we avoided further casualties.

Over the target and as far as Bethune on the return leg, the attacks were discontinued. This may have been because the cloud on this part of the route was less favourable to the defence or, perhaps, because the original attackers had exhausted their ammunition. Whatever the reason, it proved to be a short-lived respite, and a fresh onslaught soon developed. In the very first attack I saw the number four aircraft of Blue section, on the opposite side of the bombers, go down in flames after a determined attack by two Messerschmitts which had dived through the covering Spitfires.

"Look out, Toddy Red, they're coming in again." Red Four's urgent voice jerked me into action. This time, keyed up and ready, I broke so quickly that I managed to get behind a Hun as he dived away below me and, casting discretion to the winds, I stayed astern of him long enough to get a telling burst into the Messerschmitt's ugly belly before the inevitable cry of "break" warned me of danger.

"Break. BREAK."

Too late, I felt the shock of impact on my aircraft as an unseen Hun found his target; like a crack of doom the sound of an exploding cannon shell came deafeningly through my headphones. Momentarily I panicked, but quickly realized that my aircraft was still airworthy though obviously badly damaged. Continuing in the turn I eased upwards, seeking protection in the thin cloud layer just above. Once enveloped in its wet but comforting folds, I throttled back to an economical cruising speed, and with my head buried in the cockpit intent on the instrument panel, I set course for home. I could see that, although the oil pressure was normal, the coolant temperature was much too high. An immediate reduction in engine revolutions seemed to stop the needle climbing higher in the danger zone but when after a few minutes there-was no drop in temperature I realized that I had either been hit in the radiator or a glycol pipe line was punctured. However, there seemed a reasonable chance that I would be able to reach the Channel where I could bale out in the hope of being picked up by an air-sea rescue launch. Unhappily, at this point I broke free of cloud, and with ten miles to go to reach the French coast. The first desperate urge was to push the nose of the aircraft down and dive out as quickly as possible. But I knew that height was my biggest asset in the attempt to get back to England and I resisted the urge, having first ascertained that the sky around was clear of Hun fighters.

Slowly and inexorably the needle on my coolant temperature gauge climbed higher in the danger zone, but still the engine showed no signs of seizing. It couldn't run for much longer; the temperature was now 115° or only 15° less than the absolute maximum. The French coast now behind me I breathed more freely but decided, nevertheless, that as an insurance, I would go over to Channel 'C' and give a 'Mayday' call. This I did, having first informed the Controller of my intention. Glancing anxiously at my port wing I noticed that the cannon shell had left a frightening hole in the wing root and as much of my fuselage as could be seen from the cockpit was riddled with bullet holes. Ahead of me the tip of the North Foreland was, at long last, clearly within reach while the bight in the Kent coast just below Margate signified the nearness of Manston airfield. My anxious glances alternated between the gradually nearing coastline and the still mounting needle of my temperature gauge. It seemed to me to be a race between the two; could I make the former before the latter went 'off the clock'? Just as one can make the drumming wheels of a train sing a desired tune, so I willed my pulsating Merlin to beat out my prayer: "keep going a little longer", and gallantly it responded.

Now over the English coast, I was within gliding distance of Manston airfield and throttling fully back, I eased the nose down and dived towards the grass runway below. Without further use of the engine, I put her safely on the ground and as soon as she touched I switched off to avoid last minute fire, still a distinct possibility. It was only after I had vacated the cockpit that I realized that I had forgotten to cancel the 'Mayday' call which I had made as an insurance. The vehicle which came out to collect me dropped me at the Control tower where I received the expected query.

"Are you the pilot who made a 'Mayday' call?" enquired the duty pilot when I entered the tower.

"Yes I am, and I'm sorry if I have caused any bother. I was so concerned about reaching land that I forgot everything else. I'll phone Kenley Operations and get them to put matters right."

While I was on the telephone, I saw through the window a flight of Hurricanes coming in to land. "Where are they from?" I enquired.

"They are here for the day on air-sea rescue duties and were ordered off to look for you," was the unexpected reply.

"Heavens, I had better go and have a word with the leader and explain," I muttered as I left the hut to walk over to examine my Spitfire which had been towed to a nearby hangar. Surrounding the aircraft was a group of pilots from the Hurricane flight which had just landed. In answer to my query as to the whereabouts of their leader I was informed that he was phoning a report.

"Good gracious, it's Colin." Involuntarily I uttered the words as I recognized Colin Gray walking from the nearby dispersal hut towards me. We hadn't met since I said good-bye on the day of 54 Squadron's departure from Catterick six months earlier.

"In trouble again, Al? I might have guessed it was you. Why the hell didn't you cancel the 'Mayday' call?"

"Sorry, Colin, I was in such a flap I forgot."

"As usual, you have been damn lucky. Let's have a look at your aircraft?"

In addition to a cannon shell in the port wing root, there were thirty-seven bullet holes in the fuselage and wings.

Also, the top petrol tank was punctured and a glycol pipe-line severed. This latter damage was the obvious cause of the over-heating. As Colin remarked, I was damn lucky. I doubt if the engine could have kept going much longer with the coolant system so severely punctured.

"What are you doing now, Colin?" I asked.

"I've got a flight of Hurricanes operating on this 'Turbinlite' night fighter scheme. You know, a twin-engined night fighter carries a searchlight and is accompanied by a Hurricane which is supposed to shoot down the bomber found and illuminated by the night fighter. It's a pretty unrewarding task and I don't think it will last much longer; the problem of bad weather operations with the paired aircraft is insuperable."

"It certainly doesn't sound your cup of tea. Perhaps when it does pack up you will get a squadron."

"Hope so. Well cheerio, Al, we must get back to Tangmere. Hope to see you again ere long. See if you can stay out of trouble for a bit."

I departed from Manston in a Magister aircraft later that day; the second time I had returned to base from Manston in a training type aircraft, having set out in a Spitfire.

"Thought we had lost you that time, Al," Johnny Kent greeted me as I entered his office to report my safe return. "It was a sticky trip, wasn't it? I suppose you heard that the wing lost five aircraft and three pilots for a score of three Messerschmitts destroyed and a further six probably destroyed or damaged; on balance, there wasn't much in it."

"I take it the Blenheims all returned?" I asked.

"Yes, of course, we always bring 'em back alive," answered Johnny lightheartedly. "Why don't you take the day off tomorrow, Al? Tommy Williams is fully capable of running the squadron in your absence and you can nip off for a game of golf without having to worry about things."

"Suits me, sir," I answered. I had started to play golf again for the first time since the outbreak of war and was only too keen to get out on the beautiful Tandridge course where we played. Among the golfing fraternity at Kenley there were two experts, Pam Barton and Dick Burton.

Pam, who was the English ladies champion of pre-war fame, was a WAAF Officer at Kenley, and it was an afternoon well spent to play golf with such an exceptional player. What a nice girl Pam was and how pleasant to watch her hit those screaming drives straight down the fairway. It was sad that she should have been killed in an unfortunate flying accident the following year. Dick Burton, who was at Kenley for a short time only, did not play there that I remember. John Ozanne, the Squadron Intelligence Officer, was another keen player and it was with him that I spent the next day on the links, a most welcome contrast to the excitement of the previous day. It was breaks like these that illustrate the difference in the intensity of operations as compared with that which prevailed in the backs-against-the-wall fight of 1940, and served further to emphasize the favourable pilot position now reached in fighter squadrons.

By the end of August, and after almost two months of continuous operations, one or two of the pilots were beginning to show signs of fatigue. After my *faux pas* over Pilot Officer Jack Coleman in the Battle of Britain, I was most sensitive to this aspect of command, and took great care to consult both the squadron doctor and the wing leader when I suspected a pilot of over-tiredness. Flight Lieutenant Hopkin was certainly due for a rest; he had been on operations since the early days with 54 Squadron and had had a very short rest only at Ayr with 602 Squadron. Both the doctor and Johnny Kent agreed that he should be rested and the latter asked me to speak to the appropriate 'P' Staff Officer at Group to see if there was a relief Flight Lieutenant available. I was informed that there was no substantive Flight Lieutenant available but that a number of promising Flying Officers had been recommended, and that the two I proposed from 602 Squadron were well down the list.

"Why can't I have 'Mitzi' Darling back?" I asked. ('Mitzi'

had been transferred to another squadron some few weeks previously on promotion to Flight Lieutenant.)

"No reason why not, providing you can fix it with his squadron commander, one of whose pilots is first on the list of the Flying Officers recommended for a flight. Perhaps you would contact Squadron Leader Burton and come to some arrangement."

An hour later I was on my way by Spitfire to West Hampnett, a satellite airfield of Tangmere, to speak to Billy Burton. I knew Billy well and was fairly certain he would agree to 'Mitzi's' return to 602 Squadron. It seemed reasonable that if he had recommended a Flying Officer in his squadron, he would be happy to retain him as a flight commander. And so it proved; 'Mitzi' returned to 602 Squadron after one month's absence flying with the Tangmere Wing. The Flying Officer promoted within 616 Squadron to take over 'Mitzi's' flight was none other than Johnnie Johnson, now famous as the top scoring fighter pilot of the war.

485 Squadron had now returned to Kenley from Redhill and I found the cheerful, if somewhat boisterous, company of my fellow countrymen no less hectic than that of the Australians who had relieved them at Redhill. Among the pilots, I was pleased to see Mick Shand, now fully recovered from the injuries he sustained when shot down on his second sortie with 54 Squadron.

"Hello, Mick, nice to see you fit and well again. That was a pretty flat approach you made coming in just now. Not up to 54 Squadron standards," jokingly I teased Mick.

"Ah, but you don't understand, sir," he answered. "There's a nudist camp on Warlingham hill, right in the line of approach, and I always come in low on this particular runway in the hope that I'll see something. Haven't had much luck so far."

Bill Wells, one of the flight commanders in 485 Squadron and very soon to become its Commanding Officer, had fought with 41 Squadron in the Battle of Britain where he became known as 'Hawkeye', (a nickname which has stuck to this day). Not only was Bill a remarkably good shot, but he could see aircraft in the air at extreme ranges and long before any other member of the formation spotted them. This was a wonderful advantage on offensive operations when surprise attack was the enemy's biggest asset. I was most interested to hear Bill's views on the present operations and particularly to discuss with him my frustrated efforts to get near enough to the Hun fighters.

"Frankly, Al, I fail to see how some of the squadrons shoot down the numbers they claim. On a very great number of occasions 485 Squadron has been on the same show, and in the same area of sky, and none of us has seen more than a few stray Messerschmitts. It always mystifies me therefore to find on landing that a particular squadron had destroyed a large number of enemy fighters when we were in spitting distance of that squad throughout the operation. I have, in fact, reported my beliefs to the Station Commander."

"It certainly worries me, Bill," I said. "602 Squadron is breaking about even at the moment and, as for me, I just cannot seem to get decisive results. As you know, we have had more than our share of close escorts as a squadron and that, perhaps, partly explains the reason. Mind you, I defy anyone to get results on close escort duties, unless he is an exceptional shot, and damned lucky into the bargain."

"I agree. It's difficult whatever the task, and the Kenley Wing has had more than its share of the less fruitful ones."

The question of claims is a difficult one to resolve. Unquestionably, the more experienced a pilot became the more careful he was to weigh carefully the pros and cons of a claim before submitting it as a 'destroyed'. There must have been many enemy aircraft claimed as 'probably destroyed' and others 'damaged' when, in fact, they were actually destroyed. Regrettably, the reverse was also true. In most cases, there was no intention on the part of the pilot to mislead; it was more a case of imagination, fired by the excitement of battle, causing him to dream up a picture in his mind which, in the process of telling, became so real that what started as a probable victory now became an enemy aircraft destroyed. There were, of course, definite cases of exaggeration but the offenders were usually taken to task by their fellow pilots. As the records of air fighting in the last war reveal, the RAF did over-claim but not nearly to the same extent as the Germans.

One evening, shortly after 485 Squadron's move to Kenley, I noticed a dejected-looking Pilot Officer sitting alone in the anteroom and looking as if he would rather be elsewhere. He looked a little older than the average run of officers of his rank and I assumed that he was a newly commissioned NCO pilot. (In fact, he was commissioned during pilot training at the late age of 29.) I decided therefore to have a word with him.

"What's your name?" I asked, walking over to where he sat.

"Checketts, sir," he answered, leaping to his feet.

"Why so depressed, don't you like it here?"

"Oh yes. But I was trained on Hurricanes, and Spitfires are new to me. I did my first trip this afternoon and couldn't get the approach right, my speed was always too high. In the end, Bill Compton took off and led me in to land. Now I'm afraid the squadron commander might get rid of me."

"Of course he won't. Even experienced Spitfire pilots overshoot this airfield. What did Bill say?"

"He was very nice and just said that I wasn't to worry about it."

"Come and have a drink, and we will find Bill and see what he says."

As I expected Bill was amused, not annoyed, and slapping Checketts on the back said, "Don't worry, Johnny, you managed to put her down in one piece, and that's what counts." A very relieved Pilot Officer Checketts downed his beer with relish.

As a result of this incident I took a personal interest in Johnny Checkett's career, and was pleased to see that he soon made his mark in the squadron. Later in the war he served under me as a squadron commander and by the end of hostilities he was a wing leader. Bill Compton became a flight commander very shortly after this event and within two years of the incident was appointed wing leader at Hornchurch, a post to be filled with distinction and a great deal of personal success.

Two months had passed since our arrival at Kenley and in that time the squadron had participated in about forty offensive operations. I had been on most of them, and on a number of occasions in the capacity of wing leader. As a result, I was beginning to feel a little tired and in need of a longer break than that afforded by the odd week-end and a day's golf. It will be remembered that I had chipped my coccyx in the last baling-out incident, and the injury was causing me a great deal of discomfort. The main cause of this was the hard dinghy packs, which had replaced the sorbo-cushion on the parachute pack, and on which we sat when flying. As Norman Macqueen so rightly said, "They couldn't have chosen a worse position in the dinghy pack to place the CO_2 bottle (used for inflating the dinghy); it's almost indecent." I found an hour's flying a most painful operation, and thought it was time I did something about it. It was therefore arranged that I should go into hospital for a small operation to put matters right. It did, but only temporarily. On release, I was granted ten days' leave. I spent my now customary few days with the Dumas' in Buckinghamshire before joining Joan in Birmingham. After a couple of days there, we went to stay with Joan's parents.

The ten days' break had done me good and I returned in fine fettle only to find that I was expected to speak to a gathering of workers in the HMV factory at Hayes on the following day. I was terrified at the thought of it – Lille was a minor affair compared with this undertaking – and persuaded 'Mitzi' to come along and lend me some moral support. We were royally entertained, but it was an unnerving experience. On the way back 'Mitzi' jubilantly announced that the management had promised to send me a radiogram for a job well done. The radiogram never appeared, and it was a sore point with 'Mitzi' whenever the subject of radiograms was mentioned thereafter.

Only two days after my return from leave I had yet another lucky escape. This time it was more in the nature of a lucky break or, more correctly, a near miss. I was fast becoming exasperated with myself for not getting more conclusive results in combat, especially now that we were armed with the extra firepower of the Spitfire VB's which carried two cannons and four machine guns. Despite this, and the fact that I had been in combat on numerous occasions since joining the Kenley Wing, my tally of enemy aircraft had only increased to the extent of one Messerschmitt destroyed, two probably destroyed and four damaged. On the next operation, therefore, I decided to put matters right. The wing was detailed as target support over Bethune, and I determined that if the Huns appeared I was going to pick out a target and hang on until I had shot it down. In the event, the enemy did appear and I did manage to fasten myself to a Messerschmitt 109 only to find that the Hun pilot was equally determined not to be shot down. I regret to record that despite a chase from 25,000ft down to ground level, followed by a low-level shooting match in the target area, I could only claim a 'damaged'.

Once having gone down to ground level, it would have been fatal to attempt to climb again to rejoin the squadron, so when I broke off my attacks I headed for home at full speed, hugging the tree tops to take full advantage of my camouflaged Spitfire. Unfortunately, my course for home took me over the centre of Dunkirk which came up so unexpectedly that there was no time in which to avoid the light flak hurled at me. In the circumstances, the shortest course across the town was the safest course, and I kept going straight ahead. In the minute or two it took to cross I was subjected to a really intense barrage of light-machine-gun fire but somehow escaped untouched, or so I thought. Once out to sea I should have been free from attack, but I had forgotten that the German gunners had a nasty habit of training their heavy guns horizontally, and lobbing shells in the path of the retreating aircraft. The first salvo took me by surprise and jolted me into taking immediate evasive action. One spout of water from an exploding shell was most uncomfortably close to the nose of my aircraft and I was greatly relieved when finally I flew out of range.

Safely back at base, I made a quick examination of my aircraft to find that there were only a couple of bullet holes in the tail plane. A later, and more thorough examination, revealed further damage and proved, once again, that my luck was still holding good. I was sitting in the crew room sipping a typically luke-warm and sticky cup of Naafi tea when the Flight Sergeant walked in, holding a small piece of shrapnel in his hand.

"See this, sir. It had gone through your engine cowling, leaving only a neat little hole, and lodged itself in the glycol header tank. It required a fair amount of levering to prise it free and when I pulled it out, the glycol flowed freely. In position, it made a perfect plug, rather better than if it had been engineered."

"How lucky can you get?" chorused the assembled pilots.

The piece of shrapnel was about one inch in length, sharply pointed at one end and flat-topped at the other, and had obviously come from a shell bursting in the sea near my aircraft. I carried it as a good luck talisman for the remainder of my tour with 602 Squadron.

The approach of winter, bringing with it a shorter day and less favourable weather, witnessed a gradual slowing down in the tempo of operations with a great deal more time being spent on training flying. Nevertheless, we continued to keep the Germans alert by operations whenever possible, and on a variety of new tasks. Two of our more recent tasks involved close escort to Beaufighters attacking Channel shipping and Hurricane bombers attacking coastal targets in France and the Low Countries. While engaged on one of these latter tasks, we lost our new wing leader who had only recently taken over from Johnny Kent. Norman Ryder, of 41 Squadron memory, was Johnny's relief and I personally couldn't have wished for a better choice, it was just like old times having Norman pop up at dispersal. All the more unfortunate therefore that his tour was to be a short one.

I was in Norman's office when the order arrived for the first show of the day. It was to be a Hurricane bomber attack on a target on the outskirts of Calais. Two squadrons from the Hornchurch Wing were detailed as close escort, and the Kenley Wing was ordered to do a fighter sweep in the area after the bombers had withdrawn.

"Thank heavens the Hornchurch Wing has been given the unenviable job of close escort," I said to Norman. "I don't fancy the flak around Calais on a low-level show of this sort. What about pretending to the boys when they assemble for briefing that we are down to do the close escort job? It will be amusing to watch the expressions on their faces." Norman, always keen for a good joke, agreed.

Before, however, the pilots could assemble for briefing, our little joke was played out, and in a most unhappy manner. The weather prevented the operation from taking place at the original time and it was delayed two hours, the briefing being put back accordingly. In the meantime, the tasks had been changed and the Kenley Wing was detailed to take over the close escort duties as the weather at Hornchurch was not expected to clear in time to allow their wing to get airborne to take part. It was ironic, therefore, that Norman should be shot down leading the close escort.

The escort plan was for 602 Squadron to fly on the starboard side of the Hurricanes and 485, with Norman leading them, to position on the port side. When the Hurricane leader pulled up for his attack the Spitfires were to climb with full power and cross the coast on either side of Calais and sweep out behind the bombers. All went well until the formation found itself heading straight for a German flak ship anchored off Calais. The Hurricane leader immediately turned port to avoid it and, in so doing, forced 485 Squadron to break formation to avoid collision. As a result of this unexpected manoeuvre, Norman found himself alone over the French coast, and a target for all the flak guns in the area. Before he could make good his escape, he was badly hit and had a miraculous escape from death when he crashed on the beach near Calais. He spent the remainder of the war as a prisoner; a most unlucky break, in the circumstances. As the year 1941 drew to a close, shows became less and less frequent and time off duty increased accordingly. One day I was given the day off to attend a luncheon at Hornchurch and permission was granted for me to take my service car. On the way back I stopped at the Wellington Club in London and when it came time to leave I forgot completely that I had my service car outside – we never took service transport to London – and accepted a lift to the station to catch the last train. Half-way to Lille the following morning I suddenly remembered; not only that I had left it there but that it was not immobilized. There was only one thing to do – break away from the formation, get back as quickly as possible, and dash up to London. I therefore called Tommy Williams on the RIT and told him I had to return, giving no reason. In a gradual dive, and using full throttle all the way, I returned to Kenley from where John Ozanne, who looked at me in amazement when I rushed into dispersal without an explanation, drove me to the railway station. In a side street in Knightsbridge stood the Humber brake, untouched and 'un-ticketted', the rotor-arm still in position. Sedately I drove back to Kenley, and no one was any the wiser.

Over the past few weeks a number of new faces had appeared on the station. Group Captain Prickman, who had commanded Kenley since our arrival, was relieved by none other than 'Daddy' Bouchier. He, in turn, was relieved by Victor Beamish in January. John Peel, who had returned when Norman Ryder was shot down, departed again on promotion and Finlay Boyd assumed command of the wing. In 485 Squadron, Bill Wells had taken over from Marcus Knight while in 602 Squadron Tommy Williams had gone for a well-earned rest, his place being taken by Norman Macqueen. 'Mitzi' soon followed on posting to an Operation Conversion Unit in Wales, much to his disgust. My turn soon came; towards the end of January, I was sent for by Victor Beamish, the Station Commander, who said, "Al, you are to be given a short rest. Paddy Finucane will be taking over your squadron. The AOC wishes to see you tomorrow, so will you ring up Group and fix an appointment. I believe you are to go to America for a bit; that should please you. You can get a hand-over date from Group while you are there, so fix it up with Finucane on your return."

"I am delighted about the news of an American trip, sir, but very sorry to leave Kenley. Do you know if I will come back to the Group when I return? Once out of the swim, I know how difficult it is to get back again."

"Frankly I don't know, Al, but there is every chance that you will. I should mention it to the AOC. Anyhow, if you never do another operation, you have done your share," quipped a smiling Victor.

I reported to 11 Group the next day for interview with Air Vice-Marshal Leigh-Mallory.

"Hello, Deere, take a seat and we will have a chat about future plans for you. This is a good time for you to go off for a rest because I want you back in time for next summer's operations; then we'll see about a wing. That suits you, doesn't it?"

"It certainly does, sir," I answered. "I was going to ask if I could come back into 11 Group on my return."

"We'll look after that. See P2 and he'll let you have

details of your posting to America. Look forward to seeing you on your return."

I left 11 Group feeling very pleased with life. The future looked rosy; America for a few months, and then a wing.

CHAPTER SIXTEEN

Grim Tragedy

Now that I was off operations, I was forced to admit to myself that I needed a rest. In my first tour, despite the many narrow escapes, I was always confident that I would come through all right. In contrast, throughout this one, although it was far less hectic, there was always uppermost in my mind the thought that I would be killed. Why this should be so I do not know. I don't think I was any more frightened than previously, and it can only be that I had returned to operations too soon after so many nerve-racking experiences, added to which there was the unfortunate crash-landing so soon after returning to flying. The result was a loss of confidence, not so much in my ability to meet the enemy on equal terms, but in myself (or my luck). Whatever the cause, I was sure that a complete break from the atmosphere of war, which would be afforded by a trip to America, would restore my confidence and serve as a necessary prelude to a successful tour as a wing leader.

Within two weeks of handing over 602 Squadron I was *en-route* to America aboard a ship bound for the port of Halifax. The night before I left was spent in Cardiff, the port of departure, where I was joined by Joan and 'Mitzi' for a farewell dinner. Joan had caught a direct train from Birmingham and 'Mitzi' motored in from nearby Llandow where he was an instructor at an operational conversion unit. 'Mitzi's' parting words to me were, "Don't forget, Al, when you get a wing on your return I want to come with you."

"You can rest assured I'll fix that, and as squadron commander if at all possible," I answered, in all seriousness.

The ship carrying me to Halifax was a small Norwegian one which, before the war, had been used to carry bananas from the tropics. It was well equipped therefore with cold storage facilities, and ideal for the task on which it was now employed – carrying food from Canada to England. It had a sufficient turn of speed to allow it to sail out of convoy which meant, under normal circumstances, a fairly quick trip to Halifax. As it turned out, the weather was very bad for most of the journey and she was forced to steam at a very reduced speed, well below the safety speed for the avoidance of submarine attack. Fortunately, the weather was also unfavourable for submarine operations, and the likelihood of one wasting a valuable torpedo on such a small target was remote. Our only contact with shipping in the Atlantic was a brief glimpse of a United Kingdom-bound convoy from which an escorting destroyer was detached to confirm our identity. Her captain satisfied that our Aldis lamp signals were genuine, returned with all speed to his charges, by then a faint smudge on the distant horizon.

There were eleven passengers on board, three of whom were Air Force officers: Group Captain Hess, a Czech; Flying Officer Gus Daymond, an American; and myself. The first, who had participated in the Battle of Britain as the leader of the first Czechoslovakian fighter squadron to be formed in England, was on his way to become his country's Air Attaché in Washington. Gus Daymond had served with the first Eagle Squadron in the Royal Air Force, and was returning to join the American Air Force. The other members of the party were mostly Naval officers on their way to commission a Lease-Lend destroyer in New York. All of us had been subjected to a fairly prolonged period of food rationing in wartime England and found the endless dishes at meal times most exciting, but rarely could we do justice to the fare.

After a night's stay in Halifax, brilliantly lit in contrast to the sombre black-out of Cardiff, I went by train to Montreal and thence by air to Washington. In company with Group Captain Hess, I spent a fascinating two days in the American capital visiting places of interest before reporting to the RAF Delegation for instructions. I found that my orders had been changed and instead of being seconded to the American

Navy I was to visit selected Air Force squadrons to fly the aircraft with which each squadron was equipped, and to lecture on fighter tactics. The fighter squadrons chosen were those earmarked for the Eighth and Ninth Air Forces eventually to be deployed in England.

It was a most pleasant assignment and I found unbounded enthusiasm among the squadron pilots, and also a certain amount of frustration. This was caused by dissatisfaction with the aircraft and equipment – a number of squadrons were still equipped with outdated P 40s and P 36s – and the close control exercised over the squadrons by higher headquarters. The American Air Force was then actually the Army Air Force, a part of the Army – it remained so until after the war – and it was at that time experiencing the growing pains of an expansion which was to witness a transformation in size and shape unsurpassed by any air force in World War II. Within two short years of this first contact, I was operating with the Eighth and Ninth Air Forces deployed in the United Kingdom, and was amazed at the transformation which had taken place. The growing pains were behind them, and the power and ability of the forces now carrying the air war deep into the heart of Germany by day was a fitting tribute to Billy Mitchell and his small band of American air power enthusiasts who had fought the American Army hierarchy whose chains had for so long shackled this progressive instrument of war.

Among the many pilots I met on my tour three, in particular, stood out as being of the calibre required to succeed as a fighter pilot. In fact, all three later became leading aces in the American Air Force. They were Captain Zempki and Lieutenants Schilling and Gabreski. 'Hub' Zempki was a cheerful, aggressive enthusiast dedicated to fighters; Dave Schilling, a born aviator, desperately keen to know everything about tactics, kept me talking for long hours on the subject of aerial combat; and Francis Gabreski, in contrast to the other two, a quiet and thoughtful type who had set his sights on success – he reminded me very much of Bob Tuck, already an established ace in the Royal Air Force. Dave Schilling I got to know particularly well for when he arrived in this country he was attached to me at Biggin Hill for familiarization flying and accompanied me, unofficially, on one or two operations over France. I like to think that what little advice I was able to offer helped him to achieve the success he so richly deserved. When he was killed in a motor accident in England after the war, I lost a good friend.

After six weeks of work and pleasure, the latter mostly in the very gay city of New York, I returned to Washington. It was now well into April, and much as I was enjoying myself I was already getting restless to return to operations. I therefore asked for my projected tour to the west coast of America to be cancelled in favour of my return to England. This suggestion did not meet with wholehearted approval, but fate played into my hands. At the time, Admiral Sir Dudley Pound, the First Sea Lord, was in America and was passing through Washington *en route* to Montreal, where he was to catch a plane back to England. He was flying in military aircraft, but was travelling incognito as a civilian. The journey from Montreal to England was to be made in a Liberator, a standard operational aircraft being ferried across the Atlantic. It was thought wise to provide the Admiral with an air aide, to ensure that he was well looked after on the prolonged flight across the Atlantic, usually made at heights requiring oxygen and under most unpleasant conditions in the converted bomb bay of the Liberator. My presence in Washington was fortuitous, and I got the job.

The trip across was uneventful, but cold and unpleasant, for most of the journey was made at a fairly high altitude to avoid frontal conditions over the North Sea. Our oxygen supply froze up, and it was as well that the Admiral had someone experienced in this field to make sure that he was getting supplied from the emergency bottle with which he was equipped. I was profoundly relieved when the aircraft touched down safely at Prestwick, and so was the Admiral, who had proved a most charming and interesting travelling companion. A special aircraft flew us from Prestwick to London where I parted with my charge – and his cured ham, which I had so assiduously nursed throughout our entire journey.

On the Monday following my arrival in London I hastened to Air Ministry to report my return, and to find out what was in store for me in the way of a posting. It was a great shock to find that in my absence I had been posted to a staff job in the Far East and that a posting notice to that effect had been sent to Washington with instructions that I was to proceed direct from there to my new post. Had it not been for my unexpectedly early return to act as aide to Sir Dudley Pound I would have been on my way to the Far East, very much against my will.

"If I can get Fighter Command to accept me back for a flying job can you find a substitute to go to the Far East?" I asked the personnel officer at Air Ministry.

"Yes, I think I can," he answered, "there are plenty of chaps who would be glad to go."

"Thanks, give me a day and I'll contact you again."

A phone call to the Personal Assistant to the AOC of 11 Group resulted in an interview with Air Vice-Marshal Leigh-Mallory that afternoon. My chance of a wing, temporarily shattered by the announcement of a posting to the Far East, again looked rosy.

"Hello, Deere, have a good time in America?" Air Vice-Marshal Leigh-Mallory greeted me as I entered his office. "What can I do for you?"

In answer to this query I told the Air Vice-Marshal about the posting to the Far East and reminded him of his promise of a wing on my return from America.

"I'll certainly fix it up for you to come back into the Group, but I haven't a wing to offer you at the moment What about a squadron?"

"Yes, that will be fine, sir, so long as I get back into the

Group." I answered.

"Fine, 403 Squadron at North Weald has just taken a bad knock, having lost its Commanding Officer and senior flight commander. I need someone experienced to get it in shape again; you're just the chap, Al."

"Thank you, sir, I'll do my best. Has the flight commander vacancy been filled? If not, could I have Flight Lieutenant Darling for the job?"

"Yes, let 'P' staff have his particulars, and I'll see if it can be arranged. When you have 403 Squadron on the top line again we'll see about that wing."

Thus the stage was set for an event which was to be the unhappiest experience in the whole of my war career.

I telephoned Bill Wells at Kenley from 11 Group, and surprised and delighted to learn that he was now the wing leader there. At the same time I could see that I had missed out by going to America and it mightn't be so easy getting a wing as I had imagined; there must be many new contenders on the scene.

Bill and I met that evening at the Kimul Club – a popular meeting place for fighter pilots in the war – and I was most interested to hear his views on the air war over the Channel.

"You know, Al, the introduction of the Focke-Wulf 190 fighter has made a tremendous difference to the German pilots. They have become much more aggressive, and it is no longer a question of how many we shoot down; the reverse is true and the cry is, How many did we lose today? They have definitely got the upper hand at the moment, and are likely to remain on top until we get something better than the Spitfire VB. Frankly it's bloody tough going over the other side now, and I always breathe a sigh of relief when I cross the English coast on the return journey. I bet I am not the only one, either."

"Sounds tough, Bill," I answered. "But there's no need to frighten hell out of me before I even get to my new squadron."

"Forewarned is forearmed; just you see how those Huns

dig in when they're behind the controls of a FW 190. I suppose you know that David Scott-Malden is the wing leader at North Weald?" "Yes, the AOC told me. I'm quite happy about that, David's a fairly experienced operator. He had 54 Squadron for a time, so that makes him OK by me."

The following morning I collected my kit from Kenley – where it had been stored during my absence – and that afternoon I caught a train to North Weald. I was met on arrival at the station by the surviving flight commander, Flight Lieutenant Walker, and the squadron adjutant, Flying Officer Harry Francis. On the way to the airfield I learned from 'Brad' Walker that the squadron was non-operational pending my arrival and that the pilots were mad keen to get cracking again as soon as possible.

The Station Commander, Group Captain Tom Pike, informed me on my interview that 403 Squadron would move to the satellite airfield of Rochford the next day, and that I could have up to a week, longer if I thought it necessary, to get the squadron into shape before being called upon to operate.

This arrangement suited me fine; it would give me plenty of time to get to know the pilots and to work up some squadron tactics before we went into battle. From David Scott-Malden I learned of the tactics employed by the wing on the various shows and also of the arrangements whereby I was notified at the satellite airfield of impending operations.

May 1st, 1942, witnessed my arrival at Rochford as Commanding Officer of 403 (Canadian) Squadron to commence a third tour of operations. Nostalgic memories of 54 Squadron and the many happy hours spent there with George Gribble, Johnny Allen, 'Wonky' Way and the missing comrades of my first, and most loved squadron, were recalled by my first sight of the familiar patch which was Rochford airfield. In contrast to my first sojourn at Rochford, the officers were living in the lap of luxury in a civilian house, just outside the airfield, which had been requisitioned as an Officers' Mess. The whole atmosphere of the place was more sophisticated, and a proper station headquarters was now in existence. The airfield was commanded by Cyril Gadney, the famous international rugger referee, a most helpful and popular Commanding Officer.

For the next few days I worked the squadron really hard. Three times a day, and sometimes four, I had the pilots in the air on tactical exercises until at the end of the fourth day I was satisfied that the squadron could be considered operational. The pilots – and a grand bunch of young Canadians they were too – were keen to get going on the real thing again, and so was I. A telephone call to David Scott-Malden, and 403 Squadron was booked to return to operations the following day, the 5th of May.

Excitement in the crew room was almost as if the squadron was preparing for its first-ever operation; this was in fact true of the replacement pilots who had arrived in the squadron in the last few weeks. The occasion reminded me very much of a similar occasion at Hornchurch – the evening when 54 Squadron was briefed by the Station Commander for its first operational sortie over Dunkirk. The same look of expectancy was on the faces of all the pilots as they clustered around the slate board on which I was chalking up the names of those selected for the operation. 'Brad' Walker, red-headed and smiling, as always; Pilot Officer Dough Hurst, his schoolboyish features puckered in anticipation; little Flight Sergeant Aitken, intense and expectant; Pilot Officers Parr, Somers and Wozniak standing together, hopefully and wistfully gazing at the slate board; Sergeant Murphy, an American who had hitch-hiked from his home town of Turkey Point, Michigan, to join the Canadian Air Force; and a dozen or so more, all equally eager to be in on the operation, proof positive that 403 Squadron was a fighting-fit unit once again.

If the atmosphere that prevailed at briefing was similar to that memorable 54 Squadron occasion, so, too, was the ultimate operation. There was a corresponding lack of enemy aircraft over France as the wing, acting as high cover to

Bostons, swept in and out of hostile territory. The pilots returned disappointed, and somewhat subdued, just as the 54 Squadron pilots had done from their first offensive sortie over Dunkirk.

On the 9th April, 'Mitzi' arrived to take over command of 'A' Flight. I was standing outside the dispersal hut when I saw the familiar Riley making its way towards me. 'Whining Willie', as 'Mitzi' called his beloved car, was really polished up for the occasion, and 'Mitzi's' normally sad-looking countenance was wreathed in smiles as he drew up besides me.

"Hello, 'Mitzi', you got here a damn sight sooner than I expected. I thought it would be a day or two before you managed to drag yourself away from Llandow."

"Not likely, I was packed by the time official confirmation of the posting arrived and was off like a shot the same evening. You've no idea what a tour as an instructor does to one's system Oh! It's wonderful to be back and breathe operational air again. Thanks for fixing it, Al."

"Sorry it couldn't be a squadron, 'Mitzi'. Still, if I get my wing, as I hope to do in the very near future, I think that can be fixed too. We haven't had much joy yet so you haven't missed anything in the time I've been here. I haven't yet had an opportunity to observe the FW I90 at close range, and so am unable to confirm or deny the reports of its superiority. You remember I told you on the phone that Bill Wells had said how dangerous it was and to tell you to stay in the safety of Llandow. How do you feel, scared?"

"I'm always scared, but I'll take my chance. Haven't I told you, Al, I feel quite safe flying behind you, and I mean it."

We were fairly tight on accommodation in the Mess and I arranged for 'Mitzi' to share my room on the understanding that he did not play his infernal gramophone until I was up and about in the mornings, as he was wont to do. I had visions of being awakened in the early hours by this instrument of torture blaring out 'My Heart Belongs to Daddy', 'Mitzi's' favourite tune and one which I had occasion to remember from the Kenley days when he was in the room next to mine.

As the tempo of operations gradually increased so too did the confidence of the squadron as a fighting unit. In the weeks that followed 'Mitzi's' arrival we had a few minor brushes with the FW 109s resulting in limited victories but no losses, and only the odd aircraft damaged. June 2nd was to be a different kettle of fish. The first show at 6.35am was straightforward enough, a fighter sweep with no opposition. At breakfast, taken after the show, the chatter centred around the lack of Hun reaction when there were no bombers to act as bait.

"I can't see any point in these damn fighter sweeps, they're a waste of time and effort," said a disgruntled 'Mitzi' who had not, as yet, fired his guns since joining the squadron.

"I agree, we need some bombers to stir up the hornet's nest. Perhaps this afternoon," I countered, hopefully.

At 10.30am, the squadron was airborne again and headed for rendezvous with the rest of the North Weald Wing at Thames Haven, before joining up with the Hornchurch Wing at Hastings for a two-wing fighter sweep of the St. Omer area. The North Weald Wing was to fly above the Hornchurch Wing thus forming a mass formation which would sweep into enemy territory with the object of 'seeking and destroying the enemy' as the order, detailing the operation, put it. My squadron, as the top squadron in the North Weald Wing, was at 27,000ft.

Shortly after we crossed the French coast on the way in, the Controller reported enemy activity to the raid. Varied reports on the strength of the reaction were passed over the R/T, but there was no sign of enemy fighters until about twenty miles from Le Touquet on the way out. At this point, 'Mitzi' reported a formation of about a dozen FW 190s directly behind, at the same height and closing fast. I picked them up immediately and warned the rest of the squadron to prepare for a 'break'. We had practised a manoeuvre to cope with just this sort of contingency; one section would break upwards and in the opposite direction from the other two which would turn into the attacking fighters. It will be remembered I had remarked on the effectiveness of this manoeuvre when carried out by a formation of Me 109s which I attacked near Deal in the early days of the Battle of Britain.

"They're getting close, Toby Leader," a breathless and worried Mitzi urged some action.

"OK. Blue One, I see them. Wait for the order to break."

When I judged that the Huns were about the right distance away to suit the manoeuvre I intended to carry out, I gave the order:

"Toby squadron, break left."

On my right, Yellow section broke upwards and away while, with Blue section outside me, I turned hard into the closing enemy fighters. About half-way around the break I looked for Yellow section above and to my left and was startled to see another formation of FW 190s emerging through a thin layer of stratus cloud about 2,000ft above and right on our beam. It was too late to do anything about it; the first formation of FW190s was head on to my section, which had now almost completed its turn, and there was only time for a split second burst as the Huns pulled up and above us.

"Watch out, Red Leader, more of them coming down from above and to our right."

Savagely I hauled my reluctant Spitfire around to meet this new attack and the next moment I was engulfed in enemy fighters – above, below and on both sides, they crowded in on my section. Ahead and above, I caught a glimpse of a FW 190 as it poured cannon shells into the belly of an unsuspecting Spitfire. For a brief second the Spitfire seemed to stop in mid-air, and the next instant it folded inwards and broke in two, the two pieces plummeting earthwards; a terrifying demonstration of the punch of the FW 190s four cannons and two machine-guns.

I twisted and turned my aircraft in an endeavour to avoid being jumped and at the same time to get myself into a favourable position for attack. Never had I seen the Huns stay and fight it out as these Focke-Wulf pilots were doing. In Messerschmitt 109s the Hun tactics had always followed the same pattern – a quick pass and away, sound tactics against Spitfires with their superior turning circle. Not so these FW 190 pilots, they were full of confidence.

There was no lack of targets, but precious few Spitfires to take them on. I could see my number two, Sergeant Murphy, still hanging grimly to my tail but it was impossible to tell how many Spitfires were in the area, or how many had survived the unexpected onslaught which had developed from both sides as the squadron turned to meet the threat from the rear. Break followed attack, attack followed break, and all the time the determined Murphy hung to my tail until finally, when I was just about short of ammunition and pumping what was left at a FW 190, I heard him call.

"Break right, Red One; I'll get him."

As I broke, I saw Murphy pull up after a FW 190 as it veered away from me, thwarted in its attack by his prompt action. My ammunition expended, I sought a means of retreat from a sky still generously sprinkled with hostile enemy fighters, but no Spitfires that I could see. In a series of turns and dives I made my way out until I was clear of the coast, and diving full throttle I headed for home.

About twenty miles from the English coast I overtook a lone Spitfire and was just about to pull out to one side to identify it when its hood flew off, followed a few seconds later by the pilot as he abandoned his aircraft. His parachute opened almost immediately. At that precise moment another aircraft dived into the sea over to my left, about three miles away. I could just see a parachute, very near the water and in the vicinity of the spot where the aircraft had hit the water. "He must have got out just in time," I muttered to myself as I climbed to gain height to transmit information on the position of the first pilot, now safely in his dinghy.

Having received an acknowledgement of transmission, I

flew across to the spot where I judged the second pilot would be. I had lost sight of his parachute against the hazy background over the sea and had the greatest difficulty in finding the spot where his aircraft had hit the water; this I recognized by the large oily patch it had left on the surface. Eventually I managed to locate the position of the dinghy and saw the pilot waving to attract my attention so I rocked my wings to let him know that he had been sighted. Again I gained height to broadcast his position and when this was acknowledged I flew low past the dinghy to indicate to the pilot that rescue was on the way. In the fleeting glimpse as I passed by I thought I recognized 'Mitzi', but it was impossible to be sure. By now my petrol was dangerously low and I was obliged to set course for the nearest airfield, Lympne.

When I landed I had been airborne two hours and ten minutes; there was barely enough fuel left to taxi to the refuelling point.

While my aircraft was being refuelled I checked with Manston that my messages on the two pilots had been received and was informed that action had already been taken, and the rescue boats were on the way. Indeed, when I circled the airfield prior to my return to Rochford I could see two launches headed for the area; there seemed nothing further I could do, so I returned to base.

As I taxied towards the dispersal after landing I noticed nothing unusual at first, but when I got close I was amazed, and somewhat taken aback, to see how very few Spitfires there were in the parking area. I could see 'Brad' Walker waiting to greet me, and from the look on his face I knew something dreadful had happened.

"Relieved to see you back, sir, we thought you had bought it too," was his depressing greeting.

"What do you mean, bought it too?" I queried anxiously.

"I'm afraid it's pretty bad; there's only myself and my number two back so far. The Controller thinks that there are two more at Manston – one crash-landed – but he is making a further check and will ring back as soon as he gets something definite."

I knew we had lost at least three aircraft, and feared more, but this news appalled me. "What news of 'Mitzi'?" I asked, thinking of the pilot in the second dinghy.

"Not a word," said the unusually grim-looking Harry Francis who had now joined me. I've just spoken to the Controller and he says that Sergeant Murphy is on his way back from Manston. He also confirms that the Spitfire, which crash-landed there, is ours. It's Wozniak, and he's unhurt; the Spitfire is a write-off."

"That makes it a little better," said 'Brad'. "Seven now unaccounted for. If they pick up those two in the Channel, and they turn out to be ours, it won't be quite so bad – but bad enough."

"A little, 'Brad', but not much. God, what a tragedy, I just can't believe it," I said addressing Cyril Gadney who had appeared on the scene. "Eight aircraft destroyed and, at best, five pilots missing. I must speak to the Controller to see if there is any further news from the air-sea rescue chaps."

The Controller informed me that there was still no news from the launches, and that we couldn't expect any for a bit yet. He also said that David Scott-Malden had also reported the position of one of the dinghies.

While I was telephoning, Sergeant Murphy had landed, and was excitedly relating his experiences to the others.

"Hello, Murphy, I'm damned pleased to see you back safely. How you managed to stick with me as long as you did, I don't know. Anyhow, thanks for that timely warning. Did you manage to get that Hun?"

"Hell, no. I had no sooner started firing than I was set on by a horde of the blighters. I took violent evasive action, so much so that the next thing I knew I was upside down hanging on my straps, and down to about 3,000ft. I certainly wasn't hit, but I'm not quite sure exactly how I got there. I got out all right and headed for home; I never thought I'd make it. Phew! that was some scrap – those babies can certainly fly. By the way, sir, did you get that second one you fired at?"

"Haven't a clue, Murphy, there wasn't time to see what happened. I hit him all right, but how badly is difficult to say."

There seemed little point in hanging around dispersal, and nothing could be done until we got further news, so I drove up to the Mess for lunch, accompanied by 'Brad' and Harry Francis. Lunch for me consisted of a glass of tomato juice; about the only occasion in the war when I couldn't face a meal. An hour later news was received that Flight Sergeant Aitken had been rescued from his dinghy but that there was still no news of the second dinghy. It was obvious that something had gone wrong – the two dinghies were not more than five miles apart – so I determined to take off again and join the search. 'Brad' Walker came with me, and we searched the area for one and a half hours without success. In the meantime, the haze over the Channel had thickened considerably and visibility near the sea was very poor. I could see that it was going to be almost impossible to locate the dinghy from the air, even the very distinct oil patch which had first led me to it was no longer visible. According to my reckoning, the air-sea rescue launch appeared to be much too far south, but it was difficult in the haze to gauge the distance from the coast and I wasn't too sure of my position. The search went on all that day, and the next, without success. The mystery of the dinghy, and its occupant, was never solved. Was it 'Mitzi'? I have asked myself that question a thousand times since, and always come back to the belief that it was. He has never been accounted for.

That night when I entered my room, tired out but sleepless, 'Mitzi's' gramophone, still open from its early morning use, seemed to stare at me in silent disapproval as if to say: "Remember, he felt safe with you." A fairly tough and hardened campaigner by this time, I couldn't get the thought out of my mind. 'Mitzi' had forsaken the safety of a training establishment to join me as a flight commander when by waiting a little longer he could have become a squadron commander, as had been planned when I got a wing. The wing had now become very much an if.

I awoke next morning feeling very much off colour but put it down to the stress of the previous day, and a sleepless night. At breakfast I received a message that the Station Commander at North Weald wished to see me. I flew across to North Weald later that morning, having first ascertained that there was no news of the missing dinghy. Group Captain Pike was most sympathetic and said that it had been arranged that the Squadron should move to Martlesham as a temporary expedient. While there we would be employed solely on convoy duties until our losses in pilots and aircraft had been made good. Although I would have preferred to carry straight on I appreciated the wisdom of this decision. Late that afternoon, 403 Squadron moved to Martlesham Heath airfield. I spent the next few days in bed with a mild attack of quinsy.

The body blow was delivered on the 16th June. The squadron was ordered to move to Catterick on the 18th June, and was to be replaced at North Weald by 332 (Norwegian) Squadron. It was a bitter disappointment to me, and to all the squadron pilots whose morale was in no way affected by the heavy losses we had suffered. What could I do? There was but one answer, a personal interview with the AOC. Having decided on this course of action I telephoned North Weald and asked Group Captain Pike if I could have his permission to seek an interview with Air Vice-Marshal Leigh-Mallory, and he readily agreed. That same afternoon I flew to Northolt where a car met me to take me to 11 Group Headquarters at Uxbridge.

The AOC greeted me in his usual friendly way but when I asked if 403 Squadron could stay in the Group, he became very serious.

"I'm afraid that's not possible. The squadron has suffered a heavy loss for the second time in a very short period, and Fighter Command has decided, on my recommendation, that it should be rested. You know, Deere," the AOC went on, "you aren't entirely blameless for this unfortunate incident. You are rather too fond of a fight, and take unnecessary risks."

This unexpected accusation was my first intimation that in some way I might be considered in part to blame for our severe losses on that last ill-fated trip. I didn't know what to answer; what could I say? By the damnedest piece of bad luck, my squadron had been caught in a trap, and the only way out of it was to fight. The AOC's famous dictum, 'seek and destroy the enemy', was uppermost in my thoughts; this, however, was obviously not the time to mention it. We had been beaten on that last day by a combination of superior aircraft, overwhelming odds, and skilful tactics. There seemed no point in squealing.

"I'm sorry, sir," I answered, "there was no alternative; we had to turn and fight."

"Well, that's the decision. 403 Squadron has been in the Group a long time and it is overdue for a rest."

That seemed the end of the interview so far as the fate of 403 Squadron was concerned. But what about my wing? "Now or never," I thought, as I hesitantly asked, "I've only just come back on operations as you know, sir. Would it be possible for me to stay in the south; you did say you would give me a wing?"

"No, I'm afraid it won't. You can't leave your squadron at this critical time, and will have to go to Catterick with them. I'll think about a wing."

And there the interview ended.

On the morning of the 18th June, 403 Squadron landed at Catterick. The disappointment at moving north was eased somewhat for me by the cheerful welcome I received from my many friends still serving there. But it was a sad occasion compared with those when, as a member of a victorious 54 Squadron, I had flown into this happy little station, tired but flushed with success.

Less than a week later, I received a letter from Air Vice-

Marshal Leigh-Mallory in which he asked me to convey his thanks to all members of the squadron for their faithful service in 11 Group and the hope that they would soon return south after a well-earned rest. There was no mention of my wing.

*　　*　　*

In the course of my researches at Air Ministry to gather material for this book I came across the combat reports of two of the pilots who, though they lost their aircraft, survived this epic encounter. These direct and ungarnished reports related by pilots, whose pulses still raced with the excitement of battle, convey a more vivid picture of the fight than any pen could do sixteen years later. I reproduce them as recorded, the fading signatures of the pilots bearing witness to their authenticity:

"Flying Officer Wozniak (Red Four). 'I broke with the CO and when just about to open fire I saw several FW 190s coming down on our beam. I broke left to meet them and at the same moment I felt a jolt and my radio went dead. The aircraft went into a spin at about 24,000ft but I managed to get it out only to be attacked again from the port, the starboard and then astern. Bullets hit my engine and both wings and my aircraft went into a spin again. I managed to recover at 8,000ft, where I was well clear of the fight, and made for home.' (Damage to the aircraft: large cannon hole through the fuselage near the tail which severed the radio cable and one control wire. Numerous bullets in the engine, tail plane and both wings. Aircraft a write-off.) "

"Flight Sergeant Aitken (Blue Four). 'I heard the CO call a break left and I saw enemy aircraft behind. Also just above I saw aircraft, which I think were Me 109s, coming in to attack P/O Parr (Blue Three). I gave one of these aircraft a long burst as it crossed my sights. I then felt bullets hit the armour plate at my back and bullets perforated my cockpit cover. My aircraft gave a lurch and the R/T went dead. I went into a steep turn and then levelled out and started weaving. I saw nothing more of my section. I then saw an enemy aircraft on the starboard at 500ft above and several more to the port. I attacked an enemy aircraft on the starboard as it dived towards me firing. I could see tracer passing below as I continued in the turn. I then saw tracer passing both sides of me, and coming from behind; a cannon shell hit my wing. I went into a steep diving turn and levelled out at 5,000ft and made for home. The nose of my aircraft wanted to keep coming up and I was forced to trim fully forward for straight and level flight. The engine then began to splutter and puffs of white smoke and flames came out of the exhaust. Petrol began to soak into the cockpit and the aircraft started to lose height. I then decided it was time to get out. My 'chute opened OK and it seemed only a moment before I hit the water. When in my dinghy, which I clung on to desperately in the water as I can't swim, I saw a Spitfire circling. I was picked up after about 30 minutes.' (Aircraft a complete loss.)"

CHAPTER SEVENTEEN

Wing Leader

A T first I was depressed at the turn of events; the loss of a close friend who rejoined me so recently and the shattering of my dreams of early command of a wing. As the weeks went by, however, these wounds began to heal, and brooding gave way to a determination to keep plugging away.

Not long after our arrival at Catterick the squadron was warned to prepare to move to Manston for an important operation. This seemed an ideal opportunity, and I eagerly awaited the event. The move to Manston duly took place, but after a two days' wait there the operation was postponed indefinitely (this was the landing at Dieppe). Alas for my hopes; the squadron returned to Catterick on the third day.

We had not long returned north when I was unexpectedly posted to 13 Group headquarters as a staff officer. A friend of mine on the staff, Wing Commander Tom Morgan, informed me of the posting and said that it was intended I should take over from him in the near future when he left to take a wing. In the circumstances therefore I was not too unhappy as I reasoned that once having attained the rank of wing commander it would be an easier next step to getting a wing. Events didn't quite work out as I had hoped. Out of the blue I was posted to the RAF Staff College, an Air Ministry posting which there was no gainsaying. There was but one consolation in my new posting; the Staff College was in Buckinghamshire and I would thus be near enough to the centre of fighter operations to keep in close personal touch with friends at Fighter Command and No. 11 Group with a view to keeping my urgent desire to get a fighter wing before the powers that be, when my course of staff training was completed.

A very happy interlude at this time was a visit to Buckingham Palace to a tea party given by Their Majesties for Dominion officers. It was a most enjoyable occasion and

I had the great good fortune to be introduced to Princess Elizabeth (as Her Majesty then was) and Princess Margaret. I found them both very natural to talk to, and I recall how the very bright young Princess Margaret showed great interest in the fact that I was a Spitfire pilot.

Christmas 1942 saw me enmeshed in the intricacies of Staff College exercises. In common with a number of my fellow students, I had shot up rapidly from junior rank to Squadron Leader in the hurly-burly of the wartime expansion, and staff work was a complete mystery to me. Now I was at the seat of staff learning, and there was nothing for it but to get stuck in – I had to, to keep my head above water. I found the mental effort of trying to concentrate on voluminous exercise settings, with my thoughts forever wandering into the sky at the sound of an aircraft, a slow form of torture. However, I survived the three months' course, and passed out successfully.

During a break in the course I managed to get across to 11 Group headquarters where, through the intervention of Wing Commander Johnny Walker who was on the Group staff, I was introduced to the new AOC, Air Vice-Marshal Saunders. Air Vice-Marshal Saunders had a personal interest in New Zealanders, having been seconded as CAS of the RNZAF, at an early stage in the war. He told me that he had followed my career with interest and was pleased to hear I was doing well at the Staff College (news to me at the time). There was no promise of a flying job in our conversation, but I was happy to have had the opportunity of making my number with Air Vice-Marshal Leigh-Mallory's successor; the latter was now Commander-in-Chief of Fighter Command.

To say I was bitterly disappointed when, on finishing at the Staff College, I found myself returned to 13 Group headquarters as a staff officer, would be a gross under-statement of my feelings. Optimistically, I had hoped to be returned to flying, even perhaps as a wing leader. My spirits were very low, and I thought that, for me, the active war was over. Victor Beamish's words, on my departure from Kenley when I was on the crest of the wave, often came to mind: "Al, if you never do another operation in this war, you've done more than your share." Repeatedly, I told myself that I should be satisfied, I had done my share – why not sit back, enjoy life, take it easy and let other fools get shot down. But, the gnawing desire to return to flying was ever present.

In February I saw my chance to take a step forward. 'Daddy' Bouchier, now an Air Commodore, arrived at 13 Group headquarters as SASO, and I appealed to him to allow me a two weeks' attachment at Biggin Hill, where 'Sailor' Malan was now installed as Station Commander. "After all," I pleaded, "an air staff officer must keep up to date with current operations." I knew I could fix it with 'Sailor' – in fact, I had already got his verbal agreement – and it was merely a question of being allowed away from the Group for two weeks. I think memories of 54 Squadron and Hornchurch won the day, for 'Daddy' gave his consent.

At Biggin Hill, Dicky Milne, who was the wing leader, arranged for me to fly as a member of 611 Squadron. I knew how squadron commanders hated supernumeraries in their squadron and I was careful therefore not to stake my claims to leadership but to fly when, and in whatever position in the formation, the squadron commander or his flight commanders wished. As a result, I found myself flying as a number two, as a number three and in any stooge position in the squadron where there was a gap to be filled. To be frank, I can't say I was happy going through the mill again, as it were, especially having been a leader since the early days of the war. Nevertheless, I was exhilarated, in a curious sort of way, for the first time since the fateful day over Le Touquet with 403 Squadron.

At all costs I had to bag myself a Hun; somehow I felt that a flying appointment depended on it. When my fourteen days were up I hadn't fired a shot in anger. The weather had been bad throughout the period, and the wing had been on only a few abortive shows. On two occasions I managed to get myself on a 'Rhubarb' (that useless and hated operation) but even then without success; although on one occasion, when flying as a number three in a section of four, we did manage to surprise some FW 190s but we were not quite quick enough to catch them and, using their superior speed at low level, they avoided combat.

With 'Sailor's' connivance I decided to stay on for a few more days and risk the wrath of 'Daddy' on my return to 13 Group. Two days later I was in combat. I was leading a section in the wing when at 37,000ft over St. Omer I sighted a dozen FW 190s some 10,000ft below. I called Dicky Milne and told him I was taking my section down to attack. As we neared the enemy fighters they saw us and split. I singled out one, determined at all costs to get him. I had speed and height in my favour and, in contrast to the ill-fated battle with 403 Squadron, I was behind the controls of a Spitfire IX which was superior to the FW 190 above 25,000ft. To me, the fight that ensued was more important than any that had gone before – my future was at stake. I felt like a boxer entering the ring before a big fight, tense and breathless, and curiously excited. As my cannons found their mark, and bits from the disintegrating Focke-Wulf hurtled past my aircraft, there was no exhilaration at victory, no sorrow at killing, no revenge for past hurts, but merely a sense of achievement – this is what I had set out to do, and I had done it. 'Sailor' was delighted at my success. After two more uneventful days at Biggin, I was ordered to return to 13 Group.

"I'm sorry, Al, but you'll have to return," said 'Sailor' as I faced him in his office where I had gone to plead for one more day's flying. "The Group Captain Operations at 13 Group has been on the phone and he says there can be no further extension."

"Oh well, if that's the case I'd better be on my way. Thanks for having me," I answered ruefully.

"Don't give up, Al, I'll keep plugging your case. You can

come here any time you like and fly with the wing."

Installed again in my office at 13 Group, I felt that I had played my last card, and lost. Three days later I was summoned to 'Daddy's' office to be greeted by a SASO, all smiles.

"You've made it, Al, and let me say how pleased I am. You have been posted to command the Kenley Wing with effect Monday next. Congratulations and the very best of luck."

I reported for interview with Air Vice-Marshal Saunders on the Monday, as instructed, only to find that the posting had been changed and I was to become the wing leader at Biggin Hill. In between my appointment to Kenley and arrival at Group headquarters Dicky Milne had been shot down. Apparently 'Sailor' had forthwith phoned the AOC and asked for me to replace Dicky, not knowing that I had already been appointed to Kenley. The AOC kindly agreed to switch. Thus it came about that I was appointed to command the famous Biggin Hill Wing, and Johnnie Johnson was promoted to fill the vacancy at Kenley. I felt I was now on the crest of the wave again.

During the time I was out of circulation I had thought a great deal about wing tactics and now that I had at last realized my ambition to become a wing leader there were a number of changes I proposed to introduce at Biggin. In 'Sailor' Malan as Station Commander I had, to my way of thinking, the best fighter tactician and leader produced by the RAF in World War II. I was anxious therefore to put my theories to him in order to get his approval and support before putting them into practice. On the very first day of my new command I presented myself in 'Sailor's' office and launched forthwith into the subject of wing tactics.

"You're the wing leader," he said, "and the tactics you adopt are entirely a matter for you to decide. Naturally, I'm interested but I have no intention of interfering unless things go wrong. But go ahead, I'd like to hear what you've got to say."

I outlined my policy which was based on complete freedom of action down to section leaders. My aim was that the squadrons in the wing formation should be independent, yet inter-dependent, and that the same should apply to the sections. I would control the overall formation in my capacity as wing leader only in so far as routes and timings were concerned, the squadron and section leaders being free to act on their own initiative to engage enemy aircraft on sighting, first warning me that they intend to break formation. Usually the second, or top squadron in the wing was considered as the cover squadron to the lower or bottom one. In my plan I wanted the squadron commander of this squadron to feel that he had an equal part to play in spearheading the attack, and, depending on circumstances, he might well be called upon to lead it. In short, I was keen to get away from mass-controlled attack and to rely on mutual support between the squadrons and sections within the wing as the tactical basis of a more flexible and profitable form of attack.

I then went on to discuss the specific changes I intended to introduce. These covered such things as a modified form of 'finger-four' formation (as opposed to the line-astern one then in favour), a standard colour code throughout the wing, R/T discipline, and many other tactical points concerned with fighter operations. In particular, I stressed my belief that no matter what type of escort we undertook the wing must not be tied to the bomber speeds. Naturally, on close escort duties it was important to be always in sight of the bombers but the accepted tactic of flying alongside them was outmoded; it gave the bomber pilots some measure of comfort, but no protection.

"It sounds all right to me," said 'Sailor' when I concluded my explanations, "it's up to you to make it work. I don't expect we'll get any close escort work though, there are a few Spitfire VB wings still available to do that. Go ahead and discuss your proposals with the squadron commanders. You will need their wholehearted support if they are to be a success."

There were two squadrons at Biggin Hill. I now the established complement of a fighter wing – 611 and 341

(Alsace) Squadrons. The former was commanded by 'Wag' Haw, a phlegmatic and hardened campaigner who had served with the RAF Hurricane wing assisting the Russians in the defence of Murmansk. 'Wag' received the Order of Lenin for his part in these operations, and this entitled him to free use of public transport in Russia. But, as he put it, "I can't see what the hell good that will do me." Commandant René Mouchotte, who commanded the Free French Squadron, was a completely different type. Tall and thin, he was always immaculately dressed and very rarely to be seen without a long stylish cigarette holder held either between delicate fingers or gently gripping teeth. But Rene's appearance belied his true worth as a leader and a fighter pilot. He was dedicated to the liberation of his country and to him there was no joy in life so long as the Boche (he had a singularly expressive way of pronouncing the word) was on French soil. A quiet and reserved officer on the ground; an aggressive and purposeful fighter in the air. Supporting René were his two flight commanders, Captains Martell and Boudier; the former a gentle giant of sixteen and a half stone, but a killer in action, and the latter a small quiet man who was never over-excited, an ideal trait among naturally excitable Frenchmen.

Both squadron commanders readily agreed to the suggested changes and I therefore called a full wing briefing to put my plan before the pilots. After the briefing I asked the Senior Controller, Squadron Leader Bill Igoe, into my office to discuss control of the wing on freelance fighter operations. Bill had been in the RAF before the war as a fighter pilot but had been invalided out as a result of a serious flying accident, and had become a most successful business man in the City. He rejoined the day the war broke out and got himself on to controlling as the next best thing to flying, for which he was rejected. With a background of fairly recent flying experience Bill appreciated more than any other controller I knew the sort of information the pilots required passed to them in the air, and he had the personality and ability to put it over. What a bundle of Irish energy he was – whether it was on the squash court or rugger field, and he was damn good at both games – and the operation room always took on a new lease of life when he appeared. His pride and joy at the time was a control radar on the south coast which could see well into France thus enabling him to exercise close control of the wing on offensive operations. It was this aspect of control we discussed. We had a number of successful 'bounces' under Bill's control using this equipment which, though a little inaccurate in height, proved a great asset to the wing.

I was now all set to renew acquaintances with the formidable Focke-Wulfs, but this time I was better equipped. The Biggin Hill squadrons were using the Spitfire IXBs (Merlin 66), a mark of Spitfire markedly superior in performance to the FW 190 below 27,000ft. Unlike the Spitfire IXA, with which all other Spitfire IX wings in the Group were equipped, the IXB's supercharger came in at a lower altitude and the aircraft attained its best performance at 21,000ft, or at roughly the same altitude as the FW 190. At this height it was approximately 30mph faster, was better in the climb and vastly more manoeuvrable. As an all-round fighter the Spitfire IXB was supreme, and undoubtedly the best mark of Spitfire produced, despite later and more powerful versions. The call-sign allocated to me as wing leader was 'Brutus'.

When I took over at Biggin the wing needed seventeen more enemy aircraft to bring the total to 1,000 destroyed by pilots operating from the station. Even as early as March the event was eagerly awaited by all ranks on the station, and by the British Press whose reporters were continuously on our doorstep. There was little hope of reaching this target until better weather allowed more operations, and hence more reaction from the Germans. Throughout March and most of April there was little of note to record, but this slack period suited me because it afforded an ideal testing time in which to build up confidence in my new tactics.

The AOC was most anxious to keep pegging away at the

Huns despite the weather, and encouraged wing leaders to plan their own shows to take advantage of weather breaks during which there would be insufficient time to lay on a Group operation. I am pleased to say that the unrewarding 'Rhubarbs' were now frowned upon, and were not considered as part of our programme. At about this time, we heard through intelligence sources that the first Gruppe (equivalent to an RAF wing) of the famous Richthofen Geschwader had moved into Tricqueville airfield, just south of the Seine Estuary, under the command of a well-known fighter ace, Major Walter Oesau. As soon as I learned of this I telephoned Johnny Walker, who was responsible for planning operations at 11 Group, to ask if we could plan a wing show to Tricqueville airfield with the object of enticing this Gruppe into the air. Johnny readily agreed, and so did the AOG when the suggestion was put to him.

"Al, the AOC is enthusiastic and you have a free hand this afternoon. There is a fighter sweep laid on in the Caen area so, if you wish, you can tie in your timings with it," said Johnny when he rang me first thing the following morning.

"Thanks, I will make use of it, Johnny. I propose to go out at low level until about ten miles from the French coast where I intend to commence a rapid climb to 10,000ft so as to cross in above light flak height. The idea is then to dive to ground level and hedge-hop the rest of the way to Tricqueville in the hope that we'll surprise Oesau's chaps taking off. I'll let you have my timings so that you can warn the other wings."

The plan was for 611 Squadron, with me leading, to pull up to 500ft and 341 Squadron to 3,000ft when we reached a pre-determined check point some ten miles from Tricqueville. 611 Squadron would attack anything on the airfield and 341 Squadron would patrol to the south as an insurance against surprise attack from other aircraft of JG2 based at Evereux.

The Frenchmen were enthusiastic about the operation; it was an opportunity for them to show their hand in a more positive manner over one of their captured airfields.

Lieutenant Raoul Duval, in particular, was straining at the leash; he lived in the area and knew the airfield well.

From Dungeness we set a southerly course at wave-top height on a timed run to the point at which we were to commence our quick climb before crossing in east of Deauville. The timings worked out nicely and we crossed the French coast spot on the minute, to the accompaniment of some fairly accurate medium flak. Down to ground level we dived and levelling out at tree-top height sped, in a broad front, eastwards towards our target. Would we be lucky? No doubt all twenty-four pilots on the formation asked themselves this question. At the check point I eased up to 500ft, and René pulled up into a full throttle climb, veering slightly south as planned.

I first sighted the airfield when we were about five miles from it. At the same moment Rene's voice, unruffled as always, came over the R/T:

"Brutus, there are aircraft taxiing on the airfield."

From a higher vantage point René had a better view than I, but a few seconds later I saw them, visible mainly because of the sun glinting on perspex hoods as they taxied into position for take-off. But we too had been spotted; bursting red flares appeared over the airfield as a warning to the Hun pilots of danger, and they reacted instantly. Before we could get in range the aircraft were airborne and had disappeared in several directions at low level, lost to sight against the wooded background of the surrounding countryside. We were still about a mile away, and there was no point in opening fire. I cursed our bad luck, ten seconds sooner and we would have caught them with their pants down. As it was there was only the empty airfield and a miserable-looking hangar to fire at, the latter receiving a burst from me as I hurtled across in pursuit.

"Brutus from Grass-seed. Enemy aircraft coming up fast from the south, about 5,000ft," René's voice broke through on the R/T.

Veering right and climbing, I answered, "OK, Grass-seed, coming up to assist."

We met them head on in the climb, and a glorious dog-fight developed, reminiscent of my first encounter with the Hun over Calais/Marck. This time, however, we were evenly matched in numbers. The danger from collision was greater than from Hun bullets as Spitfires and Focke-Wulfs wove a chaotic pattern in the congested air space over the airfield. It was impossible to hold one's fire for more than a fleeting second without being attacked; one moment I found myself diving vertically at the ground after a retreating Hun, and the next my over-revving airscrew was clawing at the air in response to my full throttle demand as I endeavoured to spiral upwards out of range of an attacker. This time there was to be no sudden clearance of the sky, for the Huns were obviously determined to fight it out. But our petrol was running low and we had a long way to go before clearing enemy territory. I therefore gave the order to withdraw.

"Brutus calling all Turban and Grass-seed aircraft: withdraw to R/V point immediately."

We had planned a rendezvous point just off Fecamp on the coast and I now set course for there with Flying Officer Paddy Neal, my number two, still in attendance. At Fecamp, I was eventually joined by the majority of 611 Squadron, but 341 Squadron made their way out independently.

"Boy, that was some fight," Johnny Checketts, who had destroyed a FW 190, enthusiastically greeted me as I climbed out of my aircraft. "I'll bet the Hun ground crews at Tricqueville had a grandstand view. Pity we had to pull out, those Huns seemed keen."

Before driving across to 341's dispersal to check on their story, I learned that 611 Squadron had destroyed two Focke-Wulfs without loss or damage. As I pulled up in front of the Frenchmen's dispersal I noticed Chris Martell heatedly berating a Sergeant Pilot. It was very rare for Chris to lose his temper and I was interested to find out why. "What's the matter, Chris?" I asked, coming up from behind. The normally good-natured Chris looked quite embarrassed as he turned to greet me, and answered:

"Closterman here lost me in that fight and I got jumped. I'm bloody angry." And he looked it. Sergeant Closterman (author of *Le Grande Cirque*) had not long been with the squadron but should have been aware of the golden rule in the wing: a number two must never lose his leader, the only exceptions being if he himself was shot down or had to pull out because of engine failure. This may sound a harsh rule, but it paid dividends.

341 Squadron had been less fortunate than 611 and had lost two aircraft and pilots, for two FW 190s damaged. Unfortunately, one of the pilots was Raoul Duval who had been so enthusiastic about an operation so close to his home ground.

"He'll be back, you see," said Chris confidently. In the event, Chris was right. Not only did he return but he brought with him a bride whom he married while hiding in Le Havre awaiting a chance to escape back to England.

The results of the operation were a little disappointing but, as Jack Charles put it, "I'll bet those Hun pilots got one hell of a fright; a few seconds earlier and we would've mown them down." As one who had had experience of being caught taking off, I fully supported this view. If for no other reason, that fact alone made the operation worthwhile.

Towards the end of April the total enemy aircraft destroyed stood at 990. It was obvious that the great day would not long be delayed and the spotlight of publicity was centred on the event; the BBC (represented in the person of Mr Gilbert Harding) had arranged to make a sound recording, the Press were repeatedly in attendance at the station and the Air Ministry information branch were for ever on the telephone. 'Sailor', naturally shy, avoided visitors whenever possible with the result that I found myself dancing attendance on a continual flow of visitors. Fortunately, in Squadron Leader 'Spy' De la Torre, whom one could safely call the doyen of station intelligence officers, I had a man skilled in all the arts of handling irksome enquiries, so I left all callers – either in person or on the telephone – in his capable hands.

In April, both 'Wag' Haw and his senior flight commander were rested, and their places were taken by Squadron Leader Jack Charles, a Canadian who had been with me in the 54 Squadron training era at Catterick, and Johnny Checketts, newly promoted to fill the flight commander appointment. Both had been appointed on my recommendation and both were to prove invaluable as supporting leaders in the months ahead. Johnny, it will be remembered, was my protégé in the Kenley days; he had recently returned to operations after a short rest period.

On the 4th May, with the total at 994, the wing moved to Manston for refuelling prior to escorting American Flying Fortresses on an attack against the docks at Antwerp. Previously the Fortresses had been operating without escort, other than a few withdrawal cover fighters, but recent losses from determined FW 190s had caused them to revise their tactics. Their own Thunderbolt fighters were not yet fully worked-up for escort duties, and Fighter Command had been asked to provide Spitfires as escort until such time as the Thunderbolts were ready to take over the job. At Manston, the wing was joined by Johnnie Johnson and his Canadians from Kenley. Johnnie was one of the most aggressively-minded fighter pilots I ever met; full of ideas, a first-class shot and blessed with unique powers of leadership, it was inevitable that he should reach the top. His Canadian pilots would follow him anywhere.

Although the Biggin Wing was detailed as close escort I determined to adopt freelance tactics as outlined to 'Sailor'. This was the obvious course to take when escorting Fortresses who could adequately protect themselves at close quarters. As we approached the rendezvous point, over Knocke on the Belgian coast, I could see the eighty bombers away out over the Channel, leaving in their wake as they ploughed across the sky, long white ribbons of condensation trails, narrow at first then gradually widening as, caught by the strong upper winds, they spread and joined together to form a vast area of milky cloud hiding the sea below. Behind, and to my right, I could see the Kenley Wing climbing steadily to their high cover position while further back still, and beyond the bombers, the Thunderbolts struggled laboriously (they were notoriously bad on the climb) to gain height for their task of providing withdrawal support.

"How different," I thought, "80 Fortresses as against the customary dozen or so 2 Group Bostons." This was the real thing; a punch that could be felt.

Groping flak followed us to the target, largely ineffective at 25,000ft, but there were no enemy fighters in the area; a diversionary Fortress 'spoof' had been laid on to the south and this no doubt accounted for their absence. Over the islands of Walcheren on the return journey a formation of Focke-Wulfs appeared to the north and began a desultory series of attacks, only to be met by the eager, freelancing Spitfires forming the close escort. Two dived across my line of fire and I whipped into the attack only to find myself frighteningly and unexpectedly immersed in a deluge of tracer from the starboard box of Fortresses. The angle was such that they had little chance of hitting me, or the Hun, and I continued my chase. Here was my chance of a first kill as wing leader. Closing rapidly from dead astern and slightly below, I steadied my aim and pressed the firing button, continuing firing as the range shortened to within 150 yards. Dancing splodges of yellow along the enemy's fuselage signified success. The 190 wobbled under the impact, comically it seemed, burst into flames and dived away to destruction. I had destroyed the 995th aircraft for Biggin Hill.

Three days later the total still stood at 995. Bad weather had again interfered with operations, and continued to do so until the 14th May. On this day we were heavily engaged over Courtrai and Jack Charles and his number two each destroyed a FW 190, while Chris Martell sent a Me 109G to flaming destruction. Two to go. The pilots were gripped by a feverish intensity; none would take leave and all wanted to fly. Apart from the glory of being the lucky pilot to get the 1,000th Hun, there was the added attraction of a £300 cash prize, raised through a mammoth raffle which had been under way for the past six months.

The 15th May was set fine, and I had a feeling that this was the day. So much so that I telephoned Alan Mitchell, the New Zealand War Correspondent in London and a friend of mine, to ask him out for the day to witness the event. To 'Sailor' I said, "I think you should come with us today, sir, I feel confident we're going to get among them."

"Since you put it that way, I'll come," answered 'Sailor'.

In the event, the first show took place in the late afternoon and at first sight it looked as if there would be no reaction from the Hun. Twelve Bostons were to bomb Caen airfield and the Biggin Wing was to act as withdrawal cover. At 21,000ft we swept in over Fecamp, swung around behind Le Havre, crossed the Seine estuary and approached Caen from the east. On the final approach to the target area I could just pick out the retreating bombers, their positions marked by the black balls of bursting flak in their wake, and above and behind them the glinting canopies of their escort. There were no enemy fighters to be seen. As we neared our turning point, and the bombers retreated further out to sea, I wondered if my optimism had been misplaced. But no, just below and to my left two FW 190s appeared climbing hard from out of the haze. As Jack Charles was leading the section on that side I ordered him down to attack. He was quick to take advantage of the opportunity, and I saw him sliding in behind the Huns as they disappeared from my view underneath the formation.

"Tallyho, going down, Grass-seed Red," René's voice came over the R/T.

"You've got him, Jack."

"Good show, Grass-seed Leader," Boudier's voice followed so closely on the excited victory chant of Jack's number two that the kills must have been almost simultaneous.

"Turban Yellow Leader to Brutus, both enemy aircraft destroyed," in a matter of fact voice Jack announced his kills.

"I too have one, Brutus," René, not to be outdone, announced his victory.

There was no further engagements and the wing returned to Biggin to be met by an excited gathering of officers and airmen.

"Who got the thousandth?" asked 'Spy' as I stepped from my aircraft.

"Damned if I know, 'Spy', there were three shot down, but it all happened so quickly that I couldn't tell. From the R/T chatter I should say it was a draw. Perhaps 'Sailor' will be able to make a decision. Let's go and see what he says."

"You're a fine one, Al," said 'Sailor' pointing an accusing finger at me as we approached his aircraft. "Why the hell didn't you let me go after those Huns? They passed right under my nose."

"And mine too, sir, but Jack was in the best position. I must say I was tempted to have a go myself – I could do with that £300."

"Well, we'll never know for sure who got the one that mattered. I've decided that Jack and René are to share the honour and the money. I think that's the fairest thing to do, don't you 'Spy'?"

"Yes I'm sure it is, sir," answered 'Spy' who, more than any other, had looked forward to this great day. So saying, he dashed off to send the many signals and telegrams which he had long since prepared for the occasion.

Thus it came about that the 1,000th enemy aircraft destroyed by pilots operating from Biggin Hill was shared by a Canadian and a Frenchman, while a South African station commander and a New Zealander wing leader looked on.

CHAPTER EIGHTEEN

Biggin Hill

B Y a coincidence the Alsace Squadron had arranged a party in the Hyde Park Hotel for the night of 15th May; an ideal opportunity to celebrate the thousandth Hun. It was obviously going to be a late affair and I took the precaution of asking Group operations to let the Biggin Wing stand down the following morning, but was informed that the weather report was favourable and plans were already in hand for bomber operations the next day. However, I was assured that Biggin would only be used as a last resort. I kept my fingers crossed and set off for London to meet Joan who had recently moved her ambulance driving operations to Highgate. She had been there only a few days before she discovered that the most direct route to any hospital in the Southern Counties was via Biggin Hill! In the weeks that followed an AAGB ambulance was a familiar sight on the station.

The party was a huge success; on this, their first official party, the Alsace pilots had excelled themselves. Unhappily, I had counted on no operations the following morning and stayed far too late only to be awakened at dawn – it seemed I had hardly closed my eyes – with the news that the wing was to be airborne at 10.30am for Portreath, where we were to refuel prior to acting as escort to Venturas bombing Morlaix airfield in the Cherbourg Peninsula. We returned to Biggin late that evening, a very jaded team of pilots, having done four and a half hours flying during the day, but fortunately without much enemy opposition.

The official celebration for the 1,000th Hun was planned for a later date and actually took place in the first week of July in the form of a Ball at Grosvenor House. There were over a thousand guests invited, and among the many VIP's who attended were the Commanders-in-Chief of Fighter and Bomber Commands. The music was provided by three RAF bands and the cabaret by the Windmill Theatre Company. It was a memorable occasion for those at Biggin Hill, both past and present, who had helped to achieve this historic feat, whether on the ground or in the air.

The highlight of the evening was an unexpected gesture from a group of London taxi-drivers, members of the Beaufort Club, who arrived *en masse* just before the party officially ended to offer their services free of charge to the Biggin pilots and their guests. I was approached in the early hours of the morning by one of my pilots who told me that there were some taxi-drivers in the foyer asking for 'Sailor', and would I go and see them. In the foyer I found a dozen or so cabbies, elbowing their way through the departing guests, and at their head a cockney exclaiming indignantly to an obstructing doorman:

" 'Ere, cock, we're the boys from the Beaufort Club, come to offer free taxis to 'Sailor' Malan."

This spontaneous and most generous offer was gladly accepted, and I was one of the first to take advantage of it. A week later 'Sailor' returned the compliment when he invited fifty cabbies to be our guests-of-honour at Biggin Hill. They arrived in a fleet of cabs the leading one of which carried a grandfather clock strapped to the roof. This, together with a steering wheel suitably inscribed, the cabbies solemnly presented to the Mess as a memento of their visit, and both are proudly displayed in the Officers' Mess today. In the course of a most entertaining evening a cabbie related an amusing incident to me in connection with the free taxi service on the night of the Ball. Apparently he had driven a Biggin pilot and his wife all the way to Bromley only to be offered a threepenny piece as a tip by a none too sober Scotsman. A highly amused cabby concluded his story: "I asks yer, guv, a fripenny bit and we was doing it fer nuthin." That so generously offered tip was subsequently mounted and displayed in the Beaufort Club; what inscription was added to the mounting, I never did find out.

The cabbies' departure at a very late hour was quite a spectacle; it would be true to say that a dozen taxis, in line-astern formation, wove their way through the Mess gates in typical fighter pilot style. From this time onwards, Biggin pilots experienced no difficulty in obtaining a taxi in London – a ring to the Beaufort Club, whatever the hour, met with an immediate response.

The month of June was mainly concerned with escorting RAF Mitchells, Venturas and Bostons whose operations, unlike those in 1941, were no longer the bait to encourage enemy fighters into the air; their attacks were by now an undoubted thorn in the side of the German economy in occupied Europe – a small one, perhaps, compared with the American daylight effort, but effective nonetheless. Reaction from the Germans was therefore heavier than in the past and the supporting Spitfire wings were provided with some good pickings. In this phase, the Biggin Wing made good use of the Appledore control radar to effect interceptions on defending Hun fighter formations. On one occasion, and under Bill Igoe's able control, we jumped a formation of FW 190s over Abbeville and 611 Squadron, coming down from out of the sun, shot down four of the FW 190s before the Hun pilots knew they were being attacked. Afterwards I congratulated Bill on his controlling only to be answered by an unusual request.

"Al, the war is damn nearly over and I haven't yet fired a shot in anger. Can't you do something about it?"

"Not unless you want to go across the other side in the Master and fire your revolver in the general direction of Germany," I replied jokingly, and thought no more about it.

That same afternoon Bill appeared in my office. "I've fixed it, Johnny Clouston (the wing gunnery officer) has agreed to do it."

"Do what?" I asked, puzzled.

"Fly me across to the French coast in the Master."

"You're not serious, Bill?"

"You bet I am. Damned if I'm going to finish the war without firing a shot, even if it is only with a revolver from a training aircraft," answered Bill, his Irish blood really up.

"OK. If you really feel that badly about it, I'll lay it on. But don't tell anyone, not even 'Sailor'. I'll have a word with Clouston."

"Thanks, Al. Perhaps we could tie it in with the fighter sweep this afternoon. You could then give us cover on the return trip."

"That's a good idea, I'll get Clouston to arrange it that way."

I arranged for Johnny Clouston, who told me he had been browbeaten into the job much against his better judgement, to fly out at sea-level from Manston to Gris Nez (the shortest Channel crossing) and to let Bill fire his gun at whatever he saw on the coast. He was to arrange his timings so that he would arrive at Gris Nez at the same time as we planned to cross out from Lille where we were doing a fighter sweep. In the event, the wing was engaged fairly heavily in the St. Omer area, and the Master was forgotten. It returned safely to Biggin with a somewhat subdued Bill who was highly indignant that we had failed to give the promised cover; he was chased all the way across the Channel by an imaginary FW 190. However, he fired all six rounds from his colt, but claimed no hits!

During May there was a steady increase in the strength and capability of the American fighter force thus enabling the American heavies to penetrate progressively further and further into Germany until by the middle of June an impressive array of vital targets was within their orbit. On 22nd June they launched the first daylight raid against the Ruhr; from then onwards the industrial heart of Germany was under constant attack by day and night. For the first daylight raid, seven wings of RAF fighters provided the withdrawal cover force, forming an umbrella over Sleidrecht in northern Holland under which the returning forces were pleased to seek cover. Long before the bombers reached our position we sighted the formation away to the east, a formidable mass of aircraft surging steadily ahead despite repeated attacks from Hun fighters whose pilots, secure in the knowledge that they were outside Spitfire range, pressed home their attacks with unusual ferocity. Undoubtedly, a daylight attack on the Ruhr had touched their pride. By the time the Fortresses reached our position the enemy fighter attack was almost exhausted, but a running attack was maintained all the way to the coast, despite the covering Spitfires. On this, my seventieth operation as the Biggin Wing leader, I claimed my twenty-first confirmed victory.

As the American heavies ranged even further afield so the battle moved with them, and despite the hundred-gallon ventral tank now carried on the Spitfire, the RAF wing leaders found themselves groping in the rear, unable to reach the main battle area. Not so the American Thunderbolts, Lightnings and Mustangs; they were built as escort fighters, the Spitfire as a defensive fighter, therein lay the difference. Fortunately, the advent of the American Marauders in July, to swell the RAF's short-range daylight bombing force, provided a new source of fighting for the Spitfire wings, and a further problem for the German defence machine.

As in the Battle of Britain, the intensity of operations dictated that squadrons should be withdrawn from the front line for a spell of well-earned rest. After nine months at Biggin Hill 611 Squadron was moved to a northern Group and its place taken by 485 (NZ) Squadron from Tangmere. I was sorry to see Jack Charles and his boys go, but pleased that the relief squadron was 485 with which I had such close connections. Of course, 485 Squadron had changed a great deal since the Kenley days. There were many new faces among the pilots, but a few stalwarts remained: Marty Hume, Bruce Gibbs and Jack Rae, to name three who were now seasoned veterans.

For the past six months 485 Squadron had been equipped with Spitfire VB's and employed almost solely on the dreaded close escort role. The pilots were overjoyed at the move to Biggin which meant, of course, Spitfire IXB's and a more rewarding type of operation. The AOC had decided that their CO, Squadron Leader Reg Baker who had been with the squadron for two years, was due for a rest. On my recommendation Johnny Checketts was appointed to succeed him and thus became the CO of a squadron which he had joined exactly two years earlier as a 'sprog' Pilot Officer. Under Johnny, who by now had become a shrewd and highly successful destroyer of Focke-Wulfs, the squadron's success in the wing was assured.

Three months had now gone by since I assumed command of the Biggin Wing and in that time the score had risen to 1,020 enemy aircraft destroyed – or an addition of 37 under me – while our losses had fallen off in the reverse proportion; to date, the wing had lost only nine aircraft and pilots, two of whom had already returned safely to England. The new wing tactics were paying handsome dividends and the morale of the pilots was extremely high. As for me, confidence in myself as a leader, understandably shaken by past events, was fully restored. Thus far I had had no nerve-racking incidents in any way comparable with those on previous tours. However, I did get an unpleasant fright when on a fighter support task to Amiens experienced temporary engine failure well inside France.

The practice when carrying ventral tanks was to fly on them from immediately after take-off until they ran dry before switching over to main tanks. The exception to this rule was that when enemy aircraft were sighted we would change to mains immediately, irrespective of fuel used, and drop our ventrals preparatory to action. On this particular occasion the wing was at 21,000ft and about twenty miles inside France when the latter contingency arose. Immediately the Huns were sighted I gave the order to change, and took action accordingly. On the change my engine cut – not an alarming occurrence during the change over, when a small air lock in the petrol feed was not uncommon. But, on this occasion, I was really alarmed when the usual corrective action of switching on the booster pump failed to produce results. In a matter of seconds I had fallen behind the formation, and was losing height rapidly. It was obvious that this was to be no minor air lock and I therefore called René, whose squadron I was leading, and asked him to take over the wing which by now was some distance ahead and about to engage the Huns. The numbers three and four in my section, who had remained with me, I ordered to rejoin the main formation, but requested the number two to keep with me until I was down to 10,000ft, when he was to make his way home.

It was an unenviable position to be in; an unresponsive engine with a battle developing immediately above, and enemy territory below. When at 15,000ft the engine had still not responded to my efforts with the priming pump, I really gave up hope and began looking for a suitable forced-landing spot away from a built-up area, with a view to making good my escape on the ground. At 10,000ft I ordered my number two to break away. Two thousand feet lower my engine spluttered, coughed and after a few jerky movements, responded fully to my careful throttle movements. I wasted no further time in the area; down to ground level I went out as fast as my Spitfire would take me. In previous escapes there had been little time to get frightened – it was only after the event, when there was time for contemplation of what might have been, that the cold sweat of fear attacked me – but in the eight minutes or so that it had taken me to glide down to 8,000ft I had plenty of time for thought, and they were frighteningly unpleasant ones.

Soon after this incident, but not because of it, I went on ten days' leave. I was feeling a little tired and wanted to have a break before the really intensive phase expected in August and September. Joan joined me and we went down to Cornwall to stay with the Dumas' in their cottage at Port Melon. The good Cornish sea air combined with a week of home-cooked food had the desired effect, and at the end of the first week I was champing at the bit to return to operations. My desire to return was strengthened by the announcement on the radio on the evening of 26th July that the Biggin Wing had destroyed nine enemy aircraft that day without loss. This magnificent feat, for which full credit must be given to René Mouchotte who was leading in my absence, was achieved when escorting American Marauders to bomb our old adversary, the first Gruppe of the Richthofen Geschwader at Tricqueville airfield. The following day Biggin received a telegram: "Please convey my warmest congratulations to 341 and 485 Squadrons on yesterday's achievement. Nine for nought is an excellent score. Winston Churchill." In this combat that redoubtable German fighter ace Major Von Graf was reported, through intelligence sources, to have been wounded. I have been unable to find confirmation of this in post-war records.

Early in May the American VIIIth Air Force added a wing of B26 (Marauder) medium bombers to its front-line strength and plans were made to use them against transport targets and power stations in north-west Europe to supplement the RAF's daylight bombing programme. The Americans planned to operate the Marauders at low level without fighter escort – tactics which had proved successful in the Pacific, but were unlikely to be so successful against a highly organized defensive system in Europe – and to attack fringe targets in the working-up period. On their second raid, an attack against a power station at Haarlem, of the eleven Marauders dispatched, one turned back because of mechanical trouble and the rest were lost, mostly through enemy fighter opposition.

As a result of this experience General Eaker, Commanding the VIIIth Air Force, decided that the Marauders would be withdrawn temporarily from operations to train for tactical support of the ground forces in the coming invasion of the Continent. By the end of June a considerable force of Marauders had been built up in England and in early July they re-commenced a programme of bombing, with Spitfire escort, mostly against airfields and communication targets. To ensure that the Spitfire escorts to be provided, and the tactics to be used, were understood by the Americans, Wing Commander David Scott-Malden, now at Fighter Command headquarters, and I met the Marauders' commanders at Earls Colne airfield to brief them on the types of escorts we would use. We made it quite clear that there would be no question of mass close escorts tied to the bombers, but that the majority of the Spitfire wings would be freelancing in a support role, although there would be some close escort. After their abortive attempt without escort the Americans were only too keen to accept any form of escort, and were more than willing to abide by our proposals. A very happy partnership now developed and carried through until D-Day, by which time the Marauders provided a not inconsiderable portion of the Allied bombing effort.

In the operations that followed the Biggin Wing was invariably used in the high-cover role which was normally flown between 20,000 and 25,000ft an altitude band in which the Spitfire IXB excelled. On the first operation after my return from leave, the wing once again had a resounding victory over the Hun, but on this occasion against Messerschmitt 109Gs of JG 26, commanded at the time by a most able leader, Major Josef Priller. Our task on the operation was to act as high cover to 48 Marauders, flying in two boxes of 24, bombing St. Omer airfield. *En route* to the target, and over enemy territory, the still relatively inexperienced Americans split their formation; one box of 24 carrying on towards St. Omer and the other veering away to the south. I saw the close escort fighters, under their Belgian leader Michael Donnet, peel away and attach themselves to the leading box; Michael had insufficient fighters to cover both, and rightly followed the leaders. I therefore detailed 485 Squadron to break-away and provide close escort to the rear box with orders to Johnny that he was not, under any circumstances, to leave the bombers. I remained in position behind the leading box.

It was obvious that the bomber leader was having difficulty finding the target for we overshot St. Omer by quite a few miles before he realized his error, eventually returning to bomb the airfield. So far, there was no sign of Hun fighters, but I was worried about the second box of Marauders, now lost to view, with only 12 Spitfires to protect them. They would be in serious danger if subjected to a determined Focke-Wulf attack.

"Brutus calling Jubilee leader. Are you happy?" anxiously, I called Johnny.

"Hello, Brutus. Not bloody likely, these fools are wandering around somewhere south of Merville. I'm trying to turn them around. Will keep you informed."

"OK, Jubilee leader, as soon as I get this lot as far as the coast I'll return to give you a hand."

I had just reached the coast when Johnny called: "Brutus from Jubilee leader, Huns climbing up from below, about four I think. I don't think they've seen us. Can I attack?"

"What's your position, Jubilee leader?"

"Between St. Omer and the coast, coming out."

"OK, Johnny, attack with one section. I'm returning at full speed to assist."

"Going down, Jubilee Red. Blue and Yellow remain with the bombers."

After this order from Johnny to his squadron there was an interval of silence, broken a few minutes later. Again Johnny's voice came over the R/T, now tense and excited, "Come on, Gibby, have a go. You, too, numbers three and four."

It was clear from this order that Johnny was calling all four aircraft in his section to attack and was confident of handling whatever numbers opposed him. I soon found the wayward box of Marauders, and after seeing them safely to the coast, remained there to cover Johnny's withdrawal. I warned him of my height and position and a few moments later he rejoined, his section intact and in perfect formation.

"How did you get on, Johnny?"

"I got three, Brutus."

"Good for you," I answered, staggered by this reply. "What about the rest of the section?"

"Red Two, one destroyed."

"Red Three, one destroyed."

"Red Four, one destroyed."

In amazement I listened and tallied as each member of the section announced his kill. Six without loss.

"Brutus, I also got a damaged" added a triumphant Johnny.

On the ground the full story was told. When first sighted in the haze below, Johnny thought there were only four enemy fighters, but when he got close, having dived down behind and approached unseen from below, he counted eight Me 109Gs in line abreast formation, with one lagging well behind the rest. He attacked this one which blew up in a shower of metal, but still the formation flew on obviously unaware of the danger stalking them from behind. When Johnny realized this he threw discretion to the winds and ordered all four of his section to attack; this was the order I had heard over the R/T. The subsequent action was not a fight, it was a slaughter.

"It was like shooting sitting ducks," said Johnny, who was a duck-hunting enthusiast. "I just swung my sights along the line, picking off a Me 109 with each burst. When the rest of the section joined me in the sport, the sky was full of exploding Messerschmitts." Johnny's assistants in this action were: Flying Officers Bruce Gibbs and Jack Rae and Pilot Officer Tommy Tucker. A great day for all four. For this truly unique feat Johnny was eventually awarded the Distinguished Service Order.

August witnessed a quickening in the tempo of operations and throughout the month the pace steadily increased, and so too did the diversity of tasks. Dawn found us over France as high cover to Marauders; late morning, in the Caen area covering our own 2 Group bombers; early afternoon, over Holland as withdrawal cover to Fortresses returning from Germany; and late evening, on a fighter sweep in the Pas de Calais area. In many ways the tempo of operations compared with that of August 1940, although the absence of those nerve-destroying hours on readiness made the task seem less arduous. To many of the pilots the hour or two between receipt of orders and take-off time was purgatory, but I never minded it. Far rather that, when at least you knew what your orders were, than those long hours of waiting and wondering, so much a part of defensive operations. Early morning shows were most disliked by those whose nerves were affected by the wait for take-off. They could never face breakfast beforehand, a windfall for those, such as I, who could always eat before a show and thus stood to gain an extra egg for breakfast. I was no less frightened, but there was only one occasion that I recall when I couldn't eat breakfast and that was when I lifted the lid from the pot on the hot-plate to be met by the pungent odour of stewed pigs' kidneys – I ask you!

By the end of August I was really tired, and so too was René Mouchotte, as I now know. He wrote in his diary of this period: "And the sweeps go on at a terrible pace – I feel a pitiless weariness from them."* And still they went on, but rest for René was near at hand.

On August 27th, my own Spitfire was in for inspection and I borrowed one from Chris Martell's flight for the first show of the day. I was never happy flying a strange aircraft on operations, and avoided doing so whenever possible. However, this particular show was one of the first attacks against the V1 sites by Fortresses, and promised to be a rewarding trip. I wanted to be in on the expected fun, but fate decided otherwise. When just about to get airborne I had engine failure and braked to a slithering halt only just short of the end of the runway and a drop of some 30ft into the valley on the west side of the airfield. Fate is a strange

*The Mouchotte Diaries

master, and I have always been a fatalist. It was fate that my engine should have failed on this particular operation and fate that René should have been called upon to take over the lead. In the ensuing engagement over the target, René went down in the first attack, never to be heard of again.†

This was indeed a serious blow to the squadron and to France, a country which he loved passionately and which he was so near to seeing liberated – an event he had so long awaited. The French pilots were stunned by the loss of a much loved leader; France had lost one of her most gallant sons. His epitaph was written by his own hand: "If I am not to survive this war, let me at least have the satisfaction of falling to the enemy's fire."*

Fortunately for 341 Squadron, and the wing, there was an able deputy in the person of Commandant Bernard Duperier ready to take up the reins. Under his wise leadership the squadron was soon striking back with all its old vigour and skill.

Indifferent weather afforded one day's respite on the 29th, and two further shows on the 30th and again on the 31st brought August to a close. But September offered no respite. In the first five days the wing was engaged on no fewer than ten operations, ranging from a diversionary fighter sweep in the Paris area to a withdrawal cover task deep in Holland. On the sixth day, just ten days after Mouchotte went down, grim tragedy again intruded; on a high cover mission with Marauders to Amiens, Johnny Checketts was shot down. In an attack which developed about twenty miles from the target the wing was heavily engaged by Focke-Wulfs. Johnny, after destroying one FW 190, hotly pursued a second down to ground level. After an inconclusive engagement with this Focke-Wulf, during which he used all his ammunition, he

†Mouchotte's body was found six years later in a grave in Middlekirke, in Belgium, where it had been laid to rest by the local residents who had found the body on the beach, washed there by the tides. His body was repatriated in October 1944 and buried in the family vault in Paris.
*The Mouchotte Diaries

was making his way out with his number two when they were set upon by about eight Hun fighters. Against such odds, and with no ammunition, he had little chance and was eventually seen to go down in flames by his number two, Flying Officer Johnny Houlton, who had stuck with him throughout. During the fight Houlton transmitted for help and when I heard the call I returned inland – I was just crossing out at the time with my number two – but was unable to locate the scene of the fight. In the end, very short of petrol, and with no further R/T contact, I set course for England. Behind me the eastern horizon was already shrouded in night's cloak of darkness while ahead the sun, a mocking ball of fire, sank slowly to rest. Yet another friend had fallen to the enemy.

The loss of both squadron commanders within the space of two weeks, at a time when losses in the wing were very light, was an unexpected swing of the pendulum. Morale, however, was in no way affected and the pilots were as keen as ever to get at the enemy. Flight Lieutenant Marty Hume, who had been with 485 Squadron for almost two years, succeeded Johnny Checketts and Bruce Gibbs, another old member, moved up to take the flight. And operations continued as before.

By the middle of September I had recorded my 121st operation as wing leader at Biggin and a few days previously had destroyed my 22nd enemy aircraft. By now, I was not only very tired, but also feeling ill. For the past week I had been suffering from a form of dysentery (later diagnosed as Sone dysentery) and was subject to severe stomach pains. Foolishly, I refused to consult the doctor, and continued to operate. But the human frame can stand only so much; by the 15th September I was feeling so ill that I was forced to stay in bed. As a result of a visit from 'Sailor' the SMO, was summoned, and he sent for a specialist. That same evening I was admitted to East Grinstead hospital where I was again examined by a specialist who said, "Young man, we've only just got you here in time. You have developed an acute enteritis; a day or two longer and you would have been in serious trouble."

While in hospital I was surprised to receive a visit from Air Vice-Marshal Saunders, who, after enquiring about my health, said:

"I've just had a chat with your station commander and we agree that you should be rested. In fact, I think you can safely say that you've done your last operational tour."

I was neither surprised nor disappointed by this announcement. In four years of war I had done nearly 700 hours' flying on fighter operations and had destroyed 22, probably destroyed 10 and damaged 18 enemy aircraft. Besides, I had achieved my ambition to become a wing leader. I was now quite prepared to stand down.

CHAPTER NINETEEN

The Beginning of the End

W HEN finally released from hospital, after nearly
three weeks of drugs, I was sent on two weeks' sick
leave which I spent with Joan and her parents in Harrogate.
At the end of leave I was posted to command the Fighter
Wing of Central Gunnery School, thus following in the
footsteps of such famous fighter leaders as 'Sailor' Malan,
who had started the School, Jamie Rankin and Johnny
Walker, my immediate predecessor.

I was joined at CGS, by Squadron Leader Johnny
Checketts who had made his way back to England after a
miraculous escape from France. He managed to bale out of
his burning Spitfire at a very low altitude and, though badly
burned about the face and hands, eluded capture. Through the
efforts of some very loyal French villagers, two of whom
were later caught and taken off by the Gestapo, he was
hidden from the searching Germans for a full three weeks
until his burns had healed sufficiently to enable him to travel.
From then onwards he moved under the orders of the
underground organization which assisted escaping pilots,
finally reaching a small port in Brittany where he hid in the
hold of a French fishing smack. He spent nearly a week in
this wet and overcrowded accommodation – there were nine
other escapees in hiding there also – before the smack
emerged to run the gauntlet of German patrols in the offshore
waters, and make her way to the safety of a Cornish port.
Within six months of his return Johnny was back on
operations, now in command of a wing.

In March 1944 I moved to 11 Group headquarters where,
as a member of the air staff, I again found myself serving
under 'Daddy' Bouchier who was the Senior Air Staff
Officer in the Group. After barely six weeks in this job I was
surprised when one day the AOC sent for me and said: "Al,

I've just had the AOC of 84 Group on the phone and he wants me to release you to take command of the French airfield in his Group. Apparently, General Valin (Chief of Staff of the Free French Air Forces) has made a personal request for you to be in command of the French fighter squadrons when they move into France. I'm prepared to release you, if you want to go."

I jumped at the offer and a week later found myself at Merston airfield, near Chichester, in command of 145 Airfield in the 2nd Tactical Air Force, with three French fighter squadrons under me. I felt very privileged that the French should have asked for me personally, and looked forward to the day when we would celebrate their return to a liberated France.

On the afternoon of June 4th, all senior RAF officers in the 2nd Tactical Air Force, operationally concerned with the invasion, were summoned to attend at RAF Uxbridge. We were not told in advance the reason for the summons but it was obvious that the great day was at hand. When the Commander-in-Chief, Air Marshal Coningham, stepped on to the platform of the camp cinema, where some 200 officers were assembled, an expectant hush settled over the audience. After a few introductory remarks he pulled back a curtain covering a large wall map, and the secrets of Operation 'Overlord' were revealed. For so long we had wondered where and when; now we knew the answer.

After briefing, our orders were to return direct to units, to avoid all contact with the public and to remain within service bounds until after D-Day which, as the world now knows, was originally set for June 5th. Sealed orders issued to unit commanders were to be opened, and briefing of crews carried out, only on the receipt of a signalled code-word indicating that the invasion would be launched as planned. At dusk that evening I stood on the cold, blustery airfield of Selsey, to which we had recently moved, waiting and watching for the glider force to pass overhead; this would signify that the sea-borne assault would go in on the following morning. Long after the scheduled time, and when it was obvious that there had been a postponement, I gazed hopefully into the cloud-covered sky knowing in my heart that the operation could not go on in such weather conditions. The postponement meant keeping my secret for yet another night and day from the French pilots, still blissfully unaware of the nearness of the great day.

On the following evening they came, an impressive assortment of tugs towing heavily laden gliders which, straining at their steel tow-ropes, bumped and bounced in the turbulent air below banks of dark and menacing clouds. Silently I wished them "God speed" – in such weather conditions they would need it – and dashed off to call the pilots to briefing. The expressions on the faces of the Frenchmen when they heard the glad news was indescribable.

Early next morning I was on patrol over the bridgehead. As I looked down on the hundreds of ships and landing craft disgorging men and material on to the beaches I was reminded of a similar scene that I had witnessed almost exactly four years ago to the day. Then it was the evacuation of a defeated army in retreat; now it was a victorious army on the advance, storming the citadel that it had surrendered so reluctantly in that unhappy first year of the war. For the Germans, this was the beginning of the end; for me, it was the end of the beginning.

Other Goodall paperbacks from Crécy Publishing Limited

Enemy Coast Ahead
Guy Gibson VC, DSO and Bar, DFC and Bar
Wing Commander Guy Gibson gives one of the most brilliant descriptions of the
Dambusters raid by the Lancasters of 617 Squadron which he himself led.
256 pages, paperback, photograph section
9 780907 579625 £5.99

Evader
Denys Teare
A story of escape and evasion behind enemy lines
240 pages, paperback
b&w photograph section
9 780907 579485 £6.99

Keeping Watch
Pip Beck
The story of an R/T operator in Bomber Command who talked down bomber crews
returning from operations, met them off-duty and, all too often, mourned their loss.
192 pages, paperback, photograph section
9 780907 579380 £5.99

Lancaster Target
Jack Currie
The classic story of one crew's fight to survive a full tour of operations in the
night skies of wartime Europe. Flying Lancaster bombers from RAF Wickenby,
Jack Currie chronicles the life and death struggles against flak, night fighters and
perilous weather.
192 pages, paperback, photograph section
9 780907 579281 £6.99

Mosquito Victory
Jack Currie
This sequel to *Lancaster Target* graphically and humorously describes all aspects
of life as a WWII RAF bomber pilot on 'rest'. Mess life and antics intermingle
with Jack's real task of instructing trainees on the four-engined Halifax bomber
and his subsequent return to the élite Pathfinder force flying Mosquitoes of 1409
Weather Flight.
176 pages, paperback, photograph section
9 780907 579335 £5.99

Night Fighter
C.F.Rawnsley and Robert Wright
With John "Cat's-Eyes" Cunningham, "Jimmy" Rawnsley was half of one of the
RAF's leading night fighter crews, destroying over twenty enemy aircraft.
256 pages, paperback, photograph section
9 780907 579670 £5.99

Other Goodall paperbacks from Crécy Publishing Limited

Night Flyer
Lewis Brandon DSO, DFC and Bar
The exciting story of one of the most successful RAF night fighting partnerships
of the war, the book also charts the development of night fighting.
208 pages, paperback, photograph section
9 780907 579779 £5.99

No Moon Tonight
Don Charlwood
A Bomber Command classic, this is the breathtaking story of a wartime bomber
crew facing the nightly bombing of the most strongly defended targets in Nazi
Germany.
224 pages, paperback, photograph section
9 780907 579977 £5.99

Pathfinder
Air Vice-Marshal Don Bennett CB, CBE, DSO
The autobiography of the leader of the Pathfinders – the élite force designed to
carry out pioneering target-marking and precision-bombing of Nazi-occupied
Europe.
272 pages, paperback, photograph section
9 780907 579571 £5.99

Rear Gunner Pathfinders
Ron Smith DFM
The story of the air war over Germany as seen from the small Perspex bubble of a
'Tail-End Charlie' rear gunner in a Lancaster.
200 pages, paperback
photograph section
9 780907 579274 £6.99

Uncommon Valour
AG Goulding DFM
A comprehensive account of Bomber Command's part in the Second World War,
together with a personal view of the leadership of the force in those crucial years.
192 pages, paperback
photograph section
9 780859 790956 £4.99

Warburton's War
Tony Spooner
The Life of Maverick Ace Adrian Warburton, who was one of the most highly
decorated pilots of World War II.
204 pages, 'B' format paperback
198 x 128mm
20pp b&w photograph sections
9 780907 579434 £7.99

Other Goodall paperbacks from Crécy Publishing Limited

Wing Leader
Air Vice-Marshal "Johnnie" Johnson CB, CBE, DSO and Two Bars, DFC and Bar
The thrilling story of the top-scoring Allied fighter pilot of World War Two -
'Johnnie' Johnson.
320 pages, paperback, photograph section
9 780907 579878 £6.99

Wings Aflame
Doug Stokes
The acclaimed biography of Victor Beamish, the legendary Irish station
commander who flew an incredible 126 fighter sorties in the Battle of Britain.
224 pages, paperback , photograph section
9 780907 579724 £5.99

Wings Over Georgia
Jack Currie
Forerunner to the best-selling *Lancaster Target*, the story of Jack Currie's early
training in the UK, followed by a period with the US Army Air Corps and his
return to England to join Bomber Command.
156 pages, paperback, photograph section
9 780907 579113 £3.99

Crecy Publishing Ltd,
1a Ringway Trading Estate,
Shadowmoss Road,
Manchester M22 5LH, UK
Tel: 0161 499 0024
Fax: 0161 499 0298
sales@crecy.co.uk
Order online at **www.crecy.co.uk**